# Speak Gently

## Surviving Father and the Anderson School

Judy Naumburg

iUniverse, Inc.
New York   Bloomington

*Some of the names of Anderson school kids have been changed.*

*iUniverse books may be ordered through booksellers or by contacting:
iUniverse*

*1663 Liberty Drive
Bloomington, IN 47403
www.iuniverse.com
1-800-Authors (1-800-288-4677)*

*ISBN: 978-1-4502-1609-8 (sc)
ISBN: 978-1-4502-1610-4 (ebook)*

*Printed in the United States of America*

*iUniverse rev. date: 03/23/2010*

*We do not see things as they are.*
*We see them as we are.*

The Talmud

# PREFACE

Childhood, for most American children, is a time for swinging on swings, Halloween dress-ups, sibling rivalries, and bedtime stories. For many children, it is about survival. My story, though not horrific or paralyzing, began almost perfectly among the farmlands of Pennsylvania and then abruptly took a detour down a rough road that none of my family expected, and some did not survive. As grownups, we sometimes choose to hold onto the difficult memories or often fall prey to our tragedies and never quite land on our feet. I somehow managed to stand.

My mother sent me a box of leather-bound books after my daughter was born. It contained six volumes of nursery rhymes and stories entitled *My Book House*, compiled by Olive Beaupre Miller. The pages were yellowed, stained, and creased, as if they had been read a thousand times. My grandmother bought the books after Mom was born in 1923, and they were among the few personal possessions my mother was able to keep after she returned home one day and discovered her three children were gone, their belongings missing, and in their place an emptiness she'd never thought she could feel.

While attending Harvard extension school, I began writing my memoirs in the voice of that child who grew up on a farm in the 1950s. Out of curiosity, I tailored my homework assignments so that I might revisit the madness I experienced, detailing the events as accurately as I could remember, trying to preserve the voice of the child within me. Each story in *My Book House* stirred another memory. My mother had read from the same book when my brothers and I were babies in the nursery. Would sharing those vivid memories ultimately clean out the cobwebs of my heart? Could the details be confirmed and become less painful just by putting them on paper? After receiving one essay back from a teacher who praised my writing but gave me a B+, stating that the story was clearly not believable, I smiled. Perhaps his childhood had been entirely too easy.

I kept returning to the keyboard over the years, and with every chapter, I began to feel a release I never anticipated. With every story, I put another event on a shelf in my mind—not forgotten, but up high nonetheless, where it became less painful. I did not realize how cathartic my writing would become, bleeding the struggle out of me and easing my every day. I watched my "inner" child mellow and began to realize how far I had come from that sad, confused, moody, thumb-sucking young girl. Yet I am she. Propelled by I know not what, I learned to move through the rain, letting it cascade over my shoulders, and somehow survived a madness I did not choose, confusions I did not invite.

I lived in the same town as my father, and the memories were not my only pain, because we never learned to communicate with each other honestly. Every day I saw him there was tension. Often, in restaurants or concert venues, he would walk around the periphery to avoid speaking with me and my husband. By the time he was bed-ridden with cancer, I was allowed to visit him only once for fifteen minutes. No closure took place. At the time of his death, though he lived only two miles from me, he had only seen my seven-year-old son once. I did, however, learn through patience to let the anger subside and not destroy my "self."

Working with single moms and children of divorce, I also learned that my survival alone could help others. I began working with abusive parents in the early 1980s. I watched many parents and children struggle and trip, all the while becoming aware of the universality of those missteps, and I realized that the way in which parents react plays a large part in how children grow up. I taught (and lived) not to overreact to a difficult moment—not to lie down, but to stand as firmly as one could inside one's own sense of self-worth. Love is an emotion my mother never failed to embody, and I tried to learn from her.

This memoir is not written by a rock star or politician or hero, so why do I choose to self-publish? My husband convinces me that perhaps someone can read my story and keep walking down the path of life, putting one foot in front of the other without falling too hard into the quicksand of life. His optimism has helped me see life as a survival, not only of the fittest, but a survival that is possible for all of us.

I want to thank my friend Claudia Jessup for her ongoing insightful help editing. I also want to thank my friends Jane Ervin, Lynda Levy, and Elizabeth Jacobson for their readings and thoughtful comments. Most importantly, I want to thank my husband for his tireless efforts, multiple readings, and ongoing push. Without him, this memoir would remain in the bottom drawer.

Judy Naumburg

# CHAPTER 1

**Sweet and Low**

Sleep and rest, sleep and rest,
Father will come to thee soon;
Rest, rest, on mother's breast,
Father will come to thee soon;

**Alfred Tennyson**

The night I was born, the gods were crying. Heavy skies dropped a curtain of rain on my opening act. Rain pellets pounded the windshield of my parents' slate grey 1945 Ford while my father, in high-strung anticipation of my arrival, cautiously steered through the menacing downpour. I can imagine him pressing his thick glasses up onto his bald head, squinting forward through the dense early morning hour with overstressed determination. My mother probably sat stoically by his side, as they rushed to the hospital. Perhaps she even prayed silently. They probably didn't talk much.

Childbirth carries a sense of the unknown, and my night was no different. My mother had to be totally petrified, and somewhat in the dark, because her one previous birthing experience was my older brother Steve, just fifteen months ago. He was born three weeks past due date (according to the doctor), tortured my mother for over twenty-eight hours of painful labor, then tried to come out backward like everything he's done since. First, he pushed his arm out, so they shoved him back in. Then he put his butt down, as if to say he was

1

not having any of this life crap. Finally, they grabbed him with a set of metal forceps, turned him around, and wrenched him headfirst from the womb. Mom, heavily drugged for the event, missed most of the experience, except the pain and the humiliation. There were no birthing classes or pant-blows in those days. Many kids came out with a flat, mangled head like my brother's. Childbirth was something few people talked about. Women were simply expected to know.

Instead of saddle blocks, drugs, and forceps, I was bound and determined to make my entrance unassisted. Like everything I've done since, I figured I didn't need any help, so my little baby body just slipped right out, almost too quickly, before my mom or Dr. John really knew I was happening. Actually, I think my brother eased the way. He may have done that for me all my life, but I still didn't escape. I got it good. In spite of the dire weather warnings and God knows what other obstacles, I came slithering out. I'm like that.

I was born at 5:30 in the morning on Sunday, June 20, 1948, just north of Philadelphia, in the Abington Memorial Hospital. At the time, Philadelphia, designed and built by a Quaker colonist named William Penn, was the third-largest city in the United States and home of the historic Liberty Bell. I'm sure my father, the farmer, found comfort resting in the waiting room and then handed out cigars randomly at the finale. Though this was a man whom I would watch reach his arm shoulder-deep into a laboring cow's womb, he clearly had no desire for any human childbearing education or participation, tonight or any night. Woman's work. I was born on a Sunday, Father's Day, which, all in all, didn't turn out to be such a great omen.

Back home on our farm, tending to baby Steve, was my grandmother, my mother's mother. We called her Gigi. My dad called her Flossy, but her real name was Florence. She had the largest breasts and the skinniest legs I ever saw. Doctors diagnosed her with breast cancer when she was fifty-four years old, so she had to have one of those things removed and after that always looked atilt, the fake breast having a bit more perk than the real one. She must have had the largest falsie on record. A falsie for Flossy. My mom said she didn't think Gigi ever had cancer. She thought the doctors just took off one of her breasts because she had a blocked "duck" or something.

"You just slipped right out like a little eel," my mother told me more than once during my lifetime. "They laid you on my tummy, all naked and wet, and then you arched your back and looked right up at me with your dark wide eyes as if to say 'Well, here I am.' After counting all your fingers and your toes, I was the happiest person alive." Not a bad way to come into the world if you're coming.

When my mom and I were all cleaned up, my baby body all wrapped in warm blankets, Dad came in. I don't remember the conversation, but I doubt there was still much substance. He probably counted my fingers and toes, and when he reached twenty, went home. I never got the sense from him that day was the best of his life. As time went on, I got the feeling maybe I should have stayed in. But it was too late. Out was out, and that was that.

# CHAPTER 2

## The Naumburgs

How much is that doggy in the window?
The one with the waggly tail.
How much is that doggy in the window?
I do hope that doggy is for sale.

**Lita Roza**

My father was born in New York City, on January 23, 1920. His fair hair and pale skin contrasted with his dark-haired older brother, George Washington Junior, just as their personalities did. Born two years apart and different in every possible way, George and Philip were best friends and pride-filled enemies. George was very bright, quick to learn, and self-motivated. My Uncle George managed to rise to most expectations placed on him because of his birthright, oldest son of two prominent New York Jewish families, but my dad would have been better off if he had been raised on a wheat farm somewhere in Iowa. My dad had his own ideas about life.

Their younger sister, Ellin, quite simply, was a girl, and therefore a different subspecies entirely. Each child had a special nurse or governess as they grew up and a rotating inventory of maids, cooks, and butlers from many foreign countries, though the preferred second tongue was most certainly French. My dad wrote in his own memoir, entitled *Personal Reflections*, "There were always ten or fifteen around the house." The three children were raised with an endless list of expectations, a life of immense wealth, and circumvented love.

Life began in a splendid brownstone at 52 East Sixty-Fourth Street where, according to Dad, the best day was the day they moved out. The boys attended the Lincoln School on 114th Street and Morningside Park. The school was associated with Columbia University, and many wealthy kids attended. Dad recalled attending school with a Rockefeller boy; a boy from the Sears and Roebuck fame; Tom and George Goldberg, sons of Rube Goldberg, the cartoonist; and a girl named Marjorie Lewison, who "used to insist on getting completely undressed in the cloakroom."

The Naumburgs heavily supplemented all the children's educations with music lessons at the David Mannes Music School and Saturday morning programs at Carnegie Hall with Walter Damrosch. Musical prodigies were the ultimate goal, and though George played the piano and Dad played the violin, neither showed any interest in following relatives' footsteps. To cover all bases, the children also had formal riding lessons in Central Park with their cousins Bob Morgenthau and Terry Fox. The Swiss riding master, Oscar Montelle, knew that the most efficient control was with the whip.

In 1932, my father was in fifth grade. Just after the famous Lindberg kidnapping and an anonymous threatening phone call, my grandparents tightened the security around their children, as did most wealthy families living in New York at the time. The boys were then shuttled to and from school in a chauffeur-driven 1929 Model A Ford, one of the first cars made with a gearshift. The hired driver, Peter Shoe, also became their bodyguard. The family also owned a hand built Cunningham.

While my uncle successfully mastered his schooling, Dad struggled year after year, eventually being diagnosed as mirror-minded and left-handed. In those days, teachers were ill-equipped to remedy or treat with kindness his uncommon learning disability, and Dad clearly remembered being utilized in experiments with other, right-handed, normal children. His first two teachers at Lincoln actually tied his left hand behind his back and forced him to write with his right hand, assuming left-handed people were not normal. He flunked fourth grade, basically because he couldn't read. When he eventually finished at Lincoln, his seventh-grade teacher discovered the mistake and taught him how to print with a backward slant using his left hand. He never learned how to write in cursive, except his signature. He had private readers and tutors to help him through high school and college. My uncle can recall some terrible times, including one summer when my dad was fifteen. He was given an undisciplined horse and "how to" books on horse training. As my uncle remembers, "He would go into his room to read, and emerge fifteen minutes later in a rage. The frustration of wanting to know, and being unable to find out, was horrendous for him and very painful to watch."

Around 1930, my grandfather bought a three-hundred-acre country estate just outside New York City in Westchester County called Apple Bee Farm in an area called Croton-on-Hudson. The family moved to the country after the Lindberg kidnapping, and George Senior "retired" sometime during 1932. The kids attended The Scarborough School. Here my father started raising chickens. "I got up every morning, fed the birds, cleaned the houses, etc. By fall, I had broilers for sale," he recalled with little-boy enthusiasm. "George (Wacker, the farm manager) showed me how to kill and clean the chickens, and I sold out with a profit. The next year I bought some turkey eggs and put them in an incubator. We hatched fifty and I sold enough birds for Thanksgiving to pay all my bills. I had six or seven birds left for Christmas as profit. A fox got in and ate them all—and the profit."

Both my grandfather and uncle attended Exeter. My dad went to Deerfield, even though George was at Exeter and my grandfather had donated a fair amount of money to Exeter, including support for the creation of a full-time psychiatrist. Prestigious schools were available to most wealthy families at the time, regardless of grades. Exeter agreed to take my dad even though he flunked Latin, but Grandpop decided Deerfield would be a better fit.

In spite of the fact that the boys attended boarding school, and the main house had over thirty rooms, the family psychiatrist suggested that my dad and his brother have their own place to live while they were home in the country, so the two boys moved out of the main house and into a smaller two-bedroom stone house with wooden rafters built especially for them. Soon after the house for the boys was built and Dad was sent away to prep school, his parents announced their divorce. The silent shock twisted and confused my dad's world. He was a poor student and now had added emotional turmoil as well. He went to the headmaster of Deerfield, Mr. Boyden, who told him to go home and figure things out. The headmaster added that nine times out of ten the father is the "only place to look for stability," and he advised not to depend upon the mother. The next summer my dad was sent to Culver Military Academy after calling his mother a "dirty old bitch." Though Culver was supposed to be a punishment, the experience, in my dad's eyes, was positive. At Culver he learned if you tipped the black waiter, he would then tell you which foods had the saltpeter. At Culver, he learned to be a "better man."

Perhaps if his teachers hadn't tied his left hand to his side and allowed it to perform easily what his right hand had to struggle with, he would have been free to perform in less rebellious territory. Perhaps if he had been raised in a family with lower expectations he could have tended his chickens, found self-confidence in the price of his turkeys, and lived happily ever after. The gaps between what he wanted, what

7

he could perform, and what was expected would have been smaller. Is rebelliousness inherited? Baldness is.

Every summer of my early childhood, my family journeyed by car from the farmlands of Pennsylvania to see my grandparents, who lived at Apple Bee Farm. My paternal grandfather, George Washington Naumburg Senior, was aptly born on the Fourth of July, 1876, one hundred years after the birth of America. I remember the drive we made many times through miles and miles of wooded lands. Once we had passed New York City, we rarely saw a house or farm. When we reached a special spot in the road, my dad would yell, "Here we go!" much like a horse race announcer. His face lightened up with anticipation as we raced down the slim paved road and flew off a sizable bump amid silly screams. We knew then that we were almost there.

Grandpop, the grand patriarch of the family, carried on a tradition handed down to him from many generations of Jews: making money. His father, Elkan Naumburg, was the son of a Prussian gentleman. A lover of music, Elkan walked two miles every day as a young boy for violin lessons and played the piano by ear. In 1850, at age fifteen, he emigrated alone from a small town in Bavaria, called Treuchtlingen, to the United States. There he worked for two dollars a week in the dry-goods business with his uncle in Baltimore and soon became a millionaire by starting one of the largest clothing manufacturing firms in the United States. When he turned sixty, he started his own banking firm at 14 Wall Street, formalizing a longstanding practice of lending money to friends and suppliers for a small fee. Elkan's policy was to pick out capable, industrious men and extend credit to them. In this way, he cultivated many loyal customers and became very wealthy in the process.

My great-grandfather Elkan evolved, as did many other German-Jews, into a successful transplant who felt grateful for his new opportunity in the free world, and he gave much back, especially to the music world. His patriotism showed in the naming of his son, George Washington Naumburg, and also in the contribution of a limestone band shell in Central Park, free classical music concerts at the band shell, and countless other philanthropic endeavors. Elkan died in 1924 when my father was only four years old.

Also—historically common among generations of Jews—I heard nothing as a child about my great-grandmother, except her name, Bertha Wehle. My dad wrote that she died young of a brain tumor resulting, they believed, from hitting her head on the boom of a sailing boat, and that "she was a very sweet lady." I know now that Bertha was born in Prague, Bohemia, in 1843. The Jewish congregation there was considered one of the most outstanding in Europe, and her father, my great-great-grandfather, was the vice president. She came to this country and became a teacher at the Normal College, now Hunter College, in New York City. She married Elkan in 1866. They shared a love of music and cultivated a world around this bond with friends Leopold Damrosch, William Steinway, and Theodore Thomas, who played in a quartet with Elkan in their home most Sundays.

Well-educated, extremely well-cultured and refined, Bertha married a terribly successful man, solidifying a standard passed down in the form of expectations to the next generation, and eventually to me. For Bertha, I am certain the expectation was never questioned. Her happiness depended on her success in marriage, and she accepted that graciously without public question. Before she married, Bertha kept a diary, in which she expressed her loneliness and dissatisfactions. "Last Monday I made my debut by visiting a large ball at Irving Hall; it is hard for me to express the disappointment which I experienced on that occasion," she wrote in her diary in 1862. Her first entry in this dairy, called "Bertha Wehle's Book" was a poem:

I am unhappy—very much so.

Those love now who never loved before;
And those who always loved, now love no more.
Love rules the court, the camp, the grave
And men below and saints above
For love is heaven, and heaven is love.

Then she added, "Can I, in the monotony of my daily life, find enough of interest to write in a journal?" She died in 1897, at age fifty-four, of a brain tumor, but I found no mention of the sailing accident my father passed down.

My grandfather reaped the benefits of what his immigrant father sowed. A graduate of Phillip Exeter Academy, and an 1898 Summa Cum Laude graduate of Harvard, he quickly mastered his father and older brother's world of banking, investments, and insurance at E. Naumburg & Co. on Wall Street. In 1919, he and his brother, Walter, brokered $325 million worth of commercial paper, a very substantial business in 1919. When shortly thereafter the Federal Reserve Board passed a new regulation allowing banks to rediscount commercial paper themselves, thus eliminating brokers, my grandfather bought a seat on the New York Stock Exchange. His uncanny sense of business and timing (with perhaps a touch of insider trading) enabled him to coast through the great stock market crash of 1929 with his own fortune and the million-dollar inheritance from his father intact and then retire in 1931. How he managed to retire when every facet of the country was suffocating inside the worst depression of all time, I never quite understood. Maybe I evolved from a family of mattress stuffers.

The tradition that failed to thrive after my family's emigration was Judaism. Though Grandpop was the head of the finance committee for the United Jewish Appeal for almost thirty-five years and president of the Baron de Hirsch Fund from 1933 to 1964, no aspect of Judaism was observed or taught in the home. No Seders, no high holidays—no bar mitzvahs. In their contrary worlds, both my grandfather and my great-grandfather used much of their money to cross the sometimes not-so-silent barriers of exclusive private clubs, hotels, and organizations; yet, the family rarely talked about Jewish heritage and, to my knowledge, never celebrated their Jewishness.

My own magical memories of Grandpop and his world cushioned with wealth were years away from our working farm. His farm sparkled with high-stepping thoroughbreds glistening in the fields, and sun-soaked ponds alive with frogs and twelve-inch bass. Every detail was perfect: trimmed hedges, swept walkways, glimmering cars, and clean maids dressed in pressed uniforms smelling of talcum powder. For his Fourth of July birthday Grandpop held lavish picnic parties on the lawn for all my cousins and many, many friends. We all dressed in our Sunday best and remembered to say our *please*s. I remember sitting at a long glass and wrought-iron table with cousins, aunts, uncles, and friends for Grandpop's birthday party. Telegrams were read aloud from presidents, governors, and other political notables, congratulating him for his generous contributions and participation in charitable organizations.

Built in 1920 of giant moss rock covered in thick green ivy, Grandpop's mansion was surrounded by expansive lawns and woodlands overlooking the Croton reservoir. There were five master bedrooms with complete baths. Everyone kowtowed to Grandpop, whom they fondly addressed as Boss. His sitting study, with a separate bathroom and dressing room, smelled of tobacco and shoe polish. Here he proudly showed my brothers and me his gold cuff links soldiered in a velvet-lined mahogany box.

He lived in this mansion with his third wife, my father's stepmother, Cecile Lockhart, from Philadelphia. Their opulent silk and satin bedroom, adorned with fresh-cut flowers, had a feminine aura, a complete departure from the rest of the stern, dark interior. When Grandpop grew old and walked all bent over like Rumpelstiltskin, Cecile installed a little elevator chair on the grand staircase, which we were only occasionally permitted to ride at a snail's pace with complete adult supervision. There were scores of maids and cooks, nannies and gardeners whom I imagined secretly escaped from *The Sound of Music*. Apple Bee Farm was a fairy tale come true for visiting little girls.

Most of the rooms in the house held special memories for me. The dining room, paneled in dark wood, was half the size of a gymnasium. A long mahogany table dominated the center of the room. Stately windows and French doors opened onto a black slate patio overlooking the reservoir. It was in this room my grandmother Ruth threw her hand-painted French china at my grandfather, shattering plates in her uncontrollable rage. Though I never saw them together, I imagined they had a very stormy and angry marriage. Difficult to understand how so much wealth, so much help, and so much beauty could reap so much dissatisfaction.

Most of our happiest hours were spent in one of the first privately owned Olympic-sized swimming pools built in this country. An oval-pillared changing house, with granite floors, portals, statues, and fountains, ran the north length of the pool. Fragrant boxwood hedges accented the grounds.

Grandpop lived in a magnificent world of opulence and philanthropy. He was comfortable in the world he had created for himself, or so it appeared. Yet the physical presence of my grandfather remains embedded in my mind only in one way: sitting in a soft, stuffed leather chair in the living room, in front of two huge Zenith television sets, as the outside festivities were carried on without his presence. One TV was inside a mahogany cabinet. The other was freestanding. Each set had a different baseball game on. Sometimes he was asleep, but sometimes he would let you sit quietly next to him and watch. I don't remember ever sitting on his lap, and our conversations were brief. The comfort in his life was easy to feel, but I longed to behave as a child, running barefoot or rolling through the grass. I was, however, always expected to act like a proper adult while there.

Except for the glass and wrought-iron tables, and a few black-and-white photographs he took of his many trips abroad, which hung in the living room, his reality is gone from mine: no mansions, no thoroughbreds, no limousines.

We rode in one when he died, though. My father made me buy new shoes for the funeral. My feet hurt all day. My feet always hurt in dress-up shoes, and that was all I could think about. All the cousins came. They laid him to rest next to his parents in a magnificent granite crypt on a hill at The Woodlawn Cemetery in the Bronx where people like Jay Gould, Irving Berlin, Robert Moses, and Herman Melville are buried. I was too young to be impressed. My father kept his head in his hands during most of the service.

Dad told us Grandpop was the most important person in his life. "Not only a great father, but in various ways and stages my closest friend." They each had three wives. He and Grandpop each sat on many boards and they each wrote to their children through secretaries—dictated, and often unsigned. Unlike Grandpop, my father forgot his sense of family. None of his children would ever be good enough, and he never invited his children or grandchildren to his house for his birthday.

Dad had lost most of his hair by the time I was born, and we had a pretty good time kidding him about it. He had a good sense of humor about his lack of hair, but his temper snapped if anyone messed with his glasses. He called us "good-for-nothing nudniks." When we rode in the car, he would sometimes sing stupid songs: "I've Got Sixpence, Jolly, Jolly, Sixpence," or "How Much is That Doggy in the Window." Sometimes Dad roughhoused with the boys, or frenetically tickled us all. His wide, calloused hands, with part of an index finger missing from an accident with a John Deere combine, dug hard into my ribs until I cried. He never stopped when I screamed. They called me a sissy and made fun of me, until I ran crying to my room.

I never felt Dad loved me. His expectations were too big. His voice responded easily in anger. He became the parent that loomed the largest in my life, dwarfing my mom. He was the King Kong. When you go to bed, you have nightmares about King Kong, and, chances are, you don't remember the beautiful island in the Pacific.

# CHAPTER 3

### Elegant Ashes

The world is so full
of a number of things,
I'm sure we should all
be as happy as kings

**Robert Louis Stevenson**

My paternal grandmother reigned as the quintessential enigma of my childhood. She instilled awe and fear in those subjects who scrambled to win acceptance or waited for occasional morsels of gratitude to fall from the throne. Everyone continually coveted her elegant tokens, and I never quite understood why. I never understood how I filtered past the pillars of devoted subjects into her graces and became her "favorite grandchild."

Born with looks that any parent would want to hide in the kitchen, Ruth Morgenthau Knight owned everything but beauty. Her large lumpy nose covered too much of her face; gray eyes sunk deep inside her disguised loneliness. Her walnut hair had no redeeming qualities; her skin looked like the bed of a railroad track. Yet she carried herself like Queen Victoria, and her self-assurance projected a grace that anyone could respect.

She had the most incredibly good taste of anyone I have ever met. Her perfectly tailored clothes fit her thin, well-proportioned body with style. Every accessory harmonized, and there were never frayed edges. She had personal shoppers at Saks and Bergdorf's and probably other stores as well. She demanded the highest quality and got it. She made the best of what she was given and spent her money on improving herself. Her two homes exemplified her exquisite lifestyle. A New York apartment situated her among the very wealthy tenants of the Carlyle Hotel on Madison Avenue and Seventy-Sixth Street. Often, family members secretly whispered to me their desire for one of her many beautiful treasures: sculptures, homes, or paintings. Nice things, I would think, examining the hand-carved wooden statue or the original oil painting in a gold frame, but I failed to understand the envy.

Lunch at the Carlyle with "Mom" Knight presented many challenges to my brothers and me when we were young. First, we would dress as if going to a party—usually in a Lord & Taylor dress or Brooks Brothers' suit, bought especially for the occasion and black patent leather shoes, all slippery and stiff. At lunch we would sit like inanimate porcelain dolls, Mom Knight monitoring our conversation so much so that I had difficulty remembering both what I was going to say and what everyone else was talking about. We had to use the correct fork for salad and a pressed linen napkin every time a morsel of food touched our lips. We were instructed to clean our plates without a fuss if we wanted to taste even one item on the giant tiered pastry cart filled with rich, dark chocolates and perky strawberries, real cream puddings, and scrumptious individual cakes.

Blue Herons, Mom Knight's huge white house in Pound Ridge, New York, rested among thick trees and voluptuous flower gardens overlooking a private lake that mirrored the sky. I remember swimming through the dark, cool water, racing quickly to the diving dock before my imagined monsters of the deep, living in the green slimy bottom, nipped at my toes. Or we would float the surface in a tipsy canoe, out to the island and back, brothers or cousins dragging fishing lines dotted with red-and-white bobbers. On rainy days or quiet afternoons, we would fill our hours with a hall closet full of toys. My favorite thing, though, was the taste of fresh blueberries, raspberries, or blackberries, picked from her garden, served under a blanket of fresh rich cream.

I don't know if anyone really loved my grandmother, probably because she seemed incapable of love herself. Described with words like *difficult*, *didactic*, and *vitriolic*, she endeared herself to very few who knew her superficially or intimately. "Beautiful, warm and sexy are three words that never applied to mother," my father wrote in his autobiography; I presumed those were the qualities he would have liked her to have. I often wondered why he never tried to resolve his hatred for her before she died, but, sadly, he made no attempt.

My grandmother was not an easy person to love. She could be abrupt and demanding. There was always someone in the family she wouldn't talk to or who wouldn't talk to her. My Aunt Ellin maintained a ten-year silence with her mother, though she lives at Blue Herons today. "Mom" had a constant revolving door of servants, because she was incapable of nurturing a long-term relationship with any human who functioned in a subservient role. My Uncle George was the only one of three children who preserved a constant relationship with his mother. He, presumably, remained in her good graces.

The daughter of a diplomat, Henry Morgenthau Senior, ambassador to Turkey during World War I, and sister of the Secretary of the Treasury under Franklin Roosevelt, Henry Morgenthau Junior, Mom came from a family of male dominance, where women had their proper place, and love had little meaning in a world of money, power, and politics. I don't suppose she emerged from a loving, emotionally nurturing family, or she might have transferred love to her own children.

17

Everything in her elegant and proper life existed at the expense of human vulnerability and loving-kindness.

As the children of an ambassador and a thirsty political Jew in a world where Jews and politics were planets of separate galaxies, the four Morgenthau children had many expectations placed upon them. No paternal appreciation was handed down to the youngest daughter, most of it having been spent on young Henry Junior, the only boy. Family history recounts my grandmother overhearing her father portray her as "the unwanted child."

Henry Morgenthau Senior was born in Mannheim, Germany, in 1856. His family moved to New York in 1866. He graduated from Columbia Law School and formed a law partnership with fellow classmates Samson Lachman and Abraham Goldsmith. He practiced real estate law and eventually became successful in real estate investments as well, making a fair amount of money purchasing property in the Bronx and Upper Manhattan and owning a small farm on 138th Street. They also owned a large summer home in Bar Harbor, Maine.

My dad wrote about his grandfather, "Wherever Grandpa took you it was exciting because he knew everybody. On my first airplane flight in about 1935, he took me to Newark Airport, which was about sixty by sixty feet and served all of New York City. By the time I got checked in, he had everybody in the airport talking to him."

Henry became passionate about politics, eventually donating a substantial sum of money to an early presidential campaign waged by Woodrow Wilson and then becoming Wilson's campaign committee chairman. After Wilson's election, Henry Morgenthau was overlooked for a cabinet position (indeed, no Jew received a cabinet position) and turned down Wilson's offer to become ambassador to Turkey. Later, he reconsidered. His presence in that region at that time proved more important to the preservation of the Jews than he had ever expected.

Though of German descent, my great-grandfather was leery of the German presence in Turkey, specifically their influence over the Turks, who were exterminating the Armenians as well as Jews. His force as the ambassador to Turkey became pivotal to eastern history. Ben-Gurion, the first prime minister of Israel, wrote:

"My friend J. Ben-Zvi and myself were the first to be imprisoned in Jerusalem, but, thanks to Morgenthau's strong personal intervention, we were merely 'expelled forever' from Palestine and Turkey instead of being hanged ... He stayed the Turkish dictator's (Jamal Pasha) hands ... In Beirut a number of Arab leaders were hanged and Jewish leaders would have shared their fate, had it not been for the intervention of the American ambassador ...."

Some time after the birth of the idolized son Henry Junior, Josephine, the wife of Henry Senior, and my grandmother's mother, was told to tend to the girls and leave the raising of Henry to his father. From then on, she slept in the maid's room and spent much of her time either being socially involved with parties and political functions or tending to their summer retreats in such places as Duchess County, Spring Lake, New Jersey, or Bar Harbor, Maine. When Henry's post called him to Turkey, she stayed in New York to tend to her youngest daughter's introduction to society. She and her husband both spent much time in public service and philanthropy. The most religious of my great-grandparents, Josephine donated much time to the Bronx House, a Jewish settlement primarily for immigrants.

When my great-grandfather died, Temple Emmanuel on Fifth Avenue was full. He had been a man of substantial wealth who fought for the rights of Jews at home and abroad.

He struggled to become esteemed in the political world, yet worked hard for Jewish dignity in America on many fronts. For the funeral, my father had to buy a new pair of shoes.

My grandmother traveled the globe many times; she visited her father in Turkey during his years as the ambassador. She began her education in a French boarding school at age five. She spoke fluent French, German, and Italian. Her knowledge and appreciation of the world's treasures ignited many conversations, and, when I was older and lived in New York, I loved listening to her rich stories of Chinese pagodas, opium dens, camel rides, the French Alps, Far Eastern beaches, and Egyptian tombs. Our lunches often culminated in a visit to her personal shopper at Saks Fifth Avenue or Bergdorf's, where she would buy me a handsome suit or finely tailored blouse. She was the only one in my life, really, who took time to teach me the finer points of elegant living rather than assuming I should know.

Ruth often stood between my father and me, as if she were protecting me from the pain of her own father. She had a way of making me feel as though I deserved the finest life, even if I didn't want the best for myself.

My grandmother never said good-bye on the phone. She hung up before you could wallow in clumsy endings. This upset almost everyone she knew and etched into her legacies. I soon styled my conversations with no expectations of a good-bye, so the element of surprise or disappointment was eliminated. I failed to see why this annoying practice was often the topic of conversation and a source of constant anger.

Though she spent time in her private pottery studio, she focused her main energy on charities, as did many intelligent women of prominent families. She aligned herself with the United Nations Women's Committee, a halfway house for schizophrenics called Fountain House, and the Manhattan School of Music. Later in her life, she created a children's summer theatre workshop for troubled kids near her home in

Pound Ridge. She was very involved in mental health. She took a mother-hen approach to the young and mentally disturbed—perhaps in an attempt to heal her own sadness.

Contrary to her profile of elegance, she divorced my grandfather in a time when divorce brought shame and blame among respectable families, and she then married a penniless Broadway actor, John Knight. This event strangled my father because of his strong allegiance to his father and his belief that the ultimate sin had been committed—adultery. Sadly, the romantic tale faded and she divorced John after he was diagnosed with cancer and she was unable to tolerate his convalescence. I only remember Mom after she divorced John Knight. She and my grandfather were divorced well before I was born.

I was in my early twenties when she called me on the phone for the last time. She asked me to fly to Barbados and spend a week with her. I should have known by her unusual request that something was wrong. I told her I couldn't get away from work on short notice, and that I had Christmas obligations—but I have never forgiven myself for not going. No one had told me she was sick. The next fall my father called and told me she lay in a nursing home, too old to recognize anyone and too feeble to talk. "She won't know who you are," my dad warned. "Don't waste your time going to see her." I hadn't known how quickly time passed for the dying.

I didn't believe him. Obsessed with having to see her again (living with the guilt that she might not have been so lonely if I had been less selfish and gone to Barbados), I flew to New York and drove through the countryside to see her. The nursing institution, empty and sterile compared to the elegance of her normal surroundings, backed up my apprehension with a cold, ominous fear. I walked cautiously down a long, white corridor, catching glimpses of ashen statues in wheelchairs and slow-moving wind-up toys wandering aimlessly through doorways.

The nurse showed me into a warm, sunny room alive with the colors of the surrounding autumn forest, but inside were barren white walls and antiseptic floors. My grandmother lay flat on her back underneath a starched white sheet, her strapped arms filled with IVs and tags and tapes. Her eyes stared straight into the ceiling; her mouth opened in a deadly spell. She had no teeth. She had no more life to live. I blurted out, "Hi, Mom," in spite of the fear ripping at my insides. What was I afraid of? I asked myself. Dad had warned me. "Better to remember her the way she was," he had told me with his usual abrupt answer to my lifelong questionings. I had pressed on in spite of him once again.

Minutes vanished into a time warp. I stared into this woman I loved, searching for the proud, determined woman in the one now reduced to a helpless, decrepit skeleton—and I hated life. I remembered the graces she tried to teach me. I remembered her standing up for me when my father pushed too hard, wanting to keep me from "being spoiled." Summoning strength, I gently took her bony fingers covered with a soft gossamer skin, into my hands. I hoped she couldn't feel my spastic nerves, as I spoke randomly about what I had been doing, my work, my loves. Then, challenging my father once again, I gently asked her if she knew who I was. She turned slowly to me and spoke in a determined muffled voice. "Of course I know who you are," she answered. "Judy, your life is just beginning and my life is finished. Now don't stay here. Go home. You have important things to do. You must go now and live your life." Another lesson taught, even in dying. She gave me a gift and I am grateful.

"I love you," I whispered to her, as I touched her soft, fallen cheek with my lips. Suddenly I wasn't afraid. I wanted to stay, but nothing else could be done. She had once again given strength to my life. She died of stomach cancer a few months later.

Her small, informal funeral, held in a church in Pound Ridge, New York, surprised me by its austerity, especially after the pomposity of my grandfather's. Her daughter attended only briefly, and many of my cousins were absent. I stared at the curtain as the minister spoke words of condolence and thanks to a generous, community-minded woman. The roar of the cremation growled behind a closed yellow curtain.

After the ceremony, the immediate family returned to Blue Herons for brunch. Spring leaves rustled their familiar sound as we sat on the screened porch looking out over the dark, still lake. Most of the conversation had little to do with my grandmother or her "depleted" estate. The avoidance of the pertinent was glaring to me. By the time we walked through the gardens to scatter her ashes, my father and my aunt had gone home. I watched as Uncle George awkwardly held the silver urn and mumbled a last farewell. My eyes filled with tears, as he spilled the dusty ashes over the flower gardens she had cultivated over the years of her life.

Suddenly, the wind lifted the last clump of ashes, as if in defiance of being put to rest, and covered our hair and clothes with a light chalky film. I heard gasps and coughs and the brushing of clothes. My eyes stung closed, as her ashes crawled deep inside my soul. I couldn't see anything for a minute. The words and sounds I heard were distorted. I rubbed and struggled to clear my eyes of the dusty invader, my grandmother, Ruth Knight. She got in though, and she must be here with me still.

# CHAPTER 4

### Do You Think the Rain Will Hurt the Rhubarb?

Over in the meadow,
In the sand in the sun,
Lived an old mother toad
And her little toadie one.
"Wink," said the mother;
"I wink," said the one;
So they winked and they blinked
In the sand in the sun.

**Olive A. Wadsworth**

My parents met in Colorado Springs, Colorado, in 1942. Mom was a sophomore at Colorado College, and Dad was in the army, stationed at Camp Carson. They went out on a blind date, though not together. The next day, being an army man with no time to waste, my father decided his buddy's date was far superior to his own, so he called my mom and asked her out. They went to the officers' club for steaks. Men were scarce in college during the war. Many men had been killed, leaving broken hearts and dreams behind. When my mother's mother got the gist of my father's background, she began the long campaign to woo my mother into the arms of the wealthy banker's son. My dad was a first-class catch.

I can envision the panic in my mother's throat after her first visit to Apple Bee Farm, when my dad came home on leave with his bride-to-be. The Tudor-style stone mansion, separate private homes for the children, and more hired help than Franklin Delano Roosevelt had, perhaps was not the farm my mother had envisioned as she drove down the narrow lane with a bump. No doubt Dad drove fast over that very same bump he took us flying over many times. She telephoned Gigi during the first moment of stolen privacy. "Mom, I think I'm in over my head," she quivered long-distance.

"What in heaven's name do you mean?" my grand-mother scolded.

"You should see this house. There are a zillion servants, chauffeurs and limousines, and an Olympic-sized swimming pool, and, Mother, I don't think I can do this." My mother, though raised in some wealth and comfort as well, recalled being clearly overwhelmed by my father's world.

"Oh for heaven's sake, Dorothy, you'll learn to love it," my grandmother, more readily adaptable to such hardships, assured her daughter. Gigi had trouble understanding how my mother could have any doubts about my father at all.

After the war, my parents bought a modest farm in Dublin, Pennsylvania, and then moved to Doylestown just before I was born. The dairy farm swaddled me in a rich and textured childhood very few have the privilege of experiencing in today's world. We—my mom, dad, two brothers and I—lived on acres and acres of lush Pennsylvania lands, nurturing in their touch, with views that sprawled across the peaceful valley. There were few sounds of traffic, no tall buildings—only horizons. Today, bulging populations and greedy land developers swell through the shrinking countryside of America, keeping pace with frenetic urban progress, mowing down miles of thick green forests for the sake of generic shopping malls, condominiums, and destination resorts. Twenty years after I was born, my dairy farm fell to a dense development; hundreds of suburban homes and well-kept lawns sprouted where great wheat fields once shifted with the wind; hundreds of two-car garages replaced hay bales piled high in our majestic red barn; and rows of rubber-stamped roofs obliterated acres of golden wheat and alfalfa fields. I had no sense of the encroaching time when I was I child. Each moment was my existence. The future had no place in my private world.

I also had no sense of wealth, living on the farm, except when we visited my paternal grandparents. Yet I was among the privileged youth, because my family never had to worry about greedy bankers, bad crops, or where my next pair of shoes would come from. (Having a great love of naked toes, this would not have handicapped me.) I knew we were always warm and well fed, clothed, and sent off to school with all the other kids in the neighborhood. As my father's trust funds grew quietly behind the scene, so did the acreage around our modest farm, until we owned over three hundred and fifty acres, three entire farm complexes, over one hundred dairy cows and breeding bulls, over two thousand pigs and piglets, a handful of high-strung chestnut thoroughbreds, dogs, cats, and a few chickens—which usually ended up malnourished or running beheaded in circles before too long.

My father, though fairly unconcerned with childbirth or childrearing, had great passion for his farm. He graduated from Ohio State University with a degree in agriculture, which, I presume, rattled the wealthy Jewish family that nurtured him through expensive boarding schools and the finest tutors money could buy in hopes of producing a doctor or lawyer or, ideally, a banker like his father or an ambassador like his grandfather. My dad was most at home lifting bales of hay onto a lumbering flatbed trailer, fine-tuning his state-of-the-art milking barn, or calling the cows in by cupping his hands to his mouth, "Suu-eeeet, suu-eeet, su-su-eeet" as the sun slid magically behind the western woods. He grinned as he poured fresh milk into the metal pasteurizer on our kitchen counter at the end of the day. My dad lived a life of milk, manure, and fox hunting.

My earliest memory of life is an instant, lying in a crib on my back, squinting out the window at the bright white light of the sky, listening to my mother's voice carrying on without benefit of an answer. The occasional rustling of turning pages accompanied her monologue, as she read aloud the wonders of Barrie's *Peter Pan*, or Carroll's *Alice in Wonderland*, or maybe a selection from Olive Beaupre Miller's *My Book House*. I couldn't feel my mother. I could only feel the cool sheets under my arms and fingertips and the velvet vibrations of her voice, until I drifted off to sleep. I am uncertain why I remember this time in infancy, a moment not yet developed from intellectual connections or knowledge of life. The memory is steadfast in my bank and always has been.

Beneath my nursery window, I learned later, was an opulent garden, filled with peonies—giant pink and red puffballs reaching higher than my hair ribbons, cultured in part by my mother, with the assistance of ripe mounds of warm cow manure from the barns. There were acres of grassy lawns to roll on, long drooping willow branches to swing and charge through, giant oaks and maples to climb. There was a lake, a springhouse, barns, pastures, and vast woods to secretly explore. We had a perfectly wonderful swing set, on which Mom pushed me until one day she convinced me I could pump all by myself. Then I pumped so high my feet reached over my head and touched the soft cotton clouds, my stomach left in the grass below. I reached higher and higher. My bottom would go over the top of the highest bar until the chains of my swing would become slack, and a fearful thrill would fill me up. This was one of many personal goals I set for myself, secretly, just to succeed.

I grew up after the turmoil of World War II had subsided and during the blossoming reconstruction of lifestyles and economy. The average annual income in 1948 was $2,936, nearly triple the prewar average, and demand for consumer goods rose aggressively. The average price of a new home was $7,700, and a car cost $1,200. Shopping gradually became a fulfillment of pleasures, replacing the stark war-time habits of the American family when most of their hard earned dollars were spent on necessities. New gadgets, such as televisions, dishwashers, and electric stoves, flooded markets at staggering rates. Thanks to the GI Bill of Rights, war vets took advantage of academic scholarships and graduated comfortably into the country's growing work force.

America became historically prosperous. Families and lovers, united after the war, gave birth to the largest number of babies in history, collectively called the baby boomers. I, of course, am a baby boomer. I didn't particularly like being a baby boomer, but I wasn't asked. Sociologists, scientists, and reporters followed my every move in unison with thousands of others for a lifetime. I became part of an entire generation burped, bottle-fed, and spanked according to Dr. Spock, vaccinated against polio according to Dr. Salk, and glued to the Mickey Mouse Club, thanks to a cartoonist named Walt Disney. My entire generation made history every time we collectively took a step, drank from a cup, went off to first grade, dodged the draft, smoked a joint, bought a car, married, or didn't marry. Any sense of individuality was doomed if you were born in 1948.

American farmers continued to benefit from the high war prices of cattle, grains, and cotton. Our farm fulfilled my father's life purpose and sense of sport and personal accomplishment more than becoming a national farming statistic did. He loved experimenting with special dairy cow breeds, crossing the finest registered Ayrshires and Herefords and rotating his fields with wheat, corn, and alfalfa. I don't think for a minute the clothes on our backs or the food in our mouths came solely from the sale of milk or hay, but I had no sense of that then. Life remained simple, daily, and adventurous. Though warm, steamy summers meant busy days of mowing fields, baling hay and endless jugs of lemonade for migrant workers, I don't believe my father's wealth came from the size of the load.

We lived on Cold Spring Creamery Road, outside a small town called Doylestown, across the street from the Millers who owned a sprawling horse farm, where fox hunting was the main priority, and dressage the second. My dad loved the formality of the foxhunt and always kept several thoroughbreds for this purpose. He and Mr. Miller had both attended Culver Military Academy. They were both members of the Huntington Valley Hunt Club. Every year Dad traveled to Ireland for the hunt. He stayed with the Craigies, whom I never met, but he always came home with tales of the hunt.

Cold Spring Creamery Road was not an extremely wealthy area. On the contrary, my dad seemed uncomfortable around too much wealth. He preferred the reputation of living amongst chicken farmers, pig farmers, and dirt movers, hob-knobbing with 4-H'ers. At the same time, he maintained major status with the Huntington Valley Hunt Club.

Vivid memories of the farm are still the backdrop of last night's dreams, scenes fading in and out of an endless movie. I laugh unashamedly in my sleep, while running shirtless between rows of long-limbed corn, or watching a giant arc of irrigation spray shimmer in the wilting sunshine, or smelling the pungency of fresh cow manure spread over greening summer fields. I can still relive the freedom I felt galloping my pinto pony, Dinky, bareback through the wheat fields of late summer, feeling the coarse horsehair dampening between my thighs. I remember my mother making homemade jelly, hanging white pillowcases stained purple from the bulging handpicked grapes. Juices dripped for days into buckets placed carefully on the worn wooden dining room floor.

In September, as the sun came up over the golden hills and the morning air nipped our noses, my older brother and

I sometimes woke with the milking of the cows, saddled our horses in the dark, and joined the Millers to go cubbing, a fox-hunting ritual performed to strengthen the hounds before the formal season began. Though I constantly battled the doldrums of early morning, this was one of my favorite things. During cubbing, young pups were trained to follow the scent of a fox, and the elders strengthened their legs. Hundreds of beagles yelped and sniffed through the countryside, as we cantered gently over the dew-covered hills through the thinning greens of fall. I didn't have to wear scratchy jodhpurs or a tight riding helmet or canter at a thundering pace with multitudes pushing past each other for the proper positions during the formal foxhunt. When we ran the hounds, we never killed the fox. The final act was saved for the hunt, if they were lucky.

On Christmas mornings, toy-stuffed stockings hung from the old rock fireplace in the dining room, tormenting my brothers and me as we laboriously chewed wads of gooey oatmeal soaked with fresh milk and brown sugar. Once the stockings were opened, we were ushered blindfolded into a giant room full of toys, games, bicycles, records, tents, stuffed animals, and our hearts' greatest wishes; Santa's "Supermarket Sweepstakes."

We lived in a four-bedroom, four-floor, two hundred-year-old stone farmhouse, dampened by years of history lived long before our presence. After my stay in the nursery ended and Gory, my nurse, moved on to other babies in other towns, I took up residence in my own special bedroom at the top of the oak-banister staircase in the front hall next to my parents' room. Two single beds piled high with stuffed animals, a mirror-covered vanity adorned with white chiffon ruffles, a view of the lake through a friendly fat walnut tree outside my three windows, and the security of my parents next door made this an ideal room for a growing girl. Here I could hide in my world of paint-by-numbers and hollow plastic model horses.

Here I lay among my animals, sucked my thumb, perfecting the art of daydreaming and being alone.

One of my best days growing up was the day Mom and Dad brought home a little baby brother, all pink and squishy. I was almost four. My little fingers wiggled with desire to hold my new friend. I ran to the couch as instructed, my bottom pressing snug up against the back and my feet sticking out over the edge, just so I could hold the Johnson-and-Johnson's-powdered bundle in my lap and cradle him like a doll until he fussed and grew so heavy my legs and arms pricked with needles. My older brother, Steve, I am certain, never grew as fond of me as I did of baby Flip.

Steve and Flip shared the old nursery for most of our years growing up. Wallpapered with cowboys chasing cattle and bucking broncos kicking up dust, their room came alive with erector sets, Lincoln Log cabins, and plastic farm sets with little animal statues and interlocking fences. A tireless hamster ran endlessly inside a spinning tin wheel in a small glass cage, until, eventually, the hamster miraculously escaped into the walls and never appeared again. There were miniature cowboys and Indians, soldiers, forts and fences, and little plastic scuba divers we could put baking soda in to make bubbles in the bathtub. People could say we had everything we ever wanted.

When Steve was about eight, the attic was remodeled into a living complex for adolescent privacy. He had his own room and bathroom, though low-slanting ceilings invaded much of his space. His room had one tiny cramped window facing east. My father, a safety aficionado, conducted regular fire drills, instructing each of us to lower ourselves down to the ground on a little canvas seat attached to the window sill by a thick rope pulley. Dangling from the third-story window was a cross between a ride on a Ferris wheel and a tedious lifesaving exercise. Fortunately, we never experienced the real thing, though my dad treated each drill as potentially life-threatening, and there was no fooling around.

On the second floor, down the narrow creaking wooden hall from Flip's room, past the bathroom where Steve once started a fire in the clothes hamper, lived Lily, the "colored" maid. Her room smelled a little different than the rest of the house. She always had the ironing board with a spray can of starch set up in the middle of the braided rug in preparation for the next load of laundry. A few flower-printed dresses with starched white lace collars hung neatly pressed in her closet, carefully spaced. Once I snooped around when she went home for the weekend, searching for a special secret she might have hidden inside her private life, but I never found anything. She was just Lily. Her hair curled as tight as a newborn's fist, and her nose lay flat as a lizard in the sun. Hugging Lily was different than hugging my mom. As I placed my head against her skin, she felt cold and dark, like the smooth surface of the lake. I could smell the stiffness of her collar. My mom was warm and soft and textured, but Lily felt good just the same. I was always glad she was just there.

On the main floor, there was a living room, den, dining room, kitchen and pantry area, and a sunny little room for my father's office. He had a large oak desk with a brown leather-trimmed blotter and a gold-plated plaque with Lieutenant Philip Naumburg engraved on it from World War II. He also displayed a Purple Heart on a bookshelf and proudly explained he got his "ass shot off" while fighting Germans in the deep, damp trenches of France. Whenever he talked about the war, he launched into a litany of complaints, describing in flippant detail every foxhole, every lousy meal, every stinking cold night. He taught us popular war songs, "I like to go swimming with bow-legged women ..." but he always acted as if the war were now a joke. Whenever you came near his feelings, he dodged them coldly, claiming he had no memory of fear or loneliness. I felt maybe he did, but he didn't share. My father had a heart like coarse sandpaper.

The most exciting thing about the kitchen for me hid on the top shelf of the white metallic 1950s style cabinets with silver handles—cookies!: chocolate covered Marshmallows, Fig Newtons, and yummy Oreos, which you carefully twisted apart before slowly licking out the creamy white filling and smashing the chocolate wafers back together and stuffing them between your tongue and the roof of your mouth. Baby boomers collectively perfected this maneuver. My mother deliberately stashed all cookies up high, so little snooping fingers couldn't overindulge in sweets, which is exactly what I spent most of my childhood trying to do—another goal, reaching for another success. Every year I grew more determined and gained more ground. First I climbed onto a chair, so I could reach the counter. Then I stood on the counter, and, finally, when I reached the top shelf, with size and expertise at last on my side, I succeeded in maneuvering around the open cupboard while standing on the counter (without crashing onto the cold linoleum floor). My fingers closed around stacks of the crinkled packages. Holding my breath deep into my soul, I prayed I could eat them before hearing enemy footsteps. Cookies in the trenches.

In the beginning, my brothers and I went to public school. We played with the kids in the neighborhood and kids from school. There were birthday parties, piano and swimming lessons, summer camp, babysitters, and peanut butter and jelly sandwiches. Life seemed sort of normal—like TV, the next-door neighbors, and *My Three Sons*. I'm not exactly sure just what went wrong. In 1948, the year I was born, Life Magazine cost twenty cents, a telephone call cost a nickel, and a gallon of milk eighty-seven cents. There were no personal computers, no microwave ovens, Nintendo, nor cell phones. Automatic washing machines were a novelty, and Americans were grateful for the end of war. The population of the United States was one hundred fifty million. Almost five hundred thousand couples expected to be divorced in the year ahead.

I longed to be eternally happy feeling nature's spring grass under my bare feet, bursting through clouds of crispy fall leaves, or oozing cool mud through my toes on the banks of the lake during summer's heat. I did not want my childhood to end. I wonder if my father and mother remember the wonders of my youth, or perhaps I remain lost inside a child's timeless fantasy. My self-contained happiness should have been the insurance of a gentle life, but seeds of dissatisfaction can grow in any soil.

# CHAPTER 5

### The House by the Sea

Rich man,
Poor man,
Beggar man, thief,
Doctor, lawyer,
Indian chief.

**Jump-rope rhyme**

My mother was simply beautiful. She wore her long, silky, blond hair carefully pulled away from her face in a formal French twist or happy ponytail. Her eyes, ocean blue and deep in thought, were never afraid of mine. Though she had the body of Venus, she was at home digging in the garden, working with Dad in the fields, or de-boning the sunfish we proudly caught from the pond. I remember watching her sit in front of her mirrored vanity, brushing thick, black mascara onto her eyelashes with a tiny brush, gently squeezing them in an upward direction with a pink-handled eyelash curler. The lights around the mirror danced in her eyes. My mother was Grace Kelly or Ingrid Bergman. She dreamed of a house full of kids, and I thought she was happy.

Mom was a very hard worker, driving tractors, pulling flatbeds, milking cows—whatever was needed—as well as raising three kids. Most nights she sat on the couch, while we watched TV, and knit us sweaters—and all the cousins, too.

When she dropped a stitch or had to rip out a row, she always swore. She was president of the League of Women Voters and involved in local mental-health organizations.

Oscar Hammerstein lived nearby and owned a herd of purebred Angus. His foreman called one day to ask my dad about moving some cattle from Towanda, so Dad gave him a price of $150, which he thought was fair. When he told Mom, she jumped up and down, saying "Dummy, why didn't you ask him for tickets to My Fair Lady?" According to Dad, the tickets were like hen's teeth and $100 a pop, if you could find them, but by the time he got on the phone and called back, the foreman had made other arrangements.

Few stories trickled down about my mother's ancestors. No books were written about them or personal diaries published. There were no newspaper articles printed about the Sellners as there were about my dad's side. They were a quiet, proud family, with a rich colorful history of their own, though a bit less illustrious.

My mother's father, Harry Sellner, died of a heart attack when I was very young. I have no memory of him, except for a grainy, early color photograph in my mother's album; I was about six months old, dolled up in a little white dress with a full crinoline underneath, and my brother held a shiny red and green dump truck. We were posed with my grandmother and grandfather and mom in front of a Christmas tree. My grandfather had bright red photo-flashed eyes and no hair. He had a kind face, or so I thought. Both grandparents held a long overdue smile, the kind most family portraits have, from posing too long. No one knew he would be dead in less than a year.

My grandfather was the son of Rachel Stahl, age eighteen, from Elmira, New York, and her sweetheart (or husband) Jacob Cohen, age thirty, who reportedly died of tuberculosis shortly after my grandfather was born. This story has changed continually throughout my lifetime, leaving cause for wondering. Rachel very quickly remarried another older man named Henry Sellner. Little Harry took his name.

Harry Sellner was an industrious boy, who worked for Jersey Central Power and Light to help support his family while attending night school. He grew into a dedicated and focused man, eventually taking over a failing family clothing business, and then parlaying it into a twelve-store clothing chain on the East coast, called Carlton Clothiers. He met my grandmother, Florence Carolyn Bennett, when she was twenty-two and had left home to escape a raving, abusive stepmother. Her own mother had died when my grandmother was only nine. Her father then married his widowed sister-in-law—a web of intrigue woven in Newark, New Jersey.

By the time my mother was born, on December 23, 1923, in South Orange, New Jersey, Harry and Florence Sellner enjoyed an affluent lifestyle. My grandfather had mastered the clothing business. Full-time help, nannies, private schools, and dapper clothes were *ordinaire* for my mom and her brother, John Carlton Sellner. Mom described her dad as aggressive and hot-tempered. Though he was never physically abusive, my mom lived in fear of his anger. My grandmother never acknowledged anything was wrong, nor did she challenge him. She clung to my grandfather in spite of his temper, as if he were life's breath and stepping away even for a moment would bring certain death. My grandmother pruned her lips and stayed very much to herself, being more occupied with her own well-being than the children's. As in my father's world, there was plenty of help to raise the children.

After the crash of 1929, the Sellners lost everything. The Great Depression choked my grandfather's businesses, because millions of men could no longer afford nice clothes or even new clothes. My mother's young life became filled with uncertainty, despite my grandmother's attempt to portray it otherwise. My grandfather's pride prohibited him from declaring bankruptcy, so he put off his debtors and eventually found a job in the shoe department at the May Company in St. Louis, Missouri. From there, he sent checks home to support his family and slowly began paying his debts. According to my mother, my grandfather did everything he could to try and maintain a lavish, yet pared-down lifestyle at home. Several years later, he moved to Denver, family in tow, after securing a promotion as a men's clothing buyer with the May Company. Fifteen years after the crash, his debts were paid without his having to borrow a dime.

Mom spent most of her growing up in Denver, no longer in private schools and country clubs, yet comfortable just the same. After my parents married, my grandmother moved back to New Jersey. Gigi (so called because my brother couldn't pronounce grandmother) saw to it that her hardships were never great. She always had a well-kept home and surrounded herself with her original fineries and elegant-looking substitutes at simple costs. Gigi played bridge and kept individually wrapped hard candies in her purse and in a tinted amber glass jar at home. She had a martini every night before supper and, as far as I know, never worked a day in her life and probably never so much as cleaned the house, even when times were tough. She was very much a part of my growing up, arriving often at the farm in her sleek white Cadillac, with long red fingernails, and perfectly coiffed bleached hair. She had a tiny little mouth, which rounded into a circle and cooed when she saw us.

Mom describes her mother as a gentle, loving, social gadfly. I remember her as a woman of little movement. She never ran, jumped, or even moved quickly; never laughed wildly, pounded her fist, never threw a fit or football. She occasionally walked the breaststroke in the swimming pool at her home, carefully so her hair stayed dry, her mammoth watermelon breasts floating up beneath her chin. The most animated I ever remember her being, was the day my two brothers built a sand fort on top of her brand new white Cadillac, carefully parked inside our small garage to protect the paint from the harsh glare of the sun. After my mom alerted her to the problem, Gigi wriggled like Houdini chained inside a water tank, visibly seeking a way to vent her anger, but obviously unable to, until my father stepped in and relieved her seething emotions. (My father loved to rescue my grandmother. They were great friends.) Luckily, my bottom escaped the consequences that time but my brothers' bottoms did not.

On one occasion, Gigi and my mother were sipping tea in the den when my grandmother remarked how good and patient my older brother Steve was. He was playing with his Lionel train set, sprawled over two six-by-ten-foot plywood sheets in the basement. Steve spent hours assembling, moving, fixing, cars, engines, bridges, track, transformer, trees, buildings. Once he threw an engine at the farmhand's little girl and sliced her eye open. This time, he pushed the entire table crashing to the floor yelling, "goddamn, son-of-a-bitch!" My grandmother moved stiffly in her chair, shifting her eyes skyward, and then pursed her lips into her customary tiny circle. The story held an infamous position in the family's archives and came up whenever we talked about how patient my brother was. After my grandmother died at age ninety-six, Mom put some of her ashes in a metal box on the dresser so she could take her out to lunch on occasion.

When I was eight, my grandmother bought an eleven-bedroom Victorian house in Mammoth Beach, New Jersey, that had once belonged to a well-known financier and friend of the Morgenthaus', named Bernard Baruch. And so we began summers at the shore. The massive house faced the ocean, defiant against the powerful Atlantic waves. The soft white sand and deep blue salt water contrasted with the green Pennsylvania farmlands we left behind. Perhaps the contrast bled new life into my mother, or perhaps she sought only to escape my father who detested the beach and sun and generally stayed home to work the farm. Occasionally he came up on the weekends, but summers were different now. Freer. We escaped my dad's intensities, and, the best part for me was I didn't have to go off to Camp Kinnikinik.

Summers now meant burying ourselves in hot sand, eating fresh boiled lobsters and corn on the cob, licking mounds of soft frozen ice cream before the sun stole them from our cones. I remember rainy days, shushing parents, and giggling children packing into tiny spaces hidden in the gigantic house for a game of "sardines." Monopoly, Sorry, canasta, and Clue left little wanting for sunshine.

Two or three times during our summer we drove to Asbury Park, escaping into the perfect world of amusement parks. To twirl, spin, or whip until your laughter became uncontrollable, your surroundings blurred into oblivion, was to touch the essence of freedom. I never wanted to leave. I wanted to grow up in the neon lights and meet every challenge. I wanted to stay until I was old enough to ride the roller coaster, tall enough to try the Wildcat. I wanted to eat every cotton candy and win every stuffed animal. I watched my little brother silently study the spinning Wheel of Chance until he decoded the number sequences. Then he would run to my mom, beg a quarter, and win a stuffed animal.

There were two merry-go-rounds. A newer carousel commanded center stage bordering Asbury Lake. Beautiful hand-painted horses pranced in a glittering parade, pink, purple, and yellow plumes fluttering in the wind. Inside, next to the carnival booths and Skeet Ball, was the smaller, older, and faster merry-go-round. The horses had been around a billion times, worn wood showed through where the paint had chipped or rubbed away. My mom chose this carousel because there were brass rings, unlike the new one. If you grabbed the polished ring, you won a free ride. The first year, my eight-year-old arms struggled to reach the ring holder. My excitement inevitably faded inside my frustration, when I was only able to grab one dull ring every two or three times around. I wanted to ride the merry-go-round just like my mom.

Around and around the swift-moving horse carried her. She stood upright in the stirrups of a proud, pulsing horse, her blond ponytail blowing, her face feeling the perfection of the wind. As she neared the ring dispenser, she leaned out beyond the carousel, her left hand tight on the pole secured to the horse's back, arm stretched full length while her right hand extended into the night. As she reached the ring holder, her fingers curled like a magician wielding a silver dollar, sometimes hooking three or even four rings in each of her fingers. Most people could only grab one at a time. Mom examined her catch absently, then tossed the rings high into the collection bin, riding the rest of the way around with her hand on her hip. Finally, when a vibrant golden ring appeared in her palm, she raised it high in the air, smiling, her eyes shining with a peaceful, satisfied feeling I longed for.

My mother's brother, Uncle Jack, a low-income, bigoted Yul Brenner (tall, bald, and arrogant) hated cops, "niggers," and kids (though he had two of his own). He and my mom were very close. She laughed a lot when he was around, and they spoke a secret language called Libey Dibey. It was similar to Pig Latin, but had a more complex way of messing up the words. We were all well versed in Pig Latin, but we never solved the mystery of Libey Dibey. This was a part of her summer freedom.

Uncle Jack terrified us kids with his full-moon bedtime horror stories. The worst was "The Monkey's Paw." Late at night, he would gather my two cousins and the three of us onto his bed overlooking the dark ocean and wouldn't begin until we were deathly silent and still. The vision of a beloved son all dripping with blood at the front door, popped eyes dangling from their sockets, arm cut off and throat severed still sends a shiver through my memories. We weren't smart enough to leave, and one of us usually went screaming downstairs to the lap of a parent before he was through.

A public pavilion neighbored our house, supplying us with fresh friends, beach volleyball, dances, and handsome young lifeguards slathered with Sea 'n Ski. We ran to Mom (most things we did were at full pace) and begged nickels to buy frozen Milky Ways, trying not to lose money down the wooden slats into the sand. My brother Steve crawled on the sandy floors, peeking under dressing-stall doors. When our babysitter, who came with us for the summer, flirted with the lifeguards, we spied on her, hoping to catch a kiss.

On days when the clouds cast a cool shadow, we swam and built sandcastles with little regard for impending rain. One such day, late in August, the pavilion closed. Hurricane winds threatened. I was nine. A big sign hung on the lifeguard chair: "Swimming Prohibited, Beach Closed." The ocean swelled and thrashed angrily, reclaiming portions of sandy beach with each approach. Frank and Gene, lifeguards who worked at the pavilion next door, welcomed the challenge of the massive waves and had no trouble convincing my mom to join them body surfing. Her athletic body, combined with her determination, was almost equal to the raw male power of Frank and Gene. Together they swam resolute with the crest of every carefully chosen wave, bodies strong and arched, heads barely visible, perched on the foamy rim of the wave as it carried them to shore. Once again, I watched as my mom glowed while riding the waves. I could feel her determination and pride when the wave eventually delivered her softly onto the shore.

Steve and I stood watching at the edge of the driving sea. He wanted to swim too, but neither of us was allowed. He paced back and forth like a cormorant, darting in and out of the waves. At one point, my mom yelled at him to back away from the water. She knew he wanted to ride. He felt the pull of the sea and wanted to be with the big boys. I dug my toes into the softened sand, tiny sand crabs tickling my feet, content to stay on the shore. With each wave, my feet sank deeper, until they were covered with smooth sand. The tide still came in. I knew I had to grow a lot bigger before I could ride the big waves. I wiggled my toes and watched as they broke up the sand after each wave. The mist tickled my nose. I reached up for a scratch, when suddenly I felt the water rise around my knees, pulling them forward until they buckled. As I fell hard into the sand, the current reached deep around my legs and dragged me into a whirling eddy.

Around and around I spun, head thrashing against the now unbreakable sand. Salt water rushed into my nose and mouth. I held my mouth tight and grabbed desperately for the earth slipping through my fingers, offering no assistance. My lungs exploded with fear, trapping the last bit of air, but I knew if I exhaled, I would die.

Over and over I turned. My chest pounded. My muscles crackled. I reached for something to hold onto, a way to stop tumbling, but the pain of urgency became too intense, and helplessness overtook my will. I gave up and lost consciousness. The current then cradled my weightless body and together we drifted out to sea, the current and I, past the empty lifeguard stand, beyond the long rock jetty, out into a more peaceful, timeless ocean. The sky was no longer dark, the sea no longer angry. I stared at the piercing white light above, the same white light as over my crib years ago, but I no longer could feel the water. I closed my eyes and drifted away. Only now can I imagine the pain in my mother's heart when Frank pushed her violently onto the shore and yelled above the thrashing waves: "I can't save you both, for Christ's sake, Dorothy! Get back there, and don't move!"

Gene gripped Mom and Steve against his dripping body as they watched Frank disappear into the water. Though only fifteen, Frank's full-grown body, perfect and powerful because of steroids and pumping iron, coursed through the salt water as strong as any man. The three of them watched and waited from the beach for over an hour.

The next thing I remembered was a giant hairy arm, choking me, trying to strangle me. I gagged and struggled, then heard his familiar voice, "Judy, don't fight me. Relax. Just float." I heard his breathing and felt his fear and I wanted to fight, but the more I struggled, the tighter he gripped his arm around my chest until I couldn't breathe. I tried to push his arm away. *He's going to kill me*, I thought. *I'm going to die.* Again he scolded sternly, "Judy, stop. You have to float." I drifted in and out of consciousness, focusing only on the sky and the course hair on his arm as he guided my numb, tired body to shore in a steady rhythm of pull, pull, pull.

When I awoke, I shivered with a cold, penetrating chill. My body lay heavy on the sand, no longer weightlessly suspended on the moving sea. My legs were stiff. I heard voices. Someone put heavy blankets on top of me, and once again I couldn't breathe. I slowly focused on my mother, leaning next to me. A smile came over her ashen lips. I looked into her eyes to see if she was okay and took a labored breath. Then she pulled me into the warmth of her arms until I tasted the salt of her tears. I touched her arm but winced from the pain of the wrinkles on my fingertips.

The legendary rescue, the most difficult for a long time, turned Frank into a local hero. They said I was pulled out over a mile, and it took him over an hour to bring me in. Later that fall, the same waves fueled by determined hurricane winds, claimed my grandmother's house by the sea, board by board, standing defiant, yet eventually falling in defeat. At nine years old, I had no way of knowing that more of my world had washed away than the house by the sea and me.

# CHAPTER 6

### Dance with Strangers

Mary, Mary,
Quite contrary.
How does your garden grow?
With silver bells and cockle shells,
And pretty maids, all in a row.

**Mother Goose**

In the beginning, I wanted to be a boy. Born into a boy's world with two brothers, I grew increasingly intimidated, yet challenged, by their world. Girls were frailer, weaker, slower, scaredy-cats. Girls giggled too much, played with dumb dolls, and put ribbons in their hair. I wore dresses and crinolines and put ribbons in my braids on special occasions, but mostly I wanted to play baseball and ice hockey, ride bikes, and build hay forts. I wanted to be better than my brothers in everything. The more I understood the difference between boys and girls, the more I wanted simply to be a boy. Boys were the hope of the future, the bankers, the doctors, the lawyers. Boys were the pride of the family, the link to further generations. The most anyone expected out of me was a good rich husband. There were moments I understood being different from boys, and these times, of course, prevailed over the years.

I primarily wanted to be better than my brother Steve. As fast as a racecar, intent as a mole, my brother was "all boy." The only way to catch him was to outfox him, but I spent most of my childhood as his victim. How do you explain the madness of a full-throttle brother? His torture took any convenient form. Several times he was punished for his abuse: when he jumped out of the bushes, frightening my horse, Dinky, who then threw me soaring through the air and hard to the ground, knocking the wind out of me; or when he actually beat down my bedroom door while my parents were in Europe with my grandmother Ruth. I thought I was safe behind a locked door with bedcovers pulled over my head, but neither stopped the raging lunatic from pummeling the wooden door into splinters, then relentlessly jumping up and down on me until the babysitter came to the rescue. No, I don't think I was rescued from my brother, ever, but we were very close. We had to be. We were playmates, competitors, cohorts, and confidants. We were there when everyone went home, going through the same times, reacting to them in our own special ways. The older we grew, the smarter I got, and the less of a victim I became, but my young life was heavily influenced by my crazy brother Steve.

Everyone has a sexual history, and I was no exception. My sexual life basically had three roots: what my parents taught me, what I learned for myself, and what my older brother thrust upon me. The latter, of course was the most twisted and persistent from the minute I was born. He understood the sweet concrete difference between boys and girls long before I did. Steve never for a moment wanted to be a girl, of that I am most certain.

Mom shared openly and honestly about boys and girls and sex, discussing problems and questions as they arose instead of the crash course Dad tried. Dad did the well-thought-out sit-on-the-couch-and-shut-up approach, with the assistance of some clinical Kinsey opus spread out on his lap. I remember the nights he read dispassionately, never pausing to clarify or allow questions. I couldn't comprehend his vacant grownup words: fallopian tubes, testes, coitus, impregnation, and so on. Relating these words to my life was like setting up housekeeping on Mars, yet I knew from everything he didn't say that this was a world I would one day understand. I, of course, set out to explore on my own at the earliest provocation.

My first semi-sexual experience came when I was about five or six years old. The play began innocently enough, I thought, down in the old neglected springhouse. Floor-to-ceiling screened panels portrayed a Pissarro-like dotted visage of pastures, lakes, and woods beyond. A large wooden plank covered an old spring or abandoned well. A thin coating of dust covered everything: the floor, the wooden panels, every tiny metal square on the screens. Outside, the constant summer buzz of the dog-day cicadas swelled into an explosive crescendo, then ebbed back into the heat. The males vibrated their stomachs in warning—or were they mating? I hated the cicadas, with their sinister bug eyes and their haunting screams incessantly driving razors through my ears. Steve gleefully pried their ugly empty shells from deep in the tree bark and ran after me in full attack mode. I was afraid the casing would enter my soul and their screams would explode inside me. They didn't stay around for long, but their shells remained embedded in the bark, and their memory remained embedded in my brain. Scaredy cat. Scaredy cat. Siddy is a scaredy cat.

On this day, Steve and I and the next-door neighbor, Butch, were blowing blades of grass stretched in between our thumbs, wondering what to do in the heat. "Hey, I got an idea," blurted my brother in his usual administrative way. "You try to walk across this plank (poor Wendy on Captain Hook's ship) without making a squeak. If it squeaks, you have to, uh, kiss Butchie. Yeah."

"Kiss Butchie?" *Yuck*, I thought to myself.

"Yeah, either that, or we'll push you down the well," threatened Steve, coming toward me with palms flexed, eyes guarding against my contemplated escape. There were two of them, one of me. The odds weren't great. If only I were a boy.

"Come on, I dare ya." I saw them look at each other and exchange boy grins. "Chicken." I felt moisture from the heat on my forehead.

Surprisingly, what surfaced then was a bold challenge to his dare. I could do it. I knew I could. I wouldn't make a sound. *Yuck. Kiss that bristle-haired nincompoop? No way.* And so I began.

My heel touched gently down, then my toes, across the board, watching every step, slowly. The cicadas began their chorus, pulsing inside my brain. I stopped to take a deep breath and could feel the board wanting to give way under my hesitation. My look shifted. Steve sneered silently in anticipation. Captain Hook. Tick, tock. I couldn't go back. Tick, tock. I kept on. *Almost there,* I thought to myself, when suddenly a defiant tiny creak escaped under my feet. I gulped as my brother jumped up with an agitating glee. "I heard it, I heard it," he jeered. *Creep.* Butchie smiled. He didn't move. This contest was about Steve and me. We all knew it. Girls lose.

Downtrodden and painfully aware of the consequences I had invoked, I silently walked over to Butch. He was quite a bit taller than me, and older, around ten, I think. He wore sandy hair cropped short and always stood very erect. I never, ever, thought I would have to kiss this guy, but here I stood, fists clenched. "Kiss him," nudged my brother.

I closed my eyes, but when Butchie's image returned in the dark I squeezed my teeth. My whole body stood bravely, with curiosity and fear, waiting for my first boy-kiss. After an eternity, I felt his two strips of flesh touch mine, but then felt my mouth relax, and much to my surprise, a tingle brushed the skin on my arms. When I realized this awful, yucky punishment actually felt good, I ran up the hill and raced into my bedroom sanctuary.

Another small part of the ongoing education began after my brother received a Brownie camera and darkroom equipment for Christmas. Into the windowless room in the dank, haunting basement, next to his Lionel train set and his chemistry lab, went his newly acquired hobby. He began his career photographing trees, cows, people, toys, rooms, trains, and clouds, then proudly developing and displaying them for my parents' approval.

Then real boredom set in. Three hundred acres of farmland was not enough for my brother. The time came to move on toward the more stirring object of my vagina. A photograph of this poor, hairless *thing* I myself had tried to inspect through contortions with a mirror was what he was after. All this idolatry was very dull to me, frankly. My brother saw some artistic merit down there that I failed to see. We watched together as the image slowly evolved in a white plastic tray full of chemicals, each naked fold rising up in all its splendor. He did not submit these to my parents for their approval.

Simultaneously, Steve started his personal Playboy Club. The Playboy Club found a home in a tiny loft above the horse stables, behind the house. In order to gain access, you had to climb up on the dividing wall, leap across the stall, and grab onto a thin, rusty iron bar without breaking skin. If you were lucky enough to hold on, you then had to shimmy your legs above your head up into a small door. If you didn't make it, you fell into a cold pile of horse manure below. These contortions yielded a pretty safe hiding place, safe from little brothers and snooping farmhands, or so we thought.

Steve and I, and sometimes Butch or other friends, spent hours in this little loft looking at lingerie ads in Sears & Roebuck catalogues, ladies with pointy bras, girdled bottoms, garter belts and now common silk stockings. Later, when Steve grew more enterprising, he showed up with *Playboy* calendar pin-ups, *Playboy* magazines, and, of course, photos of my sacred vagina carefully hidden inside the pages. We talked about bodies and our views on sex as we knew it, and my brother occasionally borrowed anything from the den with pictures of naked bodies or sexual organs. The room was our private sex education study, but the true objective, I think, was getting away with something.

Oh yes, and then there was the highly desensitizing experience of the upper-middle-class dancing lessons. This was an education of the sexes no girl raised in the 1950s could forget. At home in the privacy of my room, bustling into abrasive crinolines layered under a chiffon or dotted-Swiss cotton party dress, I felt a-twitter with excitement, thinking about dancing and boys. My white lace socks and new black patent-leather party flats supported an invincible feeling: happy and beautiful. "Earth angel" I sang facing the mirror in my room, "Earth angel, will you be mine?" A final satin bow in my hair and I was perfect. If only I could wear just a dab of lipstick. I had to stop sucking my thumb first, Mom said. She said I would look ridiculous with a red ring around my thumb. I suppose I would have, but maybe I wouldn't suck my thumb while I had lipstick on. Just maybe I wouldn't. All the bribes had failed. I never earned the pony with the cart. I even overpowered the iodine and the thumb splints. Every time I thought about trying to quit, my thumb automatically slid back into my mouth.

When I climbed into the car, all pressed, curled, and ready for the dance, butterflies began fluttering about in my stomach. As my mom drove toward the Doylestown Country Club, they crawled up into my esophagus, growing larger and larger inside my throat, until, as we came closer and closer, the butterflies metamorphosed into mountains. My bedroom confidence folded into volcanoes of anxiety. Lava poured from tiny panic holes on my skin. Landslides of beauty and poise formed beads of sweat in my palms. Perhaps mother was right. I should have worn white gloves.

"Gloves are stupid," I had whined. "They're so *girl*." My mother had a way of being whined into submission, so I used this tactic as much as I thought I could. It didn't work with my dad.

By the time we pulled into the horseshoe shaped driveway of the pristine white club with evergreen shutters, I had all but lost my ability to breathe. Both my chin and stomach had sunk to knee level by the time we handed our coats over to the hatcheck girl, my heavily laden thighs quaking. As we walked upstairs to the ballroom and entered, my ego shattered into a thousand grains of sand on the floor, and all my confidence mutated into feeling just plain ugly. How this all transpired during one simple automobile ride was beyond me, but I never did learn the ability to transport bedroom confidence into the outside world. I just didn't do well in a girls' world.

Then the moment came. A sullen, pimply faced boy moved toward me as I stood frozen in the inevitability that he was going to ask me to dance, and the good-looking boy with thick golden hair headed off in the opposite direction. I had to say yes; those were the rules: dance or defect and set yourself up for eternal wallflowerdom. God, where were those gloves?

I expected to hear a hoot, hello, or "May I have this dance, please?" but nothing came. The young man dressed in a dark blue suit standing two feet in front of me simply raised his hands into dancing position and stared at my shoes—big owl eyes staring at my shoes. This was my clue he wanted to dance. As it turned out, when our palms met his were clammier than mine. *How long does this have to go on?* As we stepped in a monotonous box rhythm, 1-2-3-4, 1-2-3-4, I stared at his hair, black and greasy under layers of Brylcreem, traces of Right Guard floating up from his armpits—all in all he smelled like the inside of a Rexall drugstore. *I can't stay here,* I thought to myself. My thoughts wandered out the window into the woods. I would have preferred being out there riding bareback on my beautiful sorrel horse, Primrose. My true and imaginary escapes into the woods lasted throughout my childhood. My safest, happiest places were surrounded by trees. The woods were for me and Winnie the Pooh.

When the dance was over, without more than a grunt being uttered on either part, we took our places and began the instruction: how to hold hands, how to correctly place your hands on each other's waists (Oh God, too many cookies. Okay, no more, I lied to myself), how to bow and curtsy after the dance, and how to dance. Step, to the side, back, to the side, 1-2-3-4, 1-2-3-4. (I was surprised how many guys just couldn't get this right even after hours of well-designed repetition.) What in heaven's name were they thinking?

After Nabisco vanilla wafers, Ladyfingers, and red, sticky punch, we usually had a magic show (where we spent most of the time figuring out what a fake the magician was) or clown act. I sat next to my brother for protection. This didn't put much of a damper on his incredibly outgoing social skills. He confidently and decidedly asked the girls to dance, and the way he moved, girls never said no. The only time the girls asked the boys to dance was the Sadie Hawkins number, and by then everybody was pretty well coupled up, so you generally picked the guy who asked you the most, avoiding the wrath of another girl and especially avoiding the embarrassing moment when the boy would see you coming and quickly start up conversation in another direction. Familiarity was easier to deal with than rejection.

Dancing, touching, moving, smiling. Why weren't they feeling good now? I thought they should. I dreamed about them. I religiously watched Bob and Justine and Kenny and Arlene on Dick Clark's American Bandstand. Then I'd go upstairs, put the metal arm up on my Victrola, and mimic for hours their every hip swing and head-bob. I'd listen to the Supremes' "Why Do Fools Fall in Love" or "Dream, Dream,

Dream," by the Everly Brothers. Jitterbugging with a doorknob takes talent, but the limited arched swing of the door actually was liberating compared to the stiffness of my dancing school partners. At least here my feet didn't get trampled, my ego tethered, or my palms drenched. By the time Doylestown Country Club dance class was over, I felt like I'd been from "Here to Eternity."

Contrary to my parents' best wishes for future elegance, grace, and diplomacy, I ingested most of my romantic etiquette from TV and Betty and Veronica comic books, with a little Spin and Marty added for good measure. A streetwise way of loving tempted me more than the white party-glove sort of approach my father had in store for me. As my debutante persona faded, I think he hated me for failing to measure up to his view of a proper young woman, like those he grew up with in New York's high society, who rode the hunt and dressed perfectly, and had their hair done with their mothers. My mom, on the other hand, was coming into her own realization of what love should be. Neither of us understood Dad's way of loving.

# CHAPTER 7

**Cross My Heart and Hope to Die**

Rock-a-bye baby
On the tree top
When the wind blows
The cradle will rock
When the bough breaks
The cradle will fall
And down will come baby
Cradle and all

**Mother Goose**

One winter night, in the middle of my tenth year, my two brothers and I were acting up at the dinner table, while our parents struggled to maintain an order we must have secretly known they would never achieve. Steve, eleven years old and historically the perpetrator of trouble, continued in his style of entertaining anyone's attentions he could command even for a moment. Flip, age six, and easily influenced by the biggest harlequin, won the prize for most infectious laugh.

Tonight's activities, normal in scenario though not everyday behavior, consisted of borderline-acceptable behavior: silly knock-knock jokes, stuffing napkins down shirts, sticking fingers in our eyes, noses, and mouths, and then pulling them into ugly faces even a mother could hate. Our contagious tomfoolery rarely infected the grown-up reality of our parents at the dinner table. Most often we were firmly told our behavior was unfitting at dinner and to "cut it out."

"Pete and repeat were sitting on a fence," baited Steve. "Pete fell off, and who was left?"

"Finish your dinner or you won't get dessert," reminded Mom.

"Say what?" goofed my brother.

"You're so stupid," I mumbled at my brother.

"Sit up and eat or you'll both go to your room," warned Dad. "I mean it!"

For some reason, the threats didn't seem serious tonight. We weren't punished, for a change. No matter how much Steve pushed, he wasn't sent to his room. There was an underlying tension between my parents, but foolish noises filled the room—foolish nights I still remember.

After dinner, my father shifted his weight stiffly in his wooden chair, looked down at the table, and before anyone could make another wisecrack about his bald head, said, "I want everyone in the living room. Now!" The word *now* exploded larger than a lifetime.

My brothers and I raced into the living room, bounding over furniture and each other. Once a haphazard playroom, the forty-foot room had been redecorated when my dad ran for state senate in 1956. The room was as slick as a model-home showcase: bamboo fabric wallpaper matched soft, cushioned wall-to-wall carpeting; new or recovered furniture coordinated with wispily patterned curtains; shiny brass lamps and a sparkling ebony Steinway added the final touches. We could no longer play here, or put our feet up, or touch anything with our sticky fingers. For months, the couches stayed covered with clear factory plastic, and we weren't allowed to sit on them. I wondered if my dad planned on returning everything to the store for a full refund after he lost the election. Though littered just a few weeks ago with wrappings and toys, bikes and

Christmas ornaments, tonight the room showed no signs of the faded holiday. Tonight the amber-lit room glowed spotlessly.

Still giggling and out of control, we waited for my parents' arrival. My little brother slithered over the back of a stuffed silk-covered chair. "Get your feet off that chair, right now," Dad ordered, reaching roughly for Flip's arm. "Sit down now and be quiet." Like a Kodak flashcube, I felt the heat of anger explode in his voice, reaching a more intense level, and I knew the little tolerance for childish behavior he had in the past, was now gone. His anger went deeper than I had ever seen before. I pushed my bottom back on the couch quietly and waited for Mom. When she came in, her swollen face looked different to me. She wore a journal of emotions I had no time to read. Something was very wrong.

Our parents sat on opposite couches. Silent and determined, they waited and waited as the night waits for day, until the last ounce of cheerfulness vanished from our faces. Their anger or pain finally subdued us without a single word. Then, when all smiles were gone from the room and all joys safely hidden, my father said in a low, cracked voice, "Your mother and I don't love each other anymore." He cleared his throat. I quickly looked at my mother's face, now red and strained, and then at my dad's. Something awful was happening. I could feel the blood throbbing in my head. My older brother, no longer filled with mischief, sat like a plate of glass, staring down at the floor. Flip looked from face to face. A growing panic swelled inside me. A long, painful numbness absorbed us all.

"What does that mean?" I asked, wondering how this spoken detail would change our life, hoping it wouldn't. Maybe, we could just keep on the way we were until they learned to love each other again. Maybe, in time, they would change their minds.

"Your father and I are going to separate for a while. He will move out and we will stay here on the farm," said my mom. She reached her arms around me and began gently stroking unbridled strands of hair from my face, placing them gently behind my ears. Shattered. Scattered.

"How long?" I asked, again hoping to disperse any permanence of the decision.

"We don't know exactly."

"Will you get a divorce?"

"We don't know." They didn't know, but they did know.

Seconds passed, like a tank pushing slowly over rugged terrain, ominously approaching the edge of enemy territory. "Where are you going to live?" Steve asked my dad.

People, words, time became a blur. I didn't want to hear another word. Somehow, trapped in this moment of eternity, I knew life would never be the same. I ran upstairs to my room, buried my face in the pillow, and cried. I cried about a crazy childhood I had wanted to keep forever. I cried about my shattered fairy tale. I think I may have cried for a week straight. My parents were very concerned about all my crying and subsequent migraine headaches, but I couldn't stop.

How do two people who love each other, have three children together, and have a beautiful home suddenly decide one day they don't love each other? I never saw my parents fight or even raise their voices to each other, and I couldn't understand now why they were so angry, or even if they were. True, they no longer hugged each other in the hallway, but that shouldn't mean divorce. I wondered if I had somehow caused their separation. I wondered: if they could stop loving each other, could they stop loving me? Love was no longer permanent. Love was no longer family.

When you are ten years old, your parents can no longer look you in the eye. You're too big and you're too small. When they stand up, they look down on you. When they kneel down, you're too tall. You're too heavy to pick up and hold, and it's too awkward to sit on their laps because you're too heavy. Parents think you understand what you don't, and sometimes they make you feel you wouldn't understand if they told you.

That's what happened to me at ten and a half. My parents stopped looking me in the eye.

Dad moved in with his friend and business partner, Jimmy Gimmel, who lived about two miles down the road. Then he moved to an apartment in one of the big houses across the field from the farm. He spent much of his time traveling to Ireland, Israel, New York, and places unknown to us. We saw him on weekends when he was in town, but life at home definitely changed. Laughter rarely filtered through the sadness.

My mother became quiet and withdrawn. She created a more solitary life for herself in a pottery studio over the garage. I sometimes visited her and watched her sitting at her wheel, bent over a soft mound of clay. She dipped her hands into a bowl of muddy water and then wrapped them softly around the clay, her elbows propped on the side of the wheel. Her hands held steady as the embryo of a new child spun inside her palms, rising up with each rotation. She pushed the pedal of the wheel with her foot, and I stared at the spinning circled patterns of clay. When her hands cramped, she pulled away, dipped them again into the water, and carefully edged them back over the evolving shape. Sometimes she swore when her hands slipped off the clay, and I could see the frustration mangle her mouth. Sometimes she heaved the whole ball of clay back into a big vat of slips and started again.

Dinner was sad, school was sad, and I just couldn't stop crying.

Living with divorce proved more difficult to absorb than any of us had anticipated. Even though my paternal grandparents were divorced, and the country's divorce rate had skyrocketed since World War II, the concept remained socially awkward. Few kids in our whole school had experienced divorce. I became so absorbed in my family void I have no memory of fifth grade. My mother and father, no longer a unit, were now two very distant people. The longer they lived apart, the more different they became. I lived in a world of new confusion—afraid they both would one day simply disappear.

The first tangible change after my dad moved out was that he fired Lily, or, in his own written words, "Gave the colored cook the gate." He didn't seem to think she was important to us anymore. He replaced her with a large psychiatric nurse, whom he had hired from an agency out of New York that Mom Knight had recommended. Her name was Mrs. Yelsky. She was the shape of an eggplant, with a big, lumpy nose and funny black glasses. Like Mary Poppins, she was entirely too jolly for the situation. I never trusted her, and she was no Mary Poppins as far as I could see. She was given all the duties of running the house, given all the money to buy the groceries, given my father's car, and she gave my mother twenty dollars every Monday morning for spending money. I watched my mom's pain meld into the rage of a smoldering volcano. Suffering replaced living in both her and Dad; they had no tolerance for mine. My increasing neediness angered my dad. "Why can't you be like Steve and Flip?" he asked. They were taking the whole thing better, he thought. They were boys. Boys were stronger and braver, of course. It didn't matter that I no longer felt safe and there was no place I could go. Steve showed no emotion at all. Flip seemed to be sad, partly because I was, but mostly baseball kept him distracted in a world of his own.

Soon after, my dad hired a private detective to follow my mom. He suspected her of sleeping around, and Mrs. Yelsky reported to my dad during secret phone calls that my mom was out almost every night. She wanted to catch her doing anything naughty, I am certain. My mom thought this part of the whole equation was pretty ridiculous. She recounted many times a story about the night she knocked on the sleeping detective's car window, woke the sleuth-in-waiting, and told him she was leaving now, so he could follow. My father went to Europe.

My first attempt to organize my feelings resulted in hating my mother. She made him go away, I rationalized. Everything was her fault. She changed everything. To make things worse, she became quick-tempered and hard. Her hugs were no longer healing, and I felt alone. I didn't understand the changes, and there didn't seem to be anyone around to help.

Several months after the separation in early March, Mom punished me. Neither of us remembers what I did to cause the discipline, but all of us remember the punishment: she took my brand-new leather baseball mitt away and said I couldn't have it back for two months. Spring was coming, Little League had started, and she took my brand-new baseball mitt away.

Somehow, someway, I took it upon myself to deem this rash behavior totally unjustified—totally undeserved—so I decided to run away. She didn't want me, anyway. After overhearing my brothers whisper the secret whereabouts of the contraband, I stole up the steps to the attic and searched through the dark wooden eaves, where a bat or two often lived, until I found the stiff leather glove. I gathered my rescued prize possession in my arms and put my thumb in my mouth while I sat in the darkness and thought. I would be brave. I needed to leave. She wouldn't care. I'd be out of her hair. I snuck out of the house and ran quickly into the woods.

My father was my destination, of course; if Mom didn't love me, I knew for certain my father did. He had said anytime we wanted to come visit him we could. Absence makes the heart grow fonder, they say. Intent on escape, I journeyed over familiar forest and field, propelled by a ten-year-old's outrage.

In each step I found less confusion, more drive pressing through my expedition. As the sun filtered through the Pennsylvania forests, I arrived at my destination, tear-stained face caked with mud and long brown braids tangled with last year's weeds, tightly clutching a small leather baseball mitt. My mother had already called my dad to tell him of my departure and pleaded with him to bring me home for the sake of discipline, but he didn't return me. I think he felt pleased and proud that his only daughter had shown such early preference. And when I think back sadly on the situation, I'm afraid I started something awful that grew out of control.

Spring vacation, occurring shortly after my departure, gave everyone time to breathe. My Dad had Mrs. Yelsky pack my clothes and bring them up to Gimmel's house, and off we went to New York to visit my grandparents. This was the first time I think I ever went to Apple Bee Farm in the winter. There were no birthday parties, and the big pool was closed. I noticed the absence of flowers on all the tables, and the house was chilly and damp. Grandpop was glad to see me, though. He and Dad had a lot to talk about.

Things cooled down after a few days, or so I thought. The screaming phone conversations between my parents stopped. My confusion, massaged with excess attention and gifts from Dad and my grandparents, temporarily faded away. We went with my grandmother into the city to a Broadway play, to Lord & Taylor's for a shopping spree (assisted by her personal shopper), to elegant restaurants for dinner, and for the biggest treat of all, to Helena Rubinstein's Beauty Salon for my first real haircut. My almost-waist-length hair took too long to wash and dry and brush, my father and grandmother decided, and the time had come for me to take responsibility for my own hair. With a new pixie cut, I could do everything myself. I no longer needed anyone (my mom) to help me. Best of all, I had a new me in the mirror.

My Dad couldn't (or didn't) enlighten me about the separation more than had already been done. He never talked to me about his personal feelings or fears or plans, though he did make a special effort to entertain me and buy me treats. Our special vacation elevated me onto a pedestal where I reigned supreme. Supreme, that is, until I found out Mom had taken my brothers to Washington, DC for an unexpected trip. She never told me of any plans to go away. (I thought that perhaps she had planned the trip so I would miss something special, which I did.) My joyride suddenly became a reality, and I grew very homesick for my mother and my two annoying brothers, who, I realized, I had never been without.

When spring vacation ended, my dad agreed to return me home to live with my mom and finish out the school year. Though home sounded pretty good to me now, I was secretly terrified of returning to a hostile environment and ashamed of my irrational display of rebellion. As the days unfolded, my fears became reality.

I clearly remember the cold sunny day my dad pulled the car up in front of the house. We walked through the front door, strangers in our own home. No one came to greet us. My father called out. After several minutes of silence, Mrs. Yelsky came to greet us. She was all frothy and doting over my dad. My brothers were upstairs, she said. Neither mentioned my mother. When I finally did see my mother, her eyes showed animation only when she saw my hair had been cut and I now looked like an overweight elf. She secretly thought I looked very cute, I found out later, but she felt so angered by the whole episode she refused to accept the new look. She turned away, leaving the room without a word.

During the next few months, my mother and I lived in silence. She didn't look at me, and all the hugs were gone. I watched her every day, a deformed offspring shunned from the nest. For the first time in my life, I realized her hugs had been the only feel-good hugs I had ever known. My father's hugs were the same as his tickles; they were too hard, filled more with confrontation than with love. They made me too conscious of my mushrooming body and weakened female state. Now they reminded me I had no more Mommy hugs.

Mrs. Yelsky had taken over most of the household duties by now. Dad moved to Patty Clark's guesthouse on one of our farms. They had an affair. Mom spent more and more time away from the house or in her studio over the garage, throwing pots and reading. The loneliness I lived with for those months strengthened my conviction that I would never leave my mother again. I would never subject myself to such an overwhelming void, and I myself would never, ever hold a grudge. I never did leave my mother again (at least of my own volition).

# CHAPTER 8

## A Time to Sell

There was an old man
And he had a calf,
And that's half;
He took him out of the stall
And put him on the wall,
And that's all.

**Mother Goose**

*As summer came it became evident the cows had to go. They were not making any money and I was not able to give them the required attention. I decided to have an auction. I am selling not just the cows but the result of years of work. Animals I knew by name, number, pounds of milk produced, the works. I had cut off their horns, pulled their calves, held them while they bred and milked them twice a day for years. In short, it was traumatic. What was worse was that milk prices had gone to pot and most of the cows went to a butcher for 22 cents a pound. I was crushed. After the auction we had everyone who helped, plus friends, over to the pad for a barrel of beer and food prepared by Essie and Patty.*

*The children and Dorothy were at the auction. I must say Dorothy knew them all by name too. There*

Changes peppered with voids shifted with time. The cows with the big black eyes were gone, and the horses and pigs and chickens, too. Our farm became inanimate in a day. So many things I had known as a child were gone, and, at thirteen years old, it was time to grow up. As I watched the neighbors and townspeople head down our driveway with truckloads of our life, I tried to understand with my head, but sadness got in the way. I watched our family evaporate into the sunlit day.

I grew closer to my brothers, especially Steve. Our relationship became less combative, less competitive, and more tolerant. I started going up to his room in the attic and sitting on his bed, usually sucking my thumb while he tinkered with some machine or metal structure he had erected. Sometimes we talked. Sometimes we reminisced. Just sitting next to each other gave us a bond. None of us stood to win or lose, because we were all living the same empty game.

The next fall, we changed from public school to a private Quaker school called The Buckingham Friends School. Though we were all baptized Episcopalians and went to Sunday school, we moved from steeple to steeple. Since religion had never held an important place in our daily lives, I was unsure what it all meant other than coloring lots of sheep and bearded men in coloring books and praying. My father rarely went to church with us. He worked the farm seven days a week, except when he went riding.

Buckingham Friends was a beautiful rock schoolhouse set among thick trees on a hill, as most schools in Pennsylvania were. Every Monday morning we had meeting. This is how Quakers pray. We gathered at the meetinghouse, on wooden benches arranged in a rectangle, all facing each other in silence until someone shared what he or she was thinking, hopefully sharing enlightenment on some level. At the beginning of the year, there were adolescent snickers, but as the year went on, we each learned to appreciate the simplistic, magical way of sharing and praying. Even a thought as silly and minimal as, "My mom punished me," could be impetus for a round of how we felt about punishment. Most of the kids in the school were not Quakers, but in our silent meetings there was a sense of sharing and being a part of a collective whole.

In 1959, I started the sixth grade, Steve was in seventh, and Flip was four years behind me. I made friends quicker than I had at public school. My two best friends were Laurie and Ceci. Ceci was from the Funk and Wagnalls Dictionary family. She had seven brothers and sisters, all named after saints. Laurie's parents were divorced. We all three wore bras. That fact alone required much more of my attention than the increased schoolwork.

Steve made lots of friends quickly. His best friend lived with his grandfather, who had created the popular cartoon "Penny." Penny was the boy's mother, but she lived in California. His parents were divorced. Many of the kids were from wealthy, creative, and successful families living in the Bucks County area. Other than the Monday meetings and reading *The Good Earth* by Pearl S. Buck, the Quaker thing didn't much permeate our daily lives.

One fall Friday, my dad came to school. Although he still lived in the guesthouse over at the Clark farm, he traveled a lot, and I don't think we had seen him since the auction. I had no warning that he was coming to school that day. He simply walked into my classroom while I was sitting at my desk and asked me to come outside. I gave him a hug, but his rigid body repelled me. His farm manner had changed. He wore a perfectly creased gray felt hat and a formal city dress coat. I listened carefully in the dark wooden hallway, outside my classroom, while he tried to convince me to come with him to New York. His hands jingled the coins in his pockets. "We'll go to Ringling Brothers Circus," he promised.

It didn't take me long to remember the last time I had run away—how lonely I had felt in my braveness, and how long it had been since life was normal. I knew he was asking me because I went with him so easily the last time. I crossed my arms underneath my breasts and squeezed hard and didn't answer till there was a long silence. "I really don't want to go," I told him in a small voice, reliving the pain of leaving my mother. I wouldn't leave her ever again.

"Your brothers are going to come with me," he told me. He pulled his hand out of his pocket and reached for my shoulder. "You're coming with me now. Get your coat." I looked outside into the deep cold day. Rain poured down inside a dense cloud, turning midday into nightfall. I stared at the trees in the distance. I felt the damp cold seeping through.

"No," I said, once out loud, and then again and again in my head. I tried to explain why I didn't want to go, but his impatience grew as if he weren't even listening to my words. The space between us widened and another parent began a leave of absence.

"I can't believe how ungrateful you are, how ungrateful you have always been. You let your mother fill you with lies, and you can't think for yourself. I ask you to do something and you are impossible to deal with. You're a pain in the ass." He stormed out of the hallway. I slid down onto the dark pine floor, trying to organize the madness of my thoughts. I replayed the scene over and over in my head, which swelled with thoughts I couldn't arrange. What should I do? What would happen now? I didn't care if he hated me. I imagined myself going back into class, kids staring. Shaking from the cold and dampness, I slipped quietly back into the classroom, knowing I was staying while my brothers were gone. Though my insides were churning, I managed to keep calm for a while, until my teacher asked me a perfectly innocent question. Perhaps she just asked if I was all right, or maybe she wanted me mentally focused back in the subject matter.

Suddenly, I began sobbing out of control, as if he, my father, had sent a curse through me. I knew everyone was staring at me, but I couldn't stop. I covered my eyes and pushed hard against my eyelids. There was no place to hide from my new classmates. My teacher, a heavyset Quaker woman, got up from her desk, walked over to me and held me firmly by my shoulders. "Let us go outside, shall we?" she said.

"I need to call home," I begged, once back in the same hallway. "Please!" My sobbing grew worse. "My dad is taking my brothers and I just have to find my mom." Mrs. Haines slipped her arm around me and walked me quietly toward the main office.

When Mom reached the school and saw the boys were indeed gone, she raged. She raged at the principal for letting my brothers go with my dad. She raged at the teachers. She raged at the floor and the sky and the rain, and then she folded me into one of her long, lifeline hugs, a hug you grow inside of. She held me strong until her breathing calmed. She no longer spoke. We left the building, climbed into her lime green Karmann Ghia and drove home in silence. I began to understand just a little of what my mom was going through.

My Dad brought my brothers home several days later, and then he flew to Israel. My report card reflected a very dissatisfied teacher. I flunked my vocabulary test and got 69 percent on my grammar test. Mrs. Haines added, "Judy has been going downhill in both effort and achievement during

January. Her rudeness to her peers and her elders happened too often." My father used the report card later to prove my mom was a bad mother.

What I hadn't known at the time was that once before, during the late spring or early summer, my father had come to the house and taken my six-year-old brother, who had stayed home sick. (Essie must have called to tell him my mom was gone). Steve and I weren't there, but both Flip and Mom can vividly retell the story about my mother coming home, finding Flip gone, and tearing after my father and brother, thinking they were at Jimmy Gimmel's house.

Flip remembers sitting in my father's Oldsmobile and watching the dust exploding up behind my mother's car as she raced up the driveway toward him. She yanked Flip out of the car and locked him in her car as my father and Jimmy came out of the house. My mom started yelling at my dad. He grabbed my mom by her ponytail and began hitting her, while his six-foot-two, two-hundred-pound friend watched. The anger of a mother about to lose her child perhaps has more strength than any man.

My little brother recalled later watching her brush her hair out in the bathtub of a friend's house. As clumps of her ponytail fell out into her hands, Flip remembers thinking she had emerged the winner in his eyes.

My dad wrote in his memoirs, "By now things had gotten rather nasty and Dorothy had two or three warrants out for my arrest in Pennsylvania. I don't recall on what grounds they were issued."

# CHAPTER 9

## PUERTO RICO

My father brought somebody up,
To show us all asleep.
They came as softly up the stairs
As you could creep.

I shut my eyes up close, and lay
As still as I could keep;
Because I knew he wanted us
To be asleep.

**Josephine Preston Peabody**

The next time I saw my father was June 1960, a few days before my twelfth birthday. Almost a year had passed since we had a legal visit with Dad. He arranged through the lawyers to take the three of us to see our grandparents in New York. Lawyers negotiated all the custody issues, because my parents no longer spoke to each other. At this particular time, my mom needed to go to the hospital for female problems, so she agreed to the visitation. By now we missed the old bald guy, and most of the past had been forgiven, if not forgotten.

Yet our parents' separation continued defining our lives, especially mine. So much was changing. Even my developing body betrayed me. I felt an awkward self-awareness of bulging shapes and darkening pubic hairs, and I felt others' perception of me change as well. My father warned my brothers against roughhousing with me now (a warning they found as difficult to abide by as any other) and idle talk about "becoming a lady" embarrassed me in any crowd. I didn't want to be a lady. I was still a kid, never wanting to grow up. Peter Pan. Never-Never Land. Riding ponies through the woods, playing in the hayloft. I still sucked my thumb passionately, though I began keeping my habit secret from the disapproving world; especially my father, who felt compelled to yank my thumb out of my mouth if I didn't pull it out myself after he glared at me. Now I hid behind doorways and large magazines or snuck off to my room.

We visited Mom Knight, frolicking in the lake at Blue Herons with our cousins from Scarsdale. However, we didn't stay at my grandfather's for his traditional Fourth of July birthday party. Instead, we flew to San Juan, Puerto Rico. Dad told us we were going on a special trip. We suspected nothing but a warm vacation on the beach and lots of entertainment. We hadn't been to the beach since Gigi's house was destroyed by the hurricane, so we were pretty excited. Again, Dad succeeded in lavishing great new adventures, presents, and attention upon us. We stayed in a fancy suite in a high-rise hotel right on the beach. We took snorkeling lessons in the hotel swimming pool, flapping our flippers and diving to the bottom for pennies (and gold doubloons off a sunken pirate ship), and went sailing on a small Sunfish, ineptly landing on our side after a rowdy gust of wind and needing to be rescued by the sailing instructor. We all remember savoring our first bite of the island delicacy, frog's legs. The taste, much to our relief, resembled a chewy piece of chicken floating in a pool of rich, garlicky butter. Dad was happy, and being at the ocean brought out the best in us kids. We could just be kids again.

We had been in Puerto Rico for about five idyllic days when life took another detour. I remember building a sandcastle on the beach while my older brother raced in and out of the ocean. His strong, wiry body seemed tireless in the quest for physical activity, but I remained content, quietly molding the warm white sand with my fingers and palms. No matter how long I smoothed and shaped, there was always more to do, more perfection to strive for. I felt the healing heat of the sun in my hair, the sand beneath my legs. Suddenly, dark eyes glaring, Steve raged toward my castle, and, in less than ten seconds, in spite of my screams and pleas, he kicked and smashed every carefully handcrafted shape to a sad amorphous lump of beach. I threw fists and fists of sand and screamed at him as he ran away. "Creep! I hate you!"

I wilted into the sand, tired of torment and separation. The ocean breeze blew through rows of palm trees swaying in rhythm. Children of many languages, with shiny red buckets, sticky candy wrappers, and slippery inner tubes, dotted the hotel beach. Parents and honeymooners stretched in silence like lizards in the sun. I hated my brother.

Then, whether I intended to snitch on him or just wanted to see what my dad and younger brother were doing back at the hotel, I don't remember. I got up from the sand and headed back to the hotel. I entered the lobby, decorated with plush red carpet, gaudy gold-framed pictures, and ornate chandeliers—American influence in Puerto Rico. Except for the hotel cashier, who busied himself with paperwork, the lobby was empty.

I pushed the elevator button, stepped back, and traced patterns on the carpet with my big toe. Grains of sand fell from my bathing suit and freshly tanned legs. The elevator opened. I entered, walked to the back of the cubicle and turned, watching the heavy sliding doors close slowly, squeezing the world's panorama from my view. "Fourteenth floor, please," I said to the Puerto Rican bellboy, who latched the door closed with a massive brass gate, pressed the circular *14* button, and then pulled a large brass lever. I felt my stomach sink as the elevator started up. He turned slightly and smiled, and I smiled back politely. He wore a burgundy uniform, with gold trim matching the lobby, and shiny black shoes. His thick, black hair glowed with an unnatural greasy shine. I wondered again what my dad was doing, as I watched the numbers light up in sequence: 6 ... 7 ... 8 ... 9.

Suddenly I felt a jolt. The numbers stopped. The doors of the cave did not open. His hands secured the large brass lever, and he slowly turned. As he started toward me, my heart surged, and I swallowed hard. He wasn't much bigger than I was, but I felt a giant fear rip through my body. I took a step back, pressing up against the far corner of the shrinking box. He kept moving toward me until his hands reached around me. I stood paralyzed. I felt naked as his fingers touched my uncovered back, my bathing suit suddenly too small to cover my prickling skin. His uniform pressed up against my body, pushing me further into the wall. As he reached even closer, his lips pushed hard against my mouth; big, wet, slippery lips massaging mine. His tongue urged my mouth to open, but I froze in fear, my head pressed hard against the back of the elevator. He began swallowing up everything about me.

His left arm slipped deeper around my waist and he pulled me tighter as his free hand began pressing and kneading my naive, throbbing breast. Terror ripped through my every muscle. Oh God, I had to get out. I was pressed up against a wall in a soundproof box, too far to scream, no place to run. I knew even if I could push him away, there was no place to go.

When his mouth left mine, seeking new territory, I screamed as loud as I could. The noise filled the eight-by-ten-foot space, echoing around us, breaking the spell. We stood staring at each other. The infinite darkness of his eyes locked me inside.

He slowly dropped his arms, and I pushed him away. "I thought you wanted as much as me," he spoke in broken English for the first time. My heart pounded in pain.

I crossed my arms tightly against my breasts, lowered my head and mumbled, "No, um, sorry." *Why did I say sorry? What was I doing?* "Please, let me go home." Home?

To my relief, he turned away and put his now familiar hand on the lever. The elevator climbed up the shaft and I held my breath. I could no longer think. My head was spinning. I gritted my teeth against the tears welling up in my eyes. 10 ... 11 ... 12...

Finally, the door opened, and I broke into a run down the hallway. I reached the room breathless and broken, tears pouring down my face, and pounded on the door. When my dad finally opened the door I pushed it open and threw my arms tightly around his waist, trying to squeeze the fear from my body that was no longer playful, no longer mine.

"What's the matter?" my father asked. I sobbed into his chest. "Judy, what's wrong?" I held steadfast until he pushed me away at arm's length. "You're impossible. What in God's name is the matter?"

"The boy ... in the elevator," I stammered, trying to stop crying and shaking, but the sobs kept breaking my explanation. "I got on the elevator and then he stopped it. He grabbed me and kissed me." I wanted to tell him the rest. I wanted to tell him how the elevator boy touched my breast, but suddenly I was afraid to, afraid he would hate me forever if I told him that had happened.

"Settle down, Judy, stop crying!" my father said, pulling away completely. "I can't understand you." Sunlight reflected off his thick glasses. "What did you do?" he then added. I looked up, shocked at the hint of accusation, but his eyes darted in and out of mine. My sobbing stiffened, and I felt lost in confusion once again.

I stared at him briefly, unbelieving of what he had just asked me. "I just stood there. I didn't *do* anything."

"Did you say anything to him?"

"No!"

"I think we should go find him and talk to him," suggested Dad after a pause.

"Oh, no, please don't!" I answered, humiliated at the thought of ever looking into those dark, penetrating eyes again.

"Well, maybe we should talk to the manager of the hotel."

"Oh, no. No, please Dad." How could I explain? Maybe this was the way my dad tried to help, but now he didn't understand. I didn't want anyone else to know what had happened; the shame inside felt like an electric short. I started to wonder if the whole thing was my fault.

"Then I don't know what else to do, Judy. If you won't let me talk to anyone, I can't help you," my dad said, throwing his arms out to his sides. I think I wanted him to just hold me and comfort me and tell me everything would be fine and the whole thing didn't matter, but I couldn't tell him. I couldn't tell him what I wanted. I couldn't tell him anything. He just stood there, like Acrisius, ready to lock his only daughter up in a bronze tower for her remaining days.

"We have more important things to think about right now," he finally said, walking over to the other side of the room. "Go to your room and start packing," he ordered nervously. Just then, I noticed the room was filled with open suitcases, open drawers, and piles of neatly folded clothes. A new panic swelled within me. I wondered what he was talking about.

"I thought we weren't going home until Sunday," I said.

"My plans have changed. We are all going to Ponce to visit a friend of mine for a few days."

"Where's Ponce?"

"Not far," he answered briefly.

"What about my birthday?"

"You'll have your birthday in Ponce," he answered. My mind raced back to memories of past birthdays: homemade chocolate cakes with powdered sugar and egg-white icing, streamers, party games and prizes, and lots of school friends. My favorite birthday was all day at the Willow Grove Amusement Park with my friends. I really missed Mom and wished I could go home. I was afraid to have a birthday anywhere else without her.

"When are we going home?"

"I don't know. Now go to your room and pack." My head felt wedged in a vise and my stomach pumped full of lead. Everything was out of control. I went into my room. My little brother sat on his bed shuffling tiny toy cars over and under the hotel covers, his body blistered from sunburn.

"Hi," he said. Then, "Hey, what's wrong?"

"Nothing," I yelled and slammed the bathroom door. I felt my chest tighten with anger. I walked over to the mirror and saw an ugly, dirty stranger staring at me with red puffy eyes and stringy hair littered with grains of sand. I couldn't break the lock on my own horrible image. I felt the hard kiss on my lips again and watched myself cover my mouth with both hands. I pushed my palms hard against my mouth. Then I looked down. My body was disgusting. What was this body? How could it do this to me? I dropped my hands and reached for the small packet of soap behind the sink, took off the paper wrapping and began rubbing my hands and face until they burned. My stomach dry-heaved emptiness down the drain.

I started the shower and slid under the stream of hot water. I stood for a long time, afraid to take my bathing suit off. I wanted to go. I wanted to go home. I wanted to sleep in my own bed, with all my stuffed animals, next to my parents' room. I wanted to swing on my swings, climb in the haystacks, cuddle up on the couch in the den and watch *The Wonderful World of Disney*. I felt trapped in Puerto Rico, trapped in a woman's body, and trapped in a life I did not choose.

Dad recalled the trip to Puerto Rico in his memoir: "We had fun. We swam in the pool, played games in the ocean, etc.

Judy had a pass made at her by the little elevator boy and was scared to death. It was nice."

The next morning we drove to Ponce, Puerto Rico. My brothers and I dressed in matching maroon shirts with places in Puerto Rico written all over them. My brothers' shirts tucked in, but mine tied at my belly button. From the car window I watched the metamorphosis of faces and buildings; the meticulously groomed tourist hotels melted into dirty, sprawling one-story neighborhoods where people hung laundry next to their cars in their front yards, half-dressed coffee colored children played in the streets, and old men gathered around tables piled with dominoes. As we drove across San Juan toward the interior of the island, the perceptions of the Puerto Rican people I had gleaned from the resort environment slowly faded. Their faces became more determined, with tired eyes and dusty skin. The shabby houses, surrounded with broken beds, discarded tires, and a few assorted household belongings, were a part of the world I had never seen, a piece of poverty my parents had managed to shelter me from until now.

We drove through the countryside, and the island grew thick, green, and lush with rain forest and an occasional explosion of hibiscus and bougainvillea. A certain resolve came over me as we climbed the curving, narrow roads, through a tunnel of uncertainty, to the highest peak on the island. I felt once again I was being pulled out to sea by the strong moving currents of the Atlantic Ocean. Too tired to fight, too drained to cry, I stared out the window, hoping a peaceful arm of salvation would reach out and just hold me. Maybe if I didn't care, all the confusion and uncertainty would be easier to understand. That was it. I just wouldn't care.

My Dad's friend, Cookie, was a jolly, thick-waisted lady with a warm smile, dark hair, and pointy plastic-winged glasses sparkling with glitter. She greeted us with big, happy hugs when we arrived at her house, which overlooked a panorama of jungle and the ocean in the distance. She giggled like a sorority coed and instantly reminisced about my grandfather's house and the good old days back in New York. She and my father had a long history, and during most of the conversation, my brothers and I were left to assess our new surroundings.

A huge tree, surrounded by little flowing streams and tiny bridges, grew right up through the middle of her living room. Cookie had worked many years in New York City as Grandpop's personal secretary, until she escaped with her lover from the rat race of the business world to live out the rest of her life in this elegant hideaway—much to the dismay of my grandfather. When he had objected to her leaving, she told him, "Boss, you Naumburgs live forever, but Cookie's clan doesn't," and she was right. She died in her fifties from a massive heart attack. Grandpop lived till the age of ninety-four.

We stayed at Cookie's for a few days, and our originally planned departure date from the island slipped by without a word. I knew this because it was my birthday, June 20, 1960. The day of celebration, balloons and friends, amusement parks, and huge home-baked cakes was replaced by an unfamiliar world on top of a hill in Puerto Rico. An attempt to make my twelfth birthday memorable resulted in a tiny, round, chocolate cake with a small, lonely white candle, along with a few gifts picked up at the local Puerto Rican variety store. I have a feeling that even if the most lavish of parties had graced my path, I would still remember the day with the loneliness of a prison inmate.

A few days later we left the island, suspecting we were not heading home just yet. Dad answered all our concerns and nudging with, "You'll see" or "Don't ask so many questions." I remember taking plane after plane after plane, energy fading with every mile passing under us. We colored and played cards way into the night: canasta, war, slap- jack and crazy eights. Flip crawled into the lap of a friendly stewardess, dressed in navy blue, when exhaustion had depleted us all. She stroked his soft flaxen hair. Our lady of the skies. Our mother of the moment. Perhaps we would live the rest of our lives in the air, floating between lifetimes.

We arrived very late in the night, heavy from lack of sleep, at a place called Albuquerque, New Mexico. The small, deserted airport could have been anywhere in the world for all I cared. New Mexico was a state in the Southwest next to Texas. Fifth grade geography.

My father gathered our luggage and loaded it into a big fancy new town car. I had never seen or heard about the car before. He was a long way from the farm, I could tell. We drove down a long, straight road without seeing headlight or house for an hour, in a dark world with no boundaries, no trees, just a vast sky full of stars. I stared out the window into the darkness, where space felt unlimited and horizons slipped from view. There were no thick forests with hidden secrets. I didn't know how far away we were in relation to Pennsylvania, or if my mother knew we were here, or where we were going, or if we would ever go home again. Every moment was a new experience, but I didn't quite understand how to process these new things, here in the land of no memories. Though my dad was different, my brothers were here. I was less afraid as long as my brothers were here with me.

While we traveled through the dark, I became more entrapped by a heavy sadness. Loneliness sent long tentacles through my veins. Even though people were near me, dark feelings filled up the holes of my childhood. I didn't know at the time that my father was kidnapping us, my mother didn't know where we were, and we were not going home again for a long time. I knew only that I was no longer a child.

We all emerge from our youth with a unique set of memories and emotions, colored by our own perceptions and distractions. My memory of this summer, muted with trepidation, still lingers. New Mexico bewildered like the hollow craters of the moon, stung like mosquitoes on a bog. The brown, barren world covered vast open spaces without the soft brush of a maple, oak, or willow tree. There were no mourning doves in the silence of the desert. The sky burned so blue my eyes stung, and the dry, dusty afternoons coated my tongue. The evening sky glowed in the west like a forest fire. Clumps of brittle sage and piñon, spikes of giant yucca cactus, rattlesnakes, and poisonous scorpions guarded this unfamiliar land.

After spending a few nights in a small one-bedroom apartment in Santa Fe, we moved into Mrs. Moses's house on Canyon Road, a sprawling adobe mud complex with a big thick wall around it. A whole new set of circumstances was laid out for us, as if nothing had changed. Essie was there. Strange. Our toys and clothes from Pennsylvania were there. We had a new German shepherd puppy called Mr. Lucky. Our horses weren't there, but we were quickly introduced to friends who owned horses with cumbersome, dry, squeaky saddles called Western saddles, and we rode down long arroyos where dust clogged my throat, piñon branches scratched my legs, and the intense summer heat radiating from the sandy earth closed my heart.

My dad embraced a whole new life in Santa Fe. He bought a ready-mix concrete business, which he named Colony Materials, next to the railroad tracks. I supposed Colony Bulldozers, the business he had in Pennsylvania with Jimmy Gimmel, had turned into Colony Materials. Funny, because the name *Colony* came from abbreviations of Colorado and New York, where Mom and Dad were raised. Funny he should stay with a name that represented their union. Maybe the companies were connected somehow; I never asked. My dad now wore a freshly ironed cowboy shirt and a bolo tie to work. Instead of cow manure and hay-covered overalls, he came home from work covered in fine grey silt. He looked more important and less drained.

We were introduced to new friends, my dad's new girlfriend, Coe, and her three kids, and to a young, hostile

Hispanic culture that collectively despised *Anglo* kids, which I quickly learned we were. We swam in the pool at the La Fonda Hotel, and from the roof we occasionally dropped water balloons on tourists walking below. My brothers were arrested for shoplifting tools at Woolworth's on the plaza and escorted home by two policemen one hot afternoon in July.

I became increasingly unpredictable and unappreciative, gaining a reputation for being oversensitive and moody. I rejected most attempts my father made to entertain me or garner my love. My commentary during trips to the Grand Canyon or down the spectacular Narrow Gauge Railroad in Silverton, Colorado, usually included one of my three favorite retorts, "So what?", "Big deal!", or "Who cares?" I also used "Tough!" and "Shut up!" a fair amount. And I still remember the faraway feeling I nurtured, staring at the square black phone in the hallway, sucking my thumb, wondering why my mother never called. Didn't she miss us? The summer, the dark nights of New Mexico, had no definition for me. Everything passed slowly, and my feelings were still confused. Understanding was difficult. Reactions were easier. I put one foot in front of the other during my first summer in Santa Fe.

The next time I saw my mother was down a long corridor in the county courthouse on Grant Street, late in August or early in September. She wore a tailored olive colored linen suit; her hair was pulled back neatly in her customary French twist, but her face looked sallow and sad, lacking the vibrancy I remembered from my childhood and would never see again. She walked swiftly toward us with a strain in her lips, visibly struggling with her pain. She blanketed her arms around the three of us, squeezing until she once again trusted her voice. Only she knew how it felt to come home to a house empty of children, toys, and laughter. Only she knew how it felt to fight a wealthy man, now on his own turf.

"I missed you all so very much," she finally whispered.

# CHAPTER 10

### There's No Place like Home

I wouldn't be a monkey,
Doing foolish tricks;

I wouldn't be a donkey,
Full of sullen kicks;

I wouldn't be a goose,
Nor a peacock full of pride,

But I would be a big boy,
With a pocket on each side.

**Mary Mapes Dodge**

I ran my fingers along the edge of my mother's desk, absently sucking my right thumb, left forefinger stroking my upper lip. The desk was shorter, I suddenly realized, staring down at the familiar cardboard and leather blotter. The top of the desk used to be right at my waist, and now I extended my arm down to touch it. My thoughts tightened. No—I had grown. Just a summer's worth, but I had grown. A summer in Santa Fe, and now I was home.

The smooth touch of the dark wood reminded me of Primrose, my chestnut pony, petting the soft side of her long nose near her nostrils. She'd push against my fingers for more when I pulled away. The image exploded violently into the memory of her body in the middle of the street, severed foreleg lying a few feet away amid oceans of blood reflecting the moonlight. I could feel her warmth on the road radiating against my bare legs. The grassy knoll sparkled with dew where she had missed her footing and slid down onto Cold Spring Creamery Road, crashing into a motorcycle speeding by. The police lights flashed far into the distance like a lighthouse beacon over the sea. As we drove back to the house, I heard the gunshot. Later, when I lay in bed, somewhere inside nightmares, I heard the faint gunshot again and again in the distance. I hadn't known about the dead motorcyclist who had been thrown one hundred feet in the air. The front-page headlines the next day covered the accident and the wife and kids he had left behind, but I couldn't care about them as much as I did Primrose, even though my parents did. My horse was dead.

I looked around. The heavy, drawn curtains dampened the air in the den. The mounted fox-head trophy still hung among the books. All the clutter was gone. Everything was neat and in its place. The couch I used to play horsy on when Dad was out of sight remained abandoned against the wall. The once giant Zenith TV looked not so giant anymore. I walked through the house, as big as Gulliver waking up with the Lilliputians. Then I became aware of the emptiness. Paintings were gone, books were gone, things were missing. My dad had stolen *us*, but he had stolen other things, too. Gone were the mountains of stuffed animals from my twin beds, clothes from the floor of my closet, posters from the walls. Gone were the miniature barns and toy soldiers from my little brother's floor. His room smelled more of Pledge than cedar chips in a hamster's cage. I knew there were memories sprinkled in the corners, but they were afraid to jump out and welcome me.

The farm felt deserted. There were no more cows, no thoroughbreds, nor random speckled chickens. No tractors or combines. No hum of the harvest or children playing. The children were all grown up now, or they had better be. I could see the dirt floor of the corn shed. Even before harvest, the shed had always had a thin layer of yellow kernels sprinkled over the floor, except for now. The surreal stillness hovered over the farm as if *The Fly* or aliens had scared everyone away.

Essie stayed in Santa Fe, which was just fine with me. In many ways, she tried to be our mother. She took care of us, cooked special meals, and ran the household well—but she talked to each of us about our problems with the compassion of a walrus. Actually, she kind of reminded me of a walrus, but for the summer months in Santa Fe she was all we had. Many years later, I learned that Essie had convinced Dad I needed psychiatric help at this time. Because of her psychiatric training, she thrived in the task of assisting my father and grandmother in finding treatment for me with a renowned psychiatrist at Yale University. The treatment ended because my mother refused to participate. She didn't think I needed help, and she didn't want to be under scrutiny from a doctor paid by my father.

After the kidnapping, each of us drifted to our own corners, searching for love, and I was no exception.

My mother and her new boyfriend, Johnny Francis, bought a restaurant together, called the Gaslight, in Lahaska, Pennsylvania. I hated Johnny, and he cared less. He looked like a beatnik with his stupid black goatee. He treated my mom like a servant, often standing her up or ridiculing her in front of us, and I don't think he was in love with her at all. She worked days and nights at the restaurant, and in her spare time she practiced her pottery in the studio over the garage and knit sweaters, which she sold in a local boutique. I couldn't understand why she stayed with Johnny. We all tried too hard when he was around.

Steve was in eighth grade, now going steady with my best friend, Laurie. Besides me, she was the only other girl in seventh grade who wore a C bra. Steve spent most of his time trying to figure out how he could kiss Laurie, or, better yet, convince her to let him into her C bra. We had lots of sleepovers.

I went to the end of the lane. Looking back on this search, I could have chosen a safer route, but perhaps choosing the most dangerous was my antidote. A boy my father dubbed retarded lived at the end of the lane. He was a teenager, maybe fifteen. His name was Jimmy, and he reminded me of James Dean, the rebel without a cause, with slicked-back blond hair and thin face. His father worked as our sharecropper.

When we were little, we all went to public school on the school bus. At the end of the day, we would pile off the bus and sometimes into their kitchen before heading up to the main house. On the white metal table, the mom would set out homemade cookies and glasses of fresh, pasteurized milk from our cows. Their cramped, cluttered home felt too small for all of them, and every time I went inside, I couldn't wait to leave. I think Jimmy felt the same, because he usually hung around outside in the shed or on the porch. When he grew up, he had a car. He sat in the car a lot. A buffed 1953 two-tone red and white Chevy with ripped seats perched up on cinder blocks outside in the front yard. "No tires," he told me, "cuz I ain't old enough to drive." My father said he was retarded—that was why there were no tires.

I had never cared or thought about Jimmy much until now. Lots of things were different now, and I had become curious, bored, and agitated. Jimmy was sitting behind the wheel of his car.

"How come you're not in school?" I asked on my way home one day. He was supposed to be in high school. I went to a private day school.

"Din't feel like it," he answered.

"Oh," I said, starting up the lane.

"Wanna come in?" he hollered down to me.

"No, thanks."

"Why not?" he asked with a smirk.

Reading his challenge, I walked back toward the car and put my books down on the ground. Placing one foot on the edge of a cinderblock, I pulled myself into the passenger seat. "This is pretty nice," I fumbled, softly rubbing the red leather seats.

"I come here to git away from the screamin' inside," he told me. I saw in my mind a different family than the milk-and-cookie one. I saw yelling and drinking and hitting, and I felt a little closer to Jimmy.

"Why don't you like school?" I asked.

"Just don't. Do you?"

"Yeah. I think I do. There's nothing else to do, and sometimes it's fun," I confessed. "How come you don't put on tires and drive away?" I knew he didn't really want to answer the question, but what else was I going to talk about? He didn't seem so bad.

"Muh dad took away muh tires 'cause I went drivin'," he finally revealed, fidgeting with a soft rabbit's-foot key chain, "when I weren't suppose to." He wasn't easy to talk to. The time between words and sentences seemed long enough to pick up and leave. He had softness about him, though, unlike my brothers.

"Well, I have to go," I said, when we had both continued the train of no thoughts for too long. He didn't seem so retarded, just quiet.

I didn't think much about Jimmy until one Saturday night after my mom had gone to Mexico with her weird brother Jack. A full moon lit up the fields like a spotlight. Flip, Steve, and I were in our black-and-white RCA world watching Ralph and Alice Cramden battle out their life's problems, Alice standing flat-footed with her hands upside down on her hips and Ralph clenching his fist or waving his finger defending himself by shouting obnoxious put-downs. She screamed at him with this whiney voice, and they went on and on until the neighbors just happened to drop by. The people in the audience thought they were all funny. Canned laughter was the people in the audience.

During a commercial, Flip jumped up and said, "Hey, there's somebody outside." I pulled the curtains from him and saw the sparkling Chevy *with wheels*—headlights dim and motor running. I got up slowly, looked around, then put on my coat and went outside, amazed the cinderblocks had turned into wheels so easily. Jimmy wasn't retarded, I said to myself again, or he couldn't drive. The night was as bright as the day.

"Want to get in?" he asked.

"Where are we going?"

"Nowhere," he assured me. I slid carefully across the smooth seats and sat closer this time to the "retarded" boy. The car felt warm and homey. He had been inside for a long time. His cookie-colored hair smelled sweet. The night light outlined the barns with a soft silver glow, and I remember thinking how surreal everything looked. So often, night passes, and we never see the magic, because we're locked inside a world of TV and light bulbs. He lit a cigarette and offered me one. I refused. I imagined I was on a date, my first date in a car.

"Sometimes I feel like there's a hole where my future is," he said. Who was this guy? What did we have to lose?

"Sometimes I feel like there's a hole my past fell into," I answered too quickly. I knew what he meant, though, living without visions and hopes. "Isn't there anything you want to be?"

"I know what I don't want to be. I don't want to be a farmer or a drunk. I don't want to break my back for some rich guy, get paid nothin', and come home just so's I can beat the crap out of my wife and kids." His two fingers on his right hand had tobacco stains. "My dad thinks I'm a sissy." *Wow,* I thought to myself.

"You hate the farm, don't you?" I was afraid to look at him, knowing the difference in our backgrounds was the hole in his future. Why was he here? I wondered if all fathers had expectations their kids couldn't live up to. My mind passed over the time my dad had wanted me to jump Primrose over a three-foot fence. I was too scared, and I hesitated, so he slapped the back of the horse hard and I went flying over the fence, holding onto the horse's mane for dear life. I learned how to jump, all right.

"Nah, it's not that, really," he said.

We sat for a long time, sometimes silent, sometimes not. He turned up the radio a bit. I wondered about being here in the car alone with him. I wasn't afraid, but I wondered what I would let him do if he wanted. I thought of the boy in the elevator. My body was no longer my own. He put his arm on the seat behind my shoulders. I felt his warmth even without the touch. I wanted to ask him how he had gotten so many muscles, but I chickened out. We started talking about family and school and then about the frustrations of life, until our words flowed slow and thick like the Delaware River. I felt grown-up and independent, and there was no fat Ralph Cramden in sight. Jimmy seemed normal, so I moved closer. His arm slipped onto my shoulder. His warmth flowed into me. I put my head down on his shoulder and felt a change from childhood games into a grown-up ache for love. I liked getting away with something bad.

Jimmy never came by for a date again. Maybe my dad found out or Mom came home. Maybe his dad found out. Maybe Jimmy lost interest. Maybe life just kept going out of control, but I held onto the night in my dreams.

Little Anthony and the Imperials could sum up the way I felt during the rest of seventh grade with three of their hits: "Tears on My Pillow," "Hurts So Bad," and "Think I'm Going

Out of My Head." I hid in my room, lifted the arm up on my record player so each song would keep on playing, over and over again. I cried. I cried when gangly Hilda Thomas in my class started a clique against me and wrote "Jewdy" on the blackboard. I cried over Gordon Ellis, who had dropped me cold after we stole into the hay loft for my first "real" kiss and I thought he loved me forever. He kissed me so long I couldn't figure out how to breathe at the same time, so when I finally pulled away and subtly inhaled, the hay dust particles rattled down my throat and sounded like a mating bullfrog. I was mortified. I cried watching Troy Donahue break Sandra Dee's heart, movie after movie. I cried when we had to go back to Santa Fe for Christmas, and they put up a plastic tree. I flunked seventh grade and had to take extra work to do on my summer in Santa Fe so I could pass, but that didn't matter. The distance between Santa Fe and home was still the same.

# CHAPTER 11

### The Splendor of the Façade

As I went to Bonner,
I met a pig
Without a wig,
Upon my word and honor.

**Mother Goose**

The splendor of the facade; I remember it well: acres of manicured lawns and luscious gardens trimmed with thick forests; two splendid white mansions high on a hilltop overlooking ivy-covered classrooms. My mother and I slowly drove through the campus, awed by the beauty and peace of the Anderson School. It was the fall of 1961, my first and only prep school interview. "With the sun shining on the lovely autumn colors ... red, purple, yellow, green, and brown," I wrote in a dribbling eighth-grade composition upon my return, "it was very pretty." Dorothy enchanted with the Land of Oz.

We never actually met any kids; I saw them from afar in a classroom and again briefly as they drove off in a school bus destined for a nonspecified field trip, and we only met one or two carefully handpicked teachers. Everything felt so attractive, so controlled and cared for. The handsome, august headmaster, Lewis Gage, moved with the dedication of a king draped in heavy robes, each step a statement, each smile an embrace. His words melted over us like a warm blanket of honey. My mother and I fell under his spell.

"Children need special care," he told us, as he sat behind a mahogany desk. "Each is an individual treated as such at Anderson. I have been here for over thirty years. It is my home." At the time, he seemed so promising, so nurturing in his elegant office. The idea of special care (holding, speaking gently, understanding) actually appealed to me. I was the first to need it but the last to admit it. Mr. Gage wove my apprehension into anticipation. The splendor of the campus and the promise of idyllic school days ahead carried me home with a renewed outlook on life. I soon would be a part of this beautiful world.

A month after my interview, I received the coveted prep school acceptance letter in the mail. I bubbled with excitement, relieved by my early acceptance into any school after almost flunking seventh grade. Even now, my grades only ranged between good and satisfactory. I had convinced myself I was lucky to get into any boarding school. Or maybe someone else convinced me of that. All my other classmates had to wait anxiously until spring to hear from their private schools, the George School, Exeter, or Choate. No one had ever heard of the Anderson School in Staatsburg, but I could let that slide because at least I was going to a boarding school. Boarding schools, after all, were the destination for the rich and successful, the well-heeled, my equals. The kids who went to public high schools were the poor ones. I never really questioned my early acceptance; I simply bathed in it.

I graduated from the Buckingham Friends School in Lahaska, Pennsylvania, with no particular claim to greatness. "Last but not least," my eighth-grade teacher read as I stood waiting for my diploma, "is our sometimes moody, yet mercurial class member, who can be a smoldering volcano, or a rose. She has a strong sense of justice, and an inadequate appreciation of herself. We think," (but they weren't certain) "she has convinced us this year of her own value as a student and a citizen, but most of all as a person with a sweet nature. If she has learned these things about herself as well as we have learned them, no more is needed for a happy life." Well. There I sat, stripped by my superiors of any protective coating, for all my peers to see, in case they might have missed such trenchant personality traits. Who was I, really? Was I what I thought or what they thought? Was I a figment of someone else's imagination or my own? This was not a graduation one should remember, and yet I did.

My voice strained to reach the high notes of our parting graduation song, "Walk on, walk on, with hope in your heart, and you'll never walk alone." Good-bye Quaker meetings. Good-bye Pearl S. Buck.

Weary of a still unresolved three-year custody battle, I grew certain life would be easier living away from home. I wondered if life at home would be easier without me. Even though my parents didn't live together, the tension remained as high strung as a Triple Crown thoroughbred. Every time my father called, or came by, or there was any reference to his existence from a phone call or something in the mail, the mixed signals darted around my mom's energy with obvious negative forces. The demon of divorce, unleashed and undisciplined, had over time etched pain-filled lines in my mother's face, once so beautiful and soft. I wondered if she would miss me or if her life would be better without me. No one to worry about. No one to nag. No one sassing back. "My daughter's away at boarding school," she could boast comfortably to friends down the street. "She's doing fine, thank you."

"No more is needed for a happy life," they had prophesized. Life wasn't that simple. I knew better.

As soon as I graduated, my mom and I prepared for my big high-school adventure. The Anderson School had a year-round program, beginning in July. The summer session consisted of a lighter schedule of morning classes and outdoor activities in the afternoon. Two-week vacations in September, December, March, and June were the only breaks. I overlooked this inconvenience, because the school had a three-to-one ratio of boys to girls. Less competition, I calculated, after having recently emerged in full Technicolor from my boy-crazed pubescence. The idea of attending an all-girls' school, as my dad had suggested many times, offended my budding teenage sensibilities, so the idea of attending a mostly boys school added to my pulsing anticipation.

The day finally came when my brothers and I piled into the car, happy with the excitement of three children going to the zoo. We drove for several hours, until the splendor of upstate New York unfolded into miles of beautiful Dutchess County farmland, where my great-uncle, Henry Morgenthau, had his country farm. The school, located near Hyde Park, New York, neighbored many splendid estates, such as the famed Vanderbilts', the opulent Ogden Mills estate, and the summer home belonging to Henry's good friend and boss Franklin D. Roosevelt. We toured the area, gawking at the exotic grounds and magnificent mansions, and then drove into the main campus of Anderson, now green and rich from summer's nurturing.

After checking in with the registration office, we drove to the girls' dormitory, inconveniently set five miles from the boys' dormitories on the main campus. Down a long serpentine lane, past thick forests of oak, maple, and elm, we found our way to Morgan Hall, settled among carefully disciplined lawns overlooking the Hudson River. Once a splendid summer estate of a wealthy banker named J. P. Morgan, my new home appealed soundly to my royal bloodline. The mansion, built of hand-chiseled stones and draped in a blanket of lush ivy, was a home for the wealthy, just like Grandpop's Apple Bee Farm. I didn't notice the bars on the basement windows.

When we arrived at the dorm, the Dean of Women, Mrs. Adams, greeted us with a crooked smile and showed us through the oversized, over polished wood-paneled lobby, dining room, and sitting area. She was a middle-aged woman with grapefruit colored hair. She had an odd assortment of prominent features, but all I could focus on were her knocked knees and her mouth. It was as if her creator sneezed right at those two times, creating indecision at the transition points of her calves and again at her chin. Half her mouth seemed frozen in a phony smile, the other half far into a distant world. She walked with the stride of a weather-beaten horse pulling a carriage around Central Park. She acted friendly enough, but I got the feeling from the moment I met her that she knew more about me than I did. She talked like a radio broadcaster, and she was my first hint that things at Anderson School just might not be so perfect. Mrs. Adams had been at Anderson since the year I was born, 1948.

We all sat down in the parlor, flanked with gigantic mirrors. I strained to catch a glimpse of the other girls coming in so I could size up the competition, while my mother carried on a timeworn conversation with the dean of women. I hadn't seen any students during my fall interview, and I felt anxious to begin my social indoctrination. My brothers, always in the high-fidget mode, did their best to behave. Small talk tended to do us all in.

When Mrs. Adams finally suggested my mother leave "now," I suddenly wanted a better sense of the Anderson School before my mother walked out the door. She was not allowed to venture upstairs to help me unpack. The boys, of course, thought the idea of running out the door was the best and left immediately at the suggestion.

"Can't she come upstairs with me and help me unpack?" I asked in a bit of panic.

"No, the rules clearly state no parents upstairs," Mrs. Adams answered, then turned to my mother. "You understand, I know. Sometimes it is difficult saying good-bye."

I expected this woman to leave us be, but she hovered over me like Snoopy on top of his doghouse, not saying a word but ready to pounce at any given moment. At this very second in my life, I became more constricted than I had ever been before. I felt a massive tightening in my chest, and my mind became fused into a small space, as if I'd fallen off a horse and not been able to get my breath, or as if I were under the waves of a raging ocean which was tugging at the sand that was giving way through my fingers. It was like everything I had known before and nothing. Perhaps I could at this very moment summon Superman to reach out and grasp the spinning earth. Slowly, with a determined grimace on his face, he would grab hold of the globe firmly until the whole world moved in the opposite direction—backward to the decision to go away to school-backward, to seventh grade and I won't flunk. Backward, and I won't run away. *Mom, I love you. Wait. Please. I ...*

Clever, these people are. Infuse with panic so thou doth not protest too much.

At this time both my mother and Mrs. Adams, I am certain, had their own personal directive and exit plans. I reluctantly kissed my mom and felt her arms around me stiffen. She would be better off without me, I was certain. I would stay strong. I gave each brother a quick good-bye, staving off tears of loneliness and a creeping panic, as they disappeared down the serpentine lane. I was on my own now, even more.

I carried my suitcase, brimming with new clothes, up the stairs and met the third-floor housemother, Mrs. Longo, a small, slick, rigid woman with shoe-polished hair all over her face. A German dictator. Maybe Polish. Maybe an officer from the concentration camps during World War II. Definitely an escapee from the Third Reich, hiding in a safe little place where she could continue the torture of little girls. *Not someone you want to get in the way of,* I thought to myself, as she showed me to my new room. I stopped next to the unmade mattress resting on its simple wooden frame. An eerie chill from the open window blew through me. "This is your room. You are fortunate you only have one roommate," Mrs. Longo stated indisputably. She turned and left, leaving me to assess my new home. I looked out the window. The view of the trees was good. I stared for a long time.

I was unpacking my trunk, when she walked into the room—Ann Goldenstein. She moved like a lumberjack. My new roommate. Her giant stride clumping across the floor commanded attention. I looked up to see her massive arms swinging by her side with military precision. She moved like a gorilla. My roommate, Ann Goldenstein. *You've got to be kidding,* I thought.

I stared down at the floor where she paced, the varnish scuffed bare from her giant shoes. I watched as she carefully put her heel down first with every step, so, no, the floor must have been worn before. After she paced twice, she plopped onto her perfectly made bed, spreading her knees apart under a new denim blue calf-length skirt, dangling her gorilla arms, which almost reached the floor. Nobody wore calf-length skirts anymore, did they? Maybe she wasn't really a girl, I mused. Inside her giant penny loafers were two perfectly polished pennies wedged into two perfectly polished leather flaps. And bobby socks. I couldn't believe it. It was the beginning of July, ninety-two degrees, 90 percent humidity, and she wore bobby socks. I was, at five feet five inches and 135 pounds, not a small fourteen-year-old. But this was a very big roommate.

"Hullo," she began. My eyes darted to my own brightly painted toenails, brazenly peering out from white summer sandals. Her bed was less than three feet from mine.

"Uh, hi," I fumbled, looking up to meet her gaze, trying to push my feet under the bed.

"My name's Ann. I'm a junior and a Morgan Hall monitor," she announced with all the arrogance of God. Suddenly, large words, with no hint of little-girl tones, started spewing rapidly from her mouth without stopping, and my mind whirled into a fog. I couldn't concentrate on her constant stream of instructions: what to do, where to go, what not to do, where not to go. She went on and on without asking or caring if anyone else wanted her to at all. She, my designated *only* roommate, Ann Goldenstein, was telling me what to do the first minute we met. Who died and left her in charge?

According to the manual written by the school, "Monitors are the leaders of Morgan Hall. The standards by which they are chosen are severe, and they are required to live up to those standards. The honor of being a monitor is probably the highest, and her duties are many and often hard. One does not enjoy reprimanding one's best friends, and this is often the case in a monitor's life. Monitors learn how to apply leadership in the school, an experience which will aid and guide them in their adult life."

When Ann's monologue faded into a muttering, her eyes darting around the room, I made up a lame excuse about the bathroom. Then I slowly walked through the empty halls, passing by rooms as I went, secretly looking for an alternative roommate. Another five minutes with that orangutan and I'd go crazy. The girl next door, sitting on her bed reading a large reference type book, weighed in at about 225 pounds and was even uglier than Ann. Her pimply face and arms were covered with dimpled, dripping flaps and folds. Everything in her room was yellow, my least favorite color. Everything in her room matched, as if each item had been made especially for her. Her bed quilt matched her socks, which matched her hair ribbon, which matched her drinking cup. I really didn't think she would do, either. I learned later she was an heir to the Florsheim shoe fortune. Go figure.

I went to the bathroom, closed the stall door, and sat down, slipping my thumb into my mouth, walking the streets of my mind. I heard girls chatting in the distance. When my thumb became wrinkled and stiff, I pulled my panties up and washed my face. I followed the sound of chatting girls into a larger room across the hall, when a girl with excessive scarring on her face yelled at me in a thick New York accent, "Hey, ya can't come in heee-ya. It's against the roo-oles." The veins in her face pulsed out at me as if accenting each word. "You have to stand outside the doo-or." I backed over the threshold and listened as she too went into a diatribe of the house rules. Her pretty, fragile roommate curled motionless on a windowsill, staring out through a window at the thick, green trees. I realized then that the door to the room had been removed.

"Oh, sorry, I didn't, uh …"

"Ya nee-ed ninety conduct points out of a hundred to pass every weeek," the girl explained, interrupting my attempts to arrange thoughts. She went on. There were demerits for messy clothes and messy rooms and messy hair. There were demerits for going into someone else's room. There were demerits for swearing. There were demerits for passing notes, whispering, holding hands and kissing (making the boy-to-girl ratio almost useless, of course). There were four demerits for the first late minute and one demerit for each additional minute; demerits for being in the wrong place at the wrong time, failing to sign in or out, talking after lights out, and fifteen demerits for not writing home on Sunday, whether you wrote home during the week or not. All the teachers marked your conduct card, so if you messed up anywhere, with anyone, any demerit could tilt your score, which rarely reached ninety even if you were perfect. Too many demerits and you were banned from all coed or extracurricular activity. I wondered how anyone could keep everything straight. I knew I was destined for trouble just for forgetting what I wasn't supposed to do. I just knew it.

I didn't break down until bedtime, hoping there might just be something during my first day that would give me hope, but as my brass ring faded, I could no longer hold back. I lay down on my bed and sobbed until my head pounded and my stomach jackknifed. Once again, all I could do was cry. I felt like a cat locked in a box ready for the river: no light, no food, no air; exhausted from the fight.

"Homesick," the Polish dictator proclaimed. I would get over it.

"Homesick," added Mrs. Padron, the other housemother, "nothing serious." Perhaps they thought I had a case of measles that itched and itched but eventually would go away—not a lasting ache in my heart from being sent down a river lined with polished paneled walls and no paths home, or out, or anywhere but here.

The next day I appealed to the dean of women. "There must be some mistake," I said to Mrs. Adams after carefully considering my situation. "I don't think I belong here, really. I think something is wrong." I tried to be polite. I just wanted to call home, which I now knew violated the rules, yet I didn't think my dad would ever make me stay here if he knew what kind of place this *really* was. I didn't tell Mrs. Adams this. She may have read it in my red and swollen eyes, because she finally let me call home.

First I called my mother. "Mom, I want to come home. Something's really wrong. I don't think I belong here."

"Oh honey, maybe you're just homesick. I know you feel sad now, but you'll feel better after a while," she told me. Had she been tipped off? Did she have a script? Where was my mom?

"No, I really want to come home, please?" A long pause came between us. Maybe she was glad to have me gone. "This school is a little strange, and I don't think I belong here." I would insist. I would prevail. I would reason. I would win.

"You've only just started, sweetheart. Give it some more time."

"No, this isn't about time. This is about a mismatch, a real mistake." Where was my logic? Where were the tools of persuasion? What could I possibly do?

"There's nothing I can do, Judy," she answered after time. "You better call your father."

"But he won't do anything," I predicted.

"Well, there's nothing I can do. You'll have to talk to your father," she ended firmly. Her change in voice surprised me. I began to suspect maybe, just maybe, she had known the truth about Anderson School. She couldn't possibly have made the decision knowing the real truth.

I tried my dad. The endless ringing echoed into the cross-country wire. I took a deep breath and thought about what I was going to say. *Don't show him you're too upset,* I thought to myself. *Try to act grown-up and he won't be mad. He can't be mad. He has to understand this time.* This wasn't a little thing like going to the movies with your friends or not picking up your room or sucking your thumb. This was life-threatening.

"Just stay through the summer," my dad answered predictably. "There's nothing I can do now. I've already paid for the summer. When you come out to Santa Fe for vacation in September, maybe we'll discuss it. You'll probably change your mind by then." Silence pushed open the gap once again between my dad and me, and then he hung up, leaving me with a vacant, helpless feeling. *Maybe he didn't hear me right. Maybe I can explain better face to face,* I thought to myself. After all, I didn't have time to tell him everything. I really didn't want to because Mrs. Adams was in the room while I was calling. *He won't make me stay here; I know it. I'll make him understand when I see him in September.* I knew I wouldn't change my mind.

Anderson School was started by Victor Vance Anderson in 1924 as an experimental school to handle troubled kids. Dr. Anderson was the American Orthopsychiatry Association's first president and wrote a book called *The Psychiatric Clinic in the Treatment of Conduct Disorders of Children and the Prevention of Juvenile Delinquency*. So, what was my diagnosis, and who had made it? Was I a juvenile delinquent in training? Did I have psychiatric disorder in my bones? I clearly was disordered, but how did I become such an American anomaly?

The average IQ of the Anderson student body was much higher than mine, yet each had a special problem. Many were adopted. There were kids with dyslexia, with facial tics, body handicaps, cerebral palsy, epilepsy, and two or three savants of varying degrees. The more severely autistic kids were on another campus, not far away, in Staatsburg-on-Hudson. A few of the girls had tried to kill themselves, usually by slitting their wrists or drug overdoses. Some of the boys lisped or stuttered. One fellow never took his thumb out of his mouth, in spite of constant public bantering. He looked like Porky Pig, really, all sort of pink and pale and puffy. They said he had an IQ over two hundred. I guess that's important, especially if you look like Porky Pig.

There were kids that had run away from home and kids that had been expelled from school. There were sexually abused kids and sexually obsessed kids, but then, most of us teenagers had that problem, I guessed. There were alcoholics and drug addicts in training. Most of the kids were rich, many Jewish, but I felt all were lost inside a life someone else had forced upon them. All I did was cry a little too much, or so I thought. Being sad wasn't a reason for being here. Really, being sad would just go away some day by itself. Being sad didn't warrant this much punishment. Or did it?

During the summer, while continuing to assess my new surroundings, I adopted a condescending attitude toward everyone, including the teachers, so I could stay linked to my past and keep my hopes alive. I documented evidence for my case and tried to have a little fun while I was at it. I knew I wasn't coming back; I knew my dad just couldn't send me back if he knew everything, so I kept my sense of humor, stayed out of trouble, remained aloof, and counted the days.

I was elected president of my class, though I had no idea why. Meanwhile, my grandmother, Mom Knight, treated me as if I were off at some elegant boarding school. She sent me a beautiful white blouse, plush royal blue towels monogrammed with JEN, and a large box of stationery printed with my name and new address:

Judith E. Naumburg
The Anderson School
Staatsburg-on-Hudson, New York

There were no zip codes, and a stamp cost four cents. It was the summer of 1962. I was fourteen years old, "not beautiful," my mom had once carefully organized my ego for me, "but you'll get by."

"You won't win any beauty contests," Dad had dug deeper, as only he could do, "but you should be able to find yourself a decent husband when the time comes." I certainly wasn't going to find a suitable husband around here, but the girl-boy ratio made me look pretty good, and, let's face it—who in their right mind turned their nose up at a little attention from the opposite sex?

Between the boys and President Kennedy's fitness program challenging everyone to swim fifty miles, which I happily completed, distractions kept me sane. The days passed quickly, and summer filled my soul, though I never lost sight of the fall. I took weekly life-saving instruction, played in coed softball games, went to Arts and Crafts, and practiced with the cheerleading team. Cheerleading was the only organized sport for the girls. I even took tennis lessons, because a wonderful sandy-haired college sophomore from Colgate showed me how to hold the racquet. I hadn't the faintest idea what love-forty meant. He was so kind and so normal; I hoped his sanity would help me stay sane.

Early in August, when the hot, moist air wrapped our strength in a straitjacket, one of the new girls slashed her wrists. She was a tall, pale Swedish girl I didn't know very well, big-boned with staccato features. First, the rumor was that she had died. Then we were told she had been expelled. Mrs. Longo, without comment or emotion, packed up the girl's clothes and belongings, darting carefully in and out of the hallway as we all watched. Though I never saw her again, the vision of her dripping wrists, frayed to the world, remained in my memory much too long.

The initial report from the guidance department (Mrs. Adams) failed to relate to my parents what I was hoping for:

> At first Judy's attitude implied some rather sullen withdrawal, but at present she is more outgoing, pleasant, and relaxed. In counseling, she has been able to relate easily, has discussed her liking for the school, but indicated some resentment at being sent to a boarding school ... to date Judy has done well in all areas.

My conduct and effort were satisfactory, and I received a ninety-two for personal appearance, table deportment, and room inspection.

Somehow, the perception that I wanted to go to boarding school, just not this one, never made the journey home. I met with Mrs. Adams once a week and stayed very certain she understood my dissatisfaction. I still felt in control and able to impress upon all concerned that this was not the best way to proceed with my high-school future. I had potential. I was too sane for Anderson.

September came, and I flew from New York to Santa Fe, where I planned to make my appeal. Dad had built a sprawling adobe home on the top of a hill just outside of town on Tano Road. My brothers and I each had our own room, each decorated in the colors and patterns of our choice. My room was blue, overlooking the horse's head at the Santa Fe ski area, an area defined by trees and light. I shared a long tiled bathroom with Essie. Every detail in the house was carefully thought out: the hand-hewn beams from Colorado, the gray penitentiary brick floors and fancy recessed lighting. We had never lived in a house built by an architect and an interior designer before. Each room had fantastic views of the mountains or sunsets. This house was a long way from Doylestown. A different man lived here, one I wasn't certain I understood. He was no longer the dairy farmer, the hay baler, the fox hunter, or the failed politician. Between his new concrete business, new home, and old girlfriend, he seemed pretty happy.

Still, I pressed on with my mission. I chose a moment when I thought he was in a good mood. Sitting on my royal blue Castro Convertible couch with pillows made to match the wispy wallpaper, in my semi self-decorated bedroom, Dad listened to my lengthy explanation. I chose every word with more care than I had chosen anything I had ever said before. "Dad, I don't think you know what kind of school this is," I explained. "You haven't actually visited the school." I knew he had only communicated with them by mail or phone. "The kids are different, kinda strange. Not just because I don't know them, but they have real problems. Like this one girl, she came to school and she wasn't there three weeks and she tried to kill herself. Slit her wrists and all. I mean, some of the kids are all right, I guess, but mostly they are pretty messed up."

"I know all about this school, Judy. The school is good for you," he answered when I had finished my explanation. "I want you to stay." An awkward silence pervaded between us. Termites of tension gnawed at whatever self-assurance I had managed to accumulate, but I didn't want to give up. In spite of his unsympathetic answer, I tried again, more carefully describing each detail of this strange little school with the strange people moving through their intricate maze of madness. I thought if I could be diplomatic enough he would understand the severity of my unhappiness. I remember the growing panic inside of me, though I don't remember exactly what we said. He looked as he had in Puerto Rico and many times before. Plastic. Hard and smooth on the outside, hollow on the inside.

"I'm not going to take you out of Anderson School," he said in conclusion, as if he never heard anything I said, as if I had never made my plea in his presence. "They can help you there and I want you to stay." No alternatives, no possibilities. He stood up as if to go.

My throat closed slowly and I pushed hard against the fear welling up inside. What could I do? What could I say to make him understand? *Oh God, don't make him mad, Judy; they'll lock you up forever.* "But I can't go back there," I blurted out in a last effort to persuade him. "Dad," I took a deep breath, "this school is for crazy kids." There, I did it. I told him the truth.

He started toward me, his face hard and angry. He blew up into the size of a hot-air balloon. A thousand miles came between us once again. He began sternly, "Judy, you *are* crazy. You are going back to this school, and I don't want to talk about it anymore. End of discussion. Period." As I watched his body turn and slam the door, I fell deep into Alice's well.

# CHAPTER 12

### Hawaiian Punch

Why do fools fall in love?
Why do birds sing so gay
And lovers await the break of the day
Why do they fall in love?

**F. Lymon/G. Goldner**

Soon after returning to Anderson School in September, I received a two-page letter from my father, typed in his business-blue ink on Colony Materials's stationery. I knew he hadn't dictated this one, because it was filled with typos and spelling mistakes. He reminded me that I had flunked seventh grade and warned that I would never amount to anything if I didn't stay with this school, where my grades were good (a 95 in Art and a 76 in Economic Citizenship for the summer). "One of the best schools in the country," he said, as if his daughter attended Andover or Deerfield. I wasn't old enough to know what was good for me, which I suppose had some truth to it. If I did anything foolish, he warned, he would never give me another cent for support of any kind. "If you end up on the street, that will be your problem," he wrote. He wanted me to be like his Sunday night waffles, beaten to a perfect consistency, measured, and poured onto a hot griddle, closed up and cooked (not too much) until I puffed into a perfect mold. Then he could eat me the rest of his life with so much maple syrup he couldn't taste me.

He also scolded me for writing my mom and asking her to send me some clothes. He thought I had asked her to buy new ones. Assuming she could pay for everything with her alimony payments, he had cut off her charge accounts. Though the court had ordered him to materially provide for us, he was angry whenever Mom took us shopping for clothes or school supplies. Money was always an issue; everything cost too much or was not necessary, unless the purchase was his idea, which almost never happened when it came to my needs. When he voiced displeasure with my mom, money was often the root of it. I didn't understand a lot of what was going on between my parents, because they constantly reacted to each other through their lawyers. Whatever one said or did, the other became angry. Anger was obvious on both sides, and little or no discussions were held as briefings for us kids. They each had their own criticisms of the other, the different injustices that darted out whenever occasions came up. Their separation was still painful, even after almost four years. Though my dad no longer had my mom followed by private detectives, and he had a nice new life for himself in Santa Fe, he still thought she was always trying to steal from him or take advantage of him. This is a trait, I learned as I grew older, that many Naumburgs have. They give a lot of money away to charities, but they are leery of their relatives and their hired help. When my parents were married, my mom signed the tax return unread. I don't know what my dad thought my mother was doing, but I never felt overindulged by either of them, especially my mom. She always seemed to be doing the best she could financially and she worked very hard.

I was my father's dandelion. I was the spot the *Cat in the Hat* couldn't get out. He wanted control, but I dared to question. He wanted to buy all my clothes and know where I was going and what I was doing, even if it didn't involve him. As if his power or control had been mocked, he had a fit whenever my mom bought me clothes or even when my grandmother bought me an electric Lady Schick Razor. (I had to send the razor back, because he thought I was too young to shave.)

I wrote my mother:

*He sent me a box from Saks Fifth Avenue that had a skirt that practically touched the ground and a shirt that would probably fit a grown man, but it doesn't fit me ... I have changed back to the crappy old me ... I am so damn homesick now, I don't know which way to turn. Who am I going to talk to? None of the staff is even worth looking at, let alone talking to. The school is really nice, I guess, but it's me. What's wrong with me? Why can I never be happy like any other normal young lady? I hate the women staff ... Isn't it against the law to open other people's mail? ... Maybe I'm just a baby, but I am scared, all over, and about stuff I don't even know myself. Please, don't ever not love me. I would die first.*

Then my mom wrote me a letter that really shocked me. Until now, she had been the only one I could write my feelings to. I felt free to tell her everything I thought, every emotion or downturn. Often, when I had questioned in the past, she would entertain me, talk to me, respond with words that soothed me, no matter how I twisted and toggled. In this letter, her tone of support and hope was gone. She no longer believed in me. I was frightened, because she was the only safe place I knew, and even though things kept happening to me, I always felt deep down inside that she believed in me. Now I was really scared. I wrote in response:

*Mother,*

*I am sorry you think I am crying wolf (in other words, a liar). There is nothing more I can do about it.*

*I don't know why, how or when you changed your mind about the school and furthermore I could care less. I am terribly sorry I got you upset. Maybe it would be better if I didn't take a weekend. I would be too concerned about getting you upset. Maybe this school will help me not be this way. I don't know. I thought we were going to get me out of this school next year, but I guess not. Maybe it's because I am doing so well in this school. What do I have to do, flunk out? Well, I might as well tell you that I am not going to. I am doing what I want to do and no one in my family will stop me again. And when I want to leave, I am leaving. Whether I flunk out or just leave.*

*Also, you changed your mind about the reading of the mail. Apparently I am lying about that too or maybe you just don't care how they help me as long as they change me.*

Faced with four years at Anderson or living the life of a fugitive, I felt there was no way to turn. I was on the subway of life, a rapid-moving transit, being pushed by a crowd, mangled into a small door, compressed by the boundaries of life, grateful perhaps that I could breathe, but, well no, *was I*? Steve was at Fountain Valley (wasn't it a normal boarding school?), and Flip lived at home with my mom, still going to Buckingham Friends School. Wait, why did Steve get to go to a "normal" prep school? He was the one who majored in photographing my vagina and blowing up the basement with chemistry sets and throwing trains at little girls' heads. He was the sex-crazed torturer escaped from the womb, almost destroying my mother on the way out and hell-bent on doing me in during our lifetime. How did the master trickster avoid slipping through the crack of global sanity? The first-born male thing again, I presumed. Brooks Brothers suits and sanity.

I wanted to click my heels three times, cross my heart and hope to die, promise "There's no place like home"—but I knew

I lived in the real world now; the fantasy of childhood had melted away like the wicked witch of the west under a bucket of water. I wanted to run away—but where? Who would take me? If I ran away again, I could end up someplace worse. I had been sentenced to jail, for correction, for rightness, because I was crazy. What *was* crazy? Crazy was out of control, and every day my emotions and heart claimed more of me. I grew obese with the fear of what I could change into. Maybe I was already out of control. "I don't care," I droned over and over, trying to make the pain go away. "I don't care."

I thought about going crazy. If I was crazy, how and when did I get that way? Was I born crazy? Did it come from mother's milk or eating Tony the Tiger's Frosted Flakes? I distantly recalled a psychiatrist's office when I was five or six, putting blocks together, playing in a silent room full of toys, then talking to a strange man with a low voice I had never seen before. My father told me I was sent there because Steve and I fought too much. My brother Steve tells me we never had a fight until Flip was born. My mother tells me I was sent to the psychiatrist because of a difficult relationship with my father and the fact that I wasn't doing well in school. How well can you do in school at five years old? I just remember being scared while waiting for the psychiatrist to come and talk to me and glad when it was all over. When I was twelve or thirteen, I met with the head of the psychiatric department at Yale University, a colleague my Uncle George arranged for me to see. This time they probably examined why I wasn't living up to my potential, why I almost flunked seventh grade, and other things I was not privy to. I looked at pages and pages of black ink blotches in contorted, splattered shapes on dull cream paper and talked about divorce with a tall, argentine-haired stranger in a big, well-lit office. He never said anything about crazy.

And I remembered the time I went to Hershey, Pennsylvania, for the Buckingham Friends School eighth-grade trip, a celebration of the end of the year for them, but a time of reflection for me on losing my boyfriend Randy, who had moved to California. During the whole eighth grade, no other boy had wanted to go with me. Pile loneliness on top of three years' worth of custody battles, puberty, migraine headaches, almost flunking seventh grade, and you got me— sitting on the ledge of our hotel window, overlooking the city lights of Hershey, smelling the sick, sweet stench of chocolate even after dark, avoiding the lights and sounds of the big amusement park off in the distance—ready to jump. But I didn't. Sitting on the ledge crying was easier than jumping. When I was thirteen, life wasn't fun anymore. There was no way out. I was a failure. Nobody loved me. I imagined myself jumping into a big vat of chocolate, drowning in the only thing I truly loved, until my friend Laurie came back into the room and interrupted my thinking.

I tried to remember being bad enough to be sentenced to "crazy." I had never been arrested, as my brothers had. I knew that when I was little my mother put me over her knees and spanked me with her shoe, but I don't remember why, and neither does she. I remembered my dad walking into the den one day, when I was pensively sucking my thumb, stroking my upper lip with my finger, lying on the floor, feet propped up on the brand-new brocade curtains. He slapped my thigh, quick as a bolt of lightning. I never felt so much piercing pain. He was very angry—but I didn't think I was crazy.

Was I crazy because I ran away? Was I crazy because I cried too much? Was I crazy because I had headaches and sucked my thumb? If I wasn't really crazy, could I catch it? Was crazy contagious? Did it crawl into your skin like ringworm? I only wanted to be good enough to go home.

The slot-box days of September were like a post office. Each slot was filled with something: classes, duties, chores, grooming, eating, homework, therapists, meetings, sleeping, disruptive tantrums, friends' love problems, and the ever-present, inane self-absorptions of others. There were no empty

111

boxes for choices: no slipping off to ride my horse with the sun beating down on my head and the heat of the horse under my thighs, no locking myself in my room and dancing with the doorknob, no climbing among my stuffed animals and daydreaming, not even a chance to head down to the den and watch Spin and Marty when I felt like relaxing. I forgot to feel grateful for all those days of running through the sprinklers and feeling the grass with my bare soles. I had run out of the choices of my childhood.

The powers that be moved me to the largest room in Morgan Hall, with three other girls: Lorraine Master, Susan Kaplan, and Valerie Temple. I was happy to be free from the ape, so I settled into my newly shared quarters. Maybe we could have some fun here.

I had never lived with three girls in the same room. Lorraine was the most vivacious, and bubbling was her specialty. She had mastered the art of denial and moved through life without fear of retributions, or so I thought.

Often, in her room, she stood at the mirror, meticulously applying thick layers of pancake makeup, eyeliner, mascara, shadow, and pink frosted lipstick that reflected the light. She had intense daylight-blue eyes, peanut skin, and a cute little-girl nose. After applying her makeup, she teased her fried bleached hair until it stood on end, a bit like Frankenstein with his finger in a socket. For the final step, she brushed her hair back smooth from her bangs and placed a small matching bow just above her bangs, leaving the back frizzed and teased. She never smoothed out the back of her hair. To her, she looked perfect, but because she couldn't see behind her, the back of her hair remained frayed and splattered to the rest of the world. From the front she looked like Barbie, puffed and perfect. From the back she looked like a mental case. When you tried to smooth her hair down or suggest she brush it a little better, she threw a fit. Lorraine had a temper.

Lorraine was the daughter of a woman in a wheelchair. She acted as if whatever crippling disease her mother had, afflicted her own body. I never really knew anyone who could snap as quickly or explode with seemingly no premeditation. I hated the day her mother came to visit. Her mom wheeled herself into the room and Lorraine transformed into an agitated, bloodthirsty pit bull, barking at her powerless mother as if she were a deformed beggar on the street. I cringed at her words. There were ways to speak to your parents, and I didn't feel yelling was the answer, but what if they didn't hear? Dialogue was most important, as my mother taught me, but Lorraine yelled at her mother for little reasons, petty little reasons I couldn't understand. But I liked Lorraine okay.

Susan was one of those girls you could put your hand through and never feel a thing. She was nice, but she didn't seem to have any substance. She agreed with everything you said. She smiled vacantly and never joined a club or activity, and though she usually had her head in a book, she also never got a passing grade, as far as I knew. Susan stayed for one year.

Valerie, with the face of a child, was the youngest of us all. She far surpassed the tic-laden neuroses of the rest of us, as she sat motionless on the windowsill and stared out. When ordered to move, she did so with minimal energy and no emotion. I never saw her study and she communicated rarely, leaving the rest of us daring to be the first to approach or cajole. Her emptiness surrounded her like Pig Pen's cloud, and did we dare move in, dare to comment or feel compelled to help? Her mom worked full-time as a child psychologist and her dad was a psychiatrist. Valerie was the experiment. Anytime you tried to talk to her, she looked up into the skies, as if heaven would send down an answer. She rarely spoke. The only time I ever saw her smile was when I told her she was lucky her parents gave her such a beautiful name. Even then, she smiled at the trees on the other side of the glass pane. Valerie didn't stay three months. I never knew where she went or what happened to her, but this was the only thing normal at Anderson School.

In spite of all the girls in my room, I soon became close friends with a girl named Candy, who lived on the second floor. Just like I did on my first day, she burst into our room with lots of energy and announced, "Hi there!"

I couldn't believe myself when I blurted out, "Uh, you're not allowed in each other's room. The rules."

"What? You *are* kidding," she said, literally backing out into the hall, wiggling her butt in the air.

"No, they're afraid we might steal each others Kotex," I said with a sly smile, playing off her humor.

"Well that would be a catastrophe. Hi, I'm Candy."

"I'm Judy. Which room are you in?"

"Downstairs; come on." She led me downstairs to the second floor. I followed like a puppy. "I just came from the main building. There was a kid there that looked like a bird. I swear to God. He was seven feet tall, weighed twenty-five pounds, and walked like an ostrich. His nose was kinda like a beak, too, come to think of it. I hope the other guys are a lot little cuter, or I'm outta here."

"Well, I was here all summer and, let me tell you, there is no Troy Donohue on this campus."

"I'd settle for James Dean." *Ah yes. The rebel without a cause. We all had a cause, really. And sometimes even a dream.* "So what's it like here?" she asked innocently. I stared at her soft strawberry hair and freckles, wondering why she was here, why she was crazy. "I mean, if you were here this summer and all, you know."

"Oh, well, it was okay, I guess." I wondered what I should really tell her—whether I should prepare her or just let her figure it out. I didn't want to scare her away.

"Looks like just a bunch of crazy kids, really." She drew me in like quicksand.

"Well, we are, I guess."

"Hah, hah. No way! You don't look so crazy."

"Wow, that's all your stuff?" I asked, noticing her four trunks on the floor. "Geez, you got a lot of stuff."

She started unpacking, as I slid down the door jamb onto the floor, keeping my butt just on the edge. "You got a boyfriend? Maybe back home or something?" she asked.

"Nah, not really. They're a little tough to sort through around here."

"Well, we just have to see what we can find. Maybe you didn't look hard enough."

"To be honest, I thought I was going home after the summer. My parents decided that wasn't such a great idea."

"How come they did that?"

"I'm still trying to figure that out myself."

"Shit, well, come on; let's go downstairs. We'll figure it out together."

Candy played the piano beautifully, and I spent hours watching her play, singing with her, learning from her, note by note, "Malaguena" and "Cast Your Fate to the Wind." She helped me graduate from "Chopsticks" with melodious chords that melted away the place of our existence. She taught me how to escape through music, and I loved listening to her play classical and pop pieces. Still, every once in a while, we frantically "chopsticked" together, laughing inside our collective madness.

Every morning, Mrs. Longo woke us at six by ringing a little brass bell, like the Salvation Army sergeant on Fifth Avenue. I hated the morning. I hated Mrs. Longo. I hated her ugliness. I knew she derived pleasure from torturing us. I often woke from my dreams and struggled to remember where I was. The linked chains of a prison reality pulled me down, as my reality adjusted into the impending day at the Anderson School.

Before we dressed or brushed our teeth, we dutifully performed our chore of the week: cleaning the disgusting white-tiled bathrooms, dry-mopping the wooden inlaid floors, dusting the banisters, washing countless mirrors, polishing the woodwork, or taking out the garbage. Cleaning the toilets made me sick. Fourteen-year-old girls do not have to know how to clean toilets. I longed for the gentle waking from my mother, the giant walnut tree outside my window, and the long walk down our lane to meet the school bus. But that was all gone now.

After our chores were graded, we showered, dressed, cleaned our own rooms, and stood motionless outside our door as Mrs. Longo or Mrs. Padron diligently went through each room for another grade. The bed had to be made just so, no wrinkles hiding in the corners, no dust on the floor, no dirty clothes on the closet floor. I watched as they performed their inspections, thinking they themselves had to be a little crazy to be doing this stuff. When we had been silently graded (we wouldn't know our grades until the end of the week), we methodically boarded a bus for the main campus.

The yellow bus snaked through the woods and out into the day, through a small town called Staatsburg-on-Hudson. Often I sat next to the window, gazing out at the world as if now it were a foreign country, someplace I would never be a part of. If there were children in the streets, I watched as they stopped and stared with curious, unblinking eyes, while we rode through their town in our yellow bus with Anderson School in big black letters on the side. I knew their parents had told them about us. They were probably waiting for us to do something weird, like maybe jump out of a moving bus. In the beginning, I felt myself sliding down into my seat or dropping my head low to avoid recognition. After a while, I stared back. The stare sent a clear message. I didn't care.

Twice a week we visited a psychiatrist or psychologist in an office next to the headmaster. The turnover was high, and I never knew who would be sitting at the mahogany throne when I entered. Dr. Chauncey Martin was the first. Chauncey had the personality of a wet dishrag. He sat behind his desk and asked how I was, and I answered, "Just fine." Each time, he small-talked for a while, and then he finally asked about my parents and the divorce. I answered, "I don't care," which he wrote down in his little book, and then I left. I never knew if he expected me to contribute anything more. I mean, how could anyone explain a lifetime in one hour?

The only shrink I remember liking was a woman who truly had escaped from Nazi Germany. She was a heavyset woman with wild hair, never quite put into place. She had been a medical physician in her homeland, before she had been forced to flee with her husband. She told me wonderful tales of narrow escapes, border crossings, and Nazis, and how they had eventually arrived at Ellis Island. She said she couldn't practice medicine here because of the great differences in the culture and language and profession, so, rather than repeating medical school, she earned a degree in psychiatry. I loved hearing her talk about herself, which we did at length after I told her I was "fine." She, too, left after one year.

In the fall, I was demoted to vice president of the freshman class. Every year from then on I was elected president. I never knew quite why this perpetuation of the highest honor was bestowed upon this uncaring, depressed little girl who still secretly sucked her thumb, sometimes until it got all saliva soaked and wrinkled. Someone had to know I sucked my thumb, I thought to myself, but I guess my obsession looked normal. Me and Porky Pig. Mrs. Adams thought I was wonderful for being elected president of the class. Not bad for a delinquent in training—or whatever I was.

But I hated myself. I was ugly. I was stupid. When I looked in the mirror, I saw the lines around my eyes were angry. Nothing felt good. My skin was too pale. My dried-cow-dung hair was boring, even when teased with a small bow at my crown. My hazel eyes committed to nothing, neither brown nor blue nor green. Nothing felt good; no one loved me. Okay, I was vice president of my class, but that wasn't the long hug I so desperately needed. I needed a healer. I needed something, but what? And where? The school grew smaller and more smothering every day. Everyone's problems were your problems. The insanity was contagious, and it was difficult to maintain any independence of thought or feeling. I was trapped. No cuffs on my wrist, but trapped just the same.

Then, one Friday night when the nights and the leaves turned crisp, my healer materialized. The god I had prayed for appeared in the flesh. A party hosted by the North Hall boys brought forth my vision of perfection. Where had I been? How had I missed him?

I stood in a large doorway absently watching a few select North Hall boys play pool. The guys were cool, tough. They had an aura of control. This was their dorm, their party. The stage was set. I moved over onto an empty stool in the corner, while four guys took turns stroking and jabbing at multicolored balls with numbers on them. They were joking and jeering with each other before each shot. The scene didn't feel like Anderson, certainly not the girl's dorm. Maybe we were in a pool hall, downtown anywhere. Darkness hid the outside world. I could pretend. I was out on my own. Bob Dylan sang in a strained voice through a speaker hung from the ceiling, his voice as jagged as the peaks of Everest. "A hard rain's gonna fall," he predicted, with words separated by pauses: angry, raspy, and determined. In between the words, more spoken than sung, "I've walked and I've crawled on six crooked highways." He played the harmonica with a flat melody as wise as the wind. "I've stepped in the middle of seven sad forests." I grew mesmerized, distracted, and challenged. "The executioner's face is always well hidden." *What was he saying? How did he know? How did he dare? Maybe he's crazy too,* I thought. Maybe if you could market craziness, you would be rich rather than locked up. Crazy wouldn't matter if you didn't care. I listened again. He was me. I was there. "Then I'll stand on the ocean until I start sinkin'." His voice was coarse, too defiant, too honest. He would never be rich, whoever this Bob Dylan was. But I understood.

Suddenly, one of the boys bent directly in front of me, pulling his cue way back behind him, gently pressing the butt close to my stomach. I forgot about Dylan and the night.

"Excuse me," he said, standing tall again, moving into a slight smile, and looking straight into me, as if challenging me. I felt my face flush. His deep green eyes shot deep inside, immobilizing me. My body burned.

"I'm sorry," I answered to my surprise. I slid against the wall for my escape, but I found my eyes unable to unlock from his.

"Don't go," he said, "just move a little." His lips curled into a smile. Nervous laughter echoed through the room.

I stood and moved a few feet so he could shoot. I watched for a few minutes longer, not wanting to appear afraid or conspicuous in any way, then left. *He really didn't need to pull his cue back that far,* I thought, as I reconstructed the incident.

I walked around, looking for another activity to take the place of the pool game. I felt an unfamiliar arm reach around my waist. "Want some punch?" It was the boy with the green eyes.

"Um, sure," I said. My answer triggered his arm to drop. I inhaled a little relief, though I had to acknowledge the electricity.

"My name's Pete; what's yours?" asked a confident voice.

"Judy," I offered. He dipped out lipstick-red punch into a Dixie cup and handed it to me.

"Hawaiian Punch," he said. My eyes automatically drifted to the bowl of chips and dip. "Want some chips?"

"No. No, thanks," I lied. I felt fat. I crossed my arms in front of my stomach. Suddenly I wanted to be thinner and prettier. My pig-pink mohair sweater made me feel too puffy. *Oh God*, I thought to myself, *I will never eat again.*

As Pete talked, we angled toward two corner chairs and sat down. He pulled his chair closer, leaning his elbows on the armrests. His hair, black as Beauty's, slicked back against his temple in a full Brylcreemed curl. His eyes were woven with the colors of summer's fields. The slight smell of Aqua Velva reached around me. It seemed as if everything about this boy-man was entrapping me. I was caught on a merry-go-round, spinning through the night, wind blowing my hair. Was this my brass ring?

"You weren't here this summer, were you?" I asked, not remembering him.

"No, were you?"

"Yeah, lucky me—my first summer and hopefully my last."

"Yeah, I know what you mean. What grade are you?"

"Freshman, and you?"

"Senior," he answered confidently. He looked like senior, I suppose.

"Were you here before?"

"Yeah, this is my third and last year."

"So, I thought everyone had to stay through the summer."

He laughed quickly at my question. "Boy, are you naïve. This school will do anything for money."

"Oh well, I'm new; I don't really know anything."

"My Dad wanted me to come home for the summer and work," he told me. As if reading my mind, he added, "The school was glad to get rid of me, because I cause too much trouble, but they can't afford not to take me back." He smiled. This was his last year. He came to Anderson after being thrown out of his high school back home.

"Rearranging the furniture?" the dorm father interrupted.

"Take a powder, Jones," answered Pete without looking up. My eyes betrayed my shock. The teacher smirked and moved on. Pete wasn't afraid of these people. *What a great way to be,* I thought to myself—*unafraid.* I smiled, taking on his confidence.

"You have a nice dimple," he said.

"Ugh, I hate it," I answered, raising my hand to cover the dimple. "My father used to sing this stupid song, 'She's got dimples on her butt ... I love her just the same.' I guess he learned it in the trenches during World War II." I wondered why that memory came up, why Dad was always ruining the moment. I thought about how my dad personally clarified compliments: "She can ride, but she can't jump" or "If she's so smart, why can't she type?" He added these when people complimented me.

We talked briefly about where we had grown up, some of our likes and dislikes, and what kids we were friendly with, till the party ended. I went home dizzily wondering about the boy with the thick black hair and the deep green eyes and the arm he put on my waist.

The next morning I sat in American History class, trying to focus on the drone of Mr. Ginsberg's dissertation about the 1765 Stamp Act. The English Parliament taxed the thirteen American colonies to help finance the British army, stationed in the New World. The colonists rebelled at the idea of "taxation without representation" and boycotted British goods. I didn't suppose they much liked the British army, either. We Americans are true descendants of rebels. Rebelliousness is inherited; printed right there in the history book.

Mr. Ginsberg was a big man. His carrot-colored hair topped his massive overweight structure like an indecision. Though he was one of the youngest teachers, he still looked old to me. When he didn't sit behind his desk or pace back and forth incessantly, he would sit on a metal stool right in front of the class, his crotch at eye level, flapping his massive thighs in and out, back and forth, knees clamping shut, then spreading wide apart. Sometimes I hardly noticed his motion. Sometimes his nervousness fused into my nerves, setting me on edge, shifting me side to side in my chair. Mr. Ginsberg was a wonderful, friendly man, but sometimes I couldn't move past the flapping thighs. Open and shut. Sometimes it was hard not to wonder what his penis looked like, the large bulge hanging heavily down the side of his leg like a wrecking ball, I assumed much like my dad's.

When the bell rang, I gathered all my books and saw Pete waiting for me outside the door. He was leaning against the wall, books cradled in his arms. I went over to him. "Hi," I gushed, trying not to smile too much.

"I'll walk you to French class."

"How did you know I had French class?" I asked.

"Just a hunch," he smiled—a smile to melt a thousand polar caps. We started slowly down the hall. In three minutes another piercing bell would sound, and we had to be seated before the bell stopped, or demerits flew. "You're not like the other girls," he said.

"Thanks. Wait, what does that mean?" I supposed being different could be advantageous, though I hadn't quite figured it all out. The concept of being different wasn't really what I aspired to at this point, but nonetheless, I stayed around for his answer.

"When you talk, you're interesting. You talk about feelings, and people and things. You wait for answers. Most girls just talk nonstop. They giggle but don't listen."

I smiled nervously. "I don't know. I grew up with two brothers, and I always liked being with boys better than girls. I never have had many girlfriends," I explained.

"I like you," he said, leaning down a little closer. He felt strong, assured in a way many boys were not. "Do you like French?" His mouth spoke the word carefully.

"Oh, uh, I don't know. No, I hate it. My dad speaks fluent French, because he lived in Nice for a while, when he was little, and my grandparents spend every winter in Monte Carlo, so I guess I'm expected to speak French too."

"Are they rich, your grandparents?"

"Yeah, I guess they are. They live in a big house in Croton, have an apartment in the city and travel a lot." He didn't seem very interested in the answer. We reached the door of French class and I stopped. Pete sauntered right in and peeked around the corner, where the French teacher, Mme. Patterson, sat. She reminded me of a glob of lime Jell-O, sitting on a plate, looking as if she could squish out the sides. She always wore a dark pillbox hat, like the one Bob Dylan sang about. Pete looked at her, then me, then wrinkled his nose and puckered his mouth for both of us to see.

"Shoo," she shrilled in a high-pitched voice, struggling to rise from behind her desk. "Shoooo, shoooo," she chanted while flipping the back of her hand toward Pete as she finally stood and waddled toward him. I started to laugh, as he headed down the hall. She grabbed my arm and pulled me into the classroom, slamming the door.

My next class was study hall, and again Pete walked me down the noisy hall. He leaned his elbow up against the doorjamb, and I moved close into the crook of his arm, without touching him. I felt the whole class watching us. A new couple. New gossip. New drama. Endless scrutiny. His gaze warmed my blood. I avoided him by focusing on his black West Side Story shoes—neat and polished and not quite dated—his cuffed black pants and thin black belt, his white shirt faintly smelling of starch. His words moved like those of a hypnotist: steady, commandeering, quiet. Then again, the loud piercing shrill of the bell. *Three minutes already*, I thought to myself. Reality can be a very stabbing thing. As I turned and walked into the classroom, I wanted more of this person, more than the three minutes allowed, more than anyone would ever allow.

When I sat down next to Lorraine, she laughed. "So it looks pretty serious, huh?"

"God, I don't know. He's nice. Why was everyone staring at us?" I asked her, spreading my plaid skirt smoothly over my knees.

She leaned over and whispered, "He really likes you."

"Do you think so?" I asked, not daring to turn my eyes back to the door just in case he was still there.

"Yeah," she paused. "I know so."

"Gee, how do *you* know?" I asked, thinking perhaps he had told her something. "Did he say anything to you?"

"He had a boner," she added flatly.

At first I didn't quite understand what she was saying. I found no hint of definition anywhere, and she wasn't offering. Silence spread between us. I desperately wanted to pretend I knew what she was talking about, but she was staring at me, waiting for an answer, some revealing expression. My desire to act cool wrestled with my curiosity, until the winner finally emerged.

"A what?" I confessed.

"A boner, you know, a hard-on," she answered.

"Uh, what's a hard-on?" I asked.

"It's when a guy's penis gets hard," she said with a ton of aplomb.

"Oh my God, you're crazy. How can you tell?" I was dying to know, or was I?

"I could see it in his pants. It means you really excite him."

"Judy and Lorraine, that's enough talking. Open your books," warned the study hall teacher. Oh God. My face flushed with hot molten lava, and I wanted to run, down the hall, down the stairs, out the door. Instead, I sat stunned in study hall with my book open, gazing through the changing fall leaves, thinking about nothing in this world except every square inch of Pete.

# CHAPTER 13

**Love and Lollipops**

Sweeter than candy on a stick ...
If you had a choice
He'd be your pick
But lollipop is mine

**Sung by the Chordettes**

*October 6, 1962*
*Dear Mother,*

*I received the coat today, thank you. It fits very well. I also got the brownies but they were stale. My roommates ate most of them anyway. I can't, because I am on what you call a starvation diet. Only I do eat something mealtimes. I just have no yearning to eat. I weigh too much. I feel sick anyway. I should lose weight for the play, anyway. My husband carries me off stage. It's a riot.*

*Oh I have bad news. I just got a cut for swearing, so there goes my first weekend. Gee I am real sorry. I just said "Oh Christ" because I was mad at our cheerleading team. Anyway, Gilbert (a monitor) heard me and she is always itching to report me (anybody for that matter).*

*Did you get my other letter? I wish you would tell me whether or not you get them. Because many of my friends don't get half the letters I write. I guess that's the way God wants it, and as you can see, my hands are tied with wet leather.*

*I am going with a new boy. You wouldn't like Pete, he's a hood and a hotrod fiend (only his dad is rich). So maybe he's not my type, etc. We get along real well so far, and we both have a lot in common. He's got a horrible reputation and many girls and staff resent me now but I don't care. I have tried so damn hard to be nice to the kids and especially the staff. So, what happens? They turn right around and spit in my face after I got cut. Why? Doesn't anybody believe that I try? Doesn't anybody believe me anymore?*

*Pete believes me. I may not love him but for all I know, I can and will never fall in love again. Falling in love means trusting and I will never trust anybody ever again. Why? I couldn't tell you.*

*I have saved $16 since I've been here. It may buy me a train ticket home and it may buy Xmas presents. I will have to wait. If I have to I will use that money to see you before you leave. I mean it.*

*I would be in cum laude this week but the second cut for swearing took me off. I am tired of trying. But I'm not giving up completely. My grades will keep me up to do the things I want to do. No more.*

*I am sorry I write these letters but you probably won't get it anyway.*

*Love and Lollipops,*
*Judy*

The play I was in was called *George Washington Slept Here*, and I had a very demanding one-line part playing a seventeen-year-old girl, only a few years older than myself. Yet even with that simple formula I was petrified and had no desire to be in the production, except for my friend Gerry, the director. He coaxed and cajoled until I conceded to risk the ultimate embarrassment: standing in front of my peers acting like a fool. Believe me, the world is eternally grateful my career never panned out, for my one line was delivered over and over in rehearsals without so much as a hint of intonation or emotion, as if a catatonic idiot had been hired for the job.

Drama helped fill the hours, along with any other activity I could sign up for, leaving less time to think or care. The basic premise of the school was to keep everyone preoccupied and eligible. Preoccupied was fine with me. There was drama, or the yearbook, or the newspaper, choir, math club, varsity club, cum laude and alpha beta, alpha beta study committee, game and entertainment committee, late committees, citizenship society, house committee, monitors, camera club, arts and crafts, geology club, waiters, cheerleading for girls, and many other sports, but only for boys. If you were eligible you could go to Friday night parties, Saturday night movies, weekend coed sports, off-campus roller skating, Shakespeare at Stratford, and trips to the Catskill Game Farm to pet penned up gazelles. You had to stay eligible, of course, avoiding cuts for swearing, passing notes, kissing or dancing too close, talking back, showing up late, not making your bed, wetting your bed, cleaning your room improperly, failing to report where you were at all times, not reporting your period, smoking at the wrong time, drinking ever, or just plain bad attitudes, spitting, not writing home, crossing the threshold into a friend's dorm room, or throwing a fit—unless, of course, you were an epileptic; then you were excused. Scoring 90 or above on conduct, at this state of my high-school career, proved impossible.. My grades were good, averaging 89, but I was finding it difficult to maneuver through the rules.

Cheerleading was also a new activity for me. Growing up on a farm with two brothers had made me a natural athlete, but there were no sports for girls at Anderson, except cheerleading. I had no trouble making the squad. Basically, anyone who could jump a foot in the air and land on two feet made the team. Dressed in black wool pleated skirts, white sweaters with large orange A's, and white laced sneakers with pointed toes, we bellowed in unison: "Give me a *T*, give me an *I*, give me a *G*, give me an *E*, give me an *R*, give me an *S*. What's that spell?" If we didn't hear a loud enough cry from the crowd, we repeated, "What's that spell?" like nobody really knew how to spell Tigers. We cartwheeled, split, wiggled, and leaped to the anemic cheers of the crowd. We also earned a few privileges (which I was beginning to ascertain was the way to go) whether we won the games or not (which we rarely did). We attended all of the home games, and because Pete was the captain of the soccer team, I plotted diligently any moment I could steal to be near him. Of course, I had to stay eligible to cheer. That was a high bar.

Shortly after soccer season started, our goalie went home. He was having mental problems. He never returned, and another player had to leave because his stepfather had died. He never returned either. Our soccer team ended with a 3 and 10 record, losing games by the scores of 1-10, 2-13, or 2-10. The yearbook blamed the losses on injuries, lack of a goalie, and the weather. Actually, our entire athletic department was a joke. According to the 1963 yearbook, "The Anderson Cross Country team compiled a disappointing record. In five dual meets and one triple meet, the Anderson squad failed to post a victory," and "Everyone breathed a sigh of relief when the 1962-63 basketball season came to an end. The varsity won only one of its twelve contests ..." and, "It is difficult to say anything at all about the baseball squad, for ... only three contests could be arranged, all of which were lost." I wasn't quite sure why we had a sports program at all, other than to keep the boys busy, and I still wasn't quite sure why I was here.

My dad wrote me a letter telling me what a good job I was doing with my grades. I didn't bother telling him it wasn't too difficult to succeed in this stupid school, for the distractions were rampant, most kids didn't care, and the rest created scenes on a regular basis. Studying actually kept me sane (but I didn't tell him that). I hid inside books, where all the little Anderson realities could not play out, and Dad and Mom had no say.

I was always happy to hear my dad compliment me about my grades. Compliments were rare from him and came succinctly dictated in blue type on business stationery. Primarily, he wrote about fox hunting in Dublin with his friends, the Craigies: how many riders there were, what the weather was like and whether they were able to capture a fox, who got the head, and who got the tail. Mrs. Craigie always had a warm meal for them in their home when the hunters returned. My dad's letter reminded me of when I had cubbed the hounds in the browning fields of Doylestown, the soft muzzle of Primrose, and the farm on Cold Spring Creamery Road. He could stay connected to the traditions of the past, because he was a grownup, but my life had been severed, and the memories were fading.

Pete took up more and more space in my new life. I savored my brief moments with him like a Reese's peanut butter cup, letting the seconds melt in my mouth slowly so I could recreate them when he was gone. Often our times together were so short our words flowed too slowly for our hearts' needs. Though I filled my hours with activities, my mind stayed focused on my new love.

In contraband notes we began searching for time to steal. While dreaming of the future, we planned the rest of our lives together as one. Our beings melded into a finite maze. Whatever he said, wrapped me in a blanket of security, and my self-confidence surged. In spite of him racing hotrods and being a self-proclaimed hood, our lives yearned for each other. We talked and talked about hopes and hurts. His mother and father were divorced, though his mother spent much of her time in an institution as a result of the split. Pete painted a vivid picture of a powerful, rich, controlling, hard-drinking father, and a lost mother inside an abusive system. The women of divorce were the victims, in most cases. I was beginning to figure out my mother, my grandmother, and Pete's mother all fell into the same crater. There was no such thing as joint custody or joint property, "no blame," or women's support groups. Women were just the losers.

"We have to stay eligible, so we can see each other more," Pete told me one Indian summer afternoon, squinting through the daylight after being inside classrooms all day. The brilliant fall colors of the campus belied its purpose, which should have been embedded in concrete and steel. "I want to be with you as much as I can," he whispered, his breath grazing my ear. "If you keep your grades up we can both be in alpha beta, and if we pass conduct we can see each other at the movie this Friday night."

What Pete didn't know was that my whole being was changing because of him. I felt daring. I felt safe inside our world. I felt challenged and focused. I couldn't remember ever feeling loved so much. I promised myself I would stop sucking my thumb, which I thought should be relatively easy now that I was dating a senior, a cool senior. I had a future now instead of just a past.

But no sooner had I garnered hope than it shattered. "Pete's been caught drinking," Lorraine told me, as she walked into the room back at Morgan Hall. I was combing my hair for dinner. I had never had an alcoholic drink in my life nor had I ever even tasted one.

"You're lame," I snapped, spinning around.

"Ask for yourself. Old knock-knees herself is downstairs and she's gloating."

"Oh Christ," I raced. "It can't be." I threw the brush onto my bed and flew downstairs. When I got to the first-floor landing, I could see Mrs. Adams, feet pointing out, hands on her puffy hips, watching me as if I were prey. I hated her, her smug, ugly face. "Your boyfriend's in hot water," she carped. When I didn't answer, she ignored my obvious devastation and went on, "He's in the dorm, drunk as a skunk. Guess you won't be seeing him for a while." My hands trembled, as I dropped onto the step. She stood for a few minutes but then turned and walked toward the door for lineup. This woman had the compassion of a bullfrog.

A heavy foreboding nailed me to the foot of the stairs. I felt the old uncaring mania filling me up again. I felt the pounding of footsteps behind me and slowly stood up. Lorraine came up behind me and stood silently next to me in line. I felt like a cistern, once full, then drained, and now emptied again.

Of course, when we got to dinner, the dining room was humming with the news. Would he be expelled? Where did he buy the liquor? Who was with him? Would anybody else get into trouble? I stared over at Dennis the clown, his best friend, but he avoided my glare. I knew he had been with Pete; he just didn't get caught. I glanced over at Ripley, another North Hall troublemaker, hoping to see an answer through his eyes. Finally, he caught me watching and just shrugged. The dining room was a stage and I was the celebrity. I didn't care. I just wanted to know the truth. Each table was arranged with one staff and students of the same sex, so I couldn't find out anything. All I knew was that Pete's chair was empty, as empty as the void in my heart.

Pete was not expelled, just grounded for a week, and I was lost again. My rock had shattered, and my strength had failed. My reason for living felt shaken and raw. The headmaster called Pete's father and told him how close Pete was to being expelled and unable to finish his senior year. The idea of not graduating actually petrified Pete, who had already spent three years at Anderson. He too could only think and talk of the day he would be in college and free.

That weekend we all drove across the Hudson River in Greyhound buses to a West Point football game, yet one more diversion. I knew nothing about football or the West Point cadets with their totem-pole postures and khaki uniforms. They looked like a herd of elk moving in monotonous precision, and they were an epiphany viewed from my world of insanity. They were the earth's mountains and I was the black hole in the starlit sky.

Instead of rooting for the khaki-colored animals, on the premise of going to the bathroom, I snuck out to a telephone booth to call my mother. I needed to touch home. I needed to feel. I was lost again here at Anderson. The phone rang and rang and rang. The ringing went on into the afternoon. Finally, I cradled the empty black receiver onto its holder and turned to face the crowd. There, standing in the classic teacher's pose, arms folded sternly on his chest, legs planted firmly on the ground, was the dean of men. Caught again. Grounded again. Punished for needing more than my share. Punished for letting my sadness out of control. Oh well, what did time off mean, when you couldn't be with someone your world depended on?

I saw Pete that next Monday at canteen, sitting with one leg up on a low rock wall. Canteen was the place where every school day kids met informally, hung out, and bought a candy bar, or bag of chips, stamps, or plastic combs. Pete was smoking and hanging with Ripley. They both wore tight, black pants, white button-down shirts, and thin ties, which were mandatory. I walked into the canteen, pretending to ignore him, hoping he would follow me, but he didn't. I chatted with the girls for a while, then decided to head over to him. I surprised myself, how angry I was. "You deserted me. You were the one who said 'stay eligible so we can be together.' You were the one who said every minute together was precious. God, why did you do it?" He took a deep drag on his cigarette.

He threw back the anger artfully, knowing I, too, had been in trouble. "You're Miss Goody Two-shoes, I suppose," he answered, after blowing the smoke into the air.

"It seems to me you wanted to get caught. Why did you drink in the dorm? What is that? Why didn't you just sneak out to the Staatsburg Tavern with a housefather and the other guys?" I asked. He and others had told me stories about boys sneaking out for a few nightcaps, occasionally with a teacher or housefather. I really didn't know how to talk to him.

Pete stood up violently, waving his arms, "Judy, you don't know goddamned anything." My blood ran hot. Was he serious? My fingers felt numb. The intense look in his eyes locked into mine like a jaguar's. I held firm until his face softened slightly. "Judy, to get favors around here, you have to suck up to somebody." He sat back down. "Sometimes, literally." His body took a different pose, more defeated, less sure.

"What does that mean?" I asked, over my head again.

He hissed harshly, "It means I've been here too long, and I need to get the hell *out*!" He yelled the last word, ignoring the attention he had attracted. Again, I was the star of *As the World Turns*. "I think we should break up," he said softly. "I'm nothin', and no good, and I'm dragging you down." Then the bell rang and panic, once again, raced through me. The soap opera was now mine. Who was this guy? I had thought he was sane, level, even, hopeful, there. Ah, perhaps, like Romeo and Juliet, we would shroud ourselves in eternal love, ending tragically with a little poison to my lips, a dagger through his chest.

"I'll talk to you later," I answered when the bell had died. My life defined by slot boxes and bells.

Our communication did continue through long, contraband notes, neither of us trusting ourselves to speak to the other, both knowing the school wouldn't allow us the time we needed to finish working things out. We lounged around inside a melodrama, unable to resolve our problems, but too much in love to let go.

On October 22, 1962, the United States' relations with Cuba took an ugly turn. The leaves had all fallen, and the nights grew bitter. The naked branches held firm against the darkening skies of winter. President Kennedy went on TV and gave a long, serious speech about Soviet missiles pointing toward America recently having been found on the island of Cuba. He called the missiles "clearly offensive weapons of sudden mass destruction," and he spoke somberly about a "nuclear strike capability against the Western Hemisphere." He was not going to ignore this dangerous situation, and he called for further action. I wondered if we at Anderson were included in the group he called his "fellow Americans." Suddenly we were faced with the possibility of war. Were our boys going to fight like our fathers had, or were we all locked up far from the "madding" crowd? My tears and anger changed to concern. Pete was soon to graduate, and, surely, once he went back into the real world, they would draft him into duty. Send the insane to the front line and clear the zone.

"Mother," I wrote, "do you realize what is happening? I'm scared. All the boys in North Hall (the older boys) are going to enlist if war is declared. Oh, I am so afraid Pete will go. He's old enough. What is going to happen, Mom? You've lived through a war; I haven't. I hope the boys don't go." Being caught up in the possibility of war, I never considered that high-school kids didn't enlist. The likelihood of any of them being shipped off to Guantanamo was next to none. This was the older boys' way of saying that anything, even war, was better than Anderson School.

And the national crisis was just what Pete and I needed to make up. I told him I would stand by him no matter what, because I loved him. The soap opera of our lives turned another page. We merged closer than ever, blending like the colors of a rainbow, declaring our eternal love for each other. Our passion took another leap. When we danced, even though we were more heavily guarded than President Kennedy at his inauguration, Pete refused to accept their boundaries and held me close. The more the teachers and house parents pulled us apart, the closer he held me when they turned their backs. I wanted to stay spun in his cocoon until life evolved into ecstasy. We danced and danced in a world I had never known, a dance of full-body touch. Nothing would shatter our love, we vowed. By Thanksgiving I had transferred most of my need for love to my tall, dark senior. My belief in him set me free from an outside world of never being good enough or right enough or pretty enough or sane.

We sat like Siamese twins during a Thanksgiving weekend movie, *Sundays and Cybele*, when most of the staff had gone home, and the remaining ones didn't spend much time monitoring anyone's behavior (which most of the couples quickly ascertained). The movie was the story of a lonely little girl whose parents had no time for her, so she created a world of her own. Every day after school she walked down to a lake in the woods to play. Black-and-white scenes flickered on the screen, unfolding a tale about a man, a wonderful man, whom the townspeople thought was crazy, or retarded. Cybele became friends with the man, and they spent many days inside a child's world, exploring, sharing in the now. I remember Pete's arm curving behind my neck, his hand reaching down inside my sweater where his fingertips touched my breast.

The story ended when the little girl, caught in a terrible downpour, became trapped near the lake where they often played. The man rescued her, brought her to his cabin, laid her on his bed, mopping her brow until she came to. The parents and the townspeople saw him through the rain-soaked window kneeling over the little girl and then shot him because they thought he was molesting her. Cybele screamed and screamed when she realized her only friend was dead—and so did I. Pete held me close, until my sobs and the injustices of the world melted away.

Then I got another cut for stealing a record. My sleazy roommate reported me, but I didn't steal it. I never stole anything, ever. No one believed me, but I couldn't prove my innocence. My roommate said she found the record in my belongings. Great. Life raged out of control, and God was on the wrong side once again. I didn't care.

# CHAPTER 14

**My Guy**

Nothin' you can do
Cuz I'm stuck like glue
To my guy

**Mary Wells**

*December 1, 1962*
*Dear Mom,*

*I got your letter today. You'll never know how good you made me feel. You straightened out a lot of doubts about things. There are a few things I have to tell you.*

*First, my cut for the stealing bit was excused because I finally got it through their heads the whole thing was a mistake. I feel a bit better now, though I lost a week of eligibility and my conscience still bothers me. I keep saying the cut was supposed to be, because the whole thing looked so obvious. I am glad they believe me and I am not tagged as a stealer.*

*Second, maybe you are right I have led you on to believe a million things I shouldn't have. I am truly sorry. I hope this doesn't destroy the faith and trust you had in me. I just had to take my hurt out on someone, and you were the closest one to me so naturally, you got* the worst of it. I know now what an ass I was and believe me, it won't happen again. However, Mom, most of the things I have told you about this school are true. They don't treat you like a human teenager should be treated. They just never understand any of us, Mom. They take us for fools sometimes and other times we are supposed to be perfect and do everything they want. But no matter how damn hard I try, I am not perfect. Anyway, I am sorry. I can take my moods out on Pete now. I can tell him everything. When we have time to discuss things out, then my mind is clear.

I wasn't quite sure how you would take this, but I figure I better tell you now … I am accepting an engagement ring from Pete for Christmas. I think it's right Mom. We won't be married till I graduate, which gives us three years to be sure. I know I love him Mom. He is really the greatest person I know. You aren't mad, are you? I know I am sure, and even if I am not, I have three years to prove myself. Believe me Mom, I have tried to discourage myself, but I can't.

You will probably think I am a fool at 14, but I know it's the right thing. Please understand. You'd think he was terrific too, if you knew him. I hope you understand. He's the same religion, and his family has consented, and Dad said he was glad. Maybe both of you don't believe me, but it's true. He is really the greatest guy. Please don't try and discourage me, my mind is made up. I love him and I am willing to wait three, four, or ten years. I hope you understand please tell me what you think.

Well, on to more newsy subjects. My academic average is going up. I got a 90 this past week. The kids saw What Ever Happened to Baby Jane last week. I didn't because I was ineligible …

The play is called off. Our director, the English teacher, got himself drunk and packed up and left. He

*couldn't stand this place anymore. (I am not making this*
*up.) He and the star of the play went off together. Gerry*
*came back and is on probation. So, no play. We are all*
*very disappointed. Oh well.*

*Well, Mom, I must go. You must know of course, I*
*read your letters a thousand times over too.*

*I love you, very much,*

*Judy*

By December, I had begun to accept life at Anderson
School as my reality. I was absorbed with love, friends, studying,
plotting daily freedoms, and learning the inside rules. I became
absorbed with the life I was creating and tried to separate
myself from my past. My favorite self-inflicted rehabilitation
was handwriting. Because I wrote so many letters, school
papers, notes, and poems to Pete, I decided to find a new
handwriting style. I began by copying my girlfriend Sharon's.
She was from New Paltz, New York, spoke with a thick New
York accent, and dated a junior track star, who became a good
friend of Pete's because they both liked drag racing, soccer, and
track. Sharon wrote with exaggerated melodic loops, and her
tilts never stayed neatly in one direction. This style of writing,
of course, radically changed my small, closed, discordant
scribbles. Then I went on to Pete's handwriting, which I
practiced copying in the margins for hours when classes were
too dull to take notes. His writing was as handsome as I'd ever
seen: letters all slanted equally determined to the right, each
capital majestic and stately, lines so straight one could swear
he used a ruler. My style became a mélange of the two, open
circles for dots, big loops on *f, g, q,* and *y.*

I began experimenting with makeup. My parents never
let me use makeup, because my dad said that eye makeup
made little girls look cheap. Then there was that problem of
the magenta ring around my thumb. No lipstick, Mom had
decreed, until ... At Anderson, many of the girls wore eye

makeup, lipstick, and fingernail polish. I borrowed eyeliner from Lorraine and practiced night after night, until my hand stopped quivering and I had mastered the art of painting a tiny line under and over my eyelashes. "You look incredible," Pete rewarded. "You just look so damn good to me." He smiled, and I knew feeling good about myself *could* happen.

My new faith came with a tiny handful of girls whose greatest sin was having too much fun and whose greatest asset was sitting up late hours talking about mothers and fathers, love, and the absence of love. These were the first people in my life I could just talk to about the hurt I felt, the sadness the therapists couldn't cure. Candy was the wildest of the girls. Sometimes we snuck up into the bathroom after everyone had gone to sleep and talked until our eyes grew heavy and our speech slurred. She was never afraid of getting caught.

And, of course, I took up smoking. Paddy, the housemother who kept the cigarettes locked in the pantry, would waddle in from the kitchen carrying a tray full of Camels and Kools and little paper cups with medicines for some of the girls. You would have thought she was pressing a two-hundred-pound barbell the way she puffed and panted. We were permitted to smoke six cigarettes a day under supervision of staff. The boys carried their own cigarettes around but were permitted to smoke only in designated areas. We had to smoke with Paddy, sitting down at a table. Walking around with a cigarette, after all, is unladylike.

As I lit up my recessed-filter Parliament from the navy blue and white package, I often thought of home. Mom smoked Parliaments. I still longed to be home, longed for a normal life, longed to know the answers I was denied. But this was a time to hear all the gossip of the day: who got in trouble, who skipped class, what event was coming up, which couple had a fight, who flirted with whom, who flunked the exams. Each time the phone rang, Paddy waddled back into the kitchen to answer it. You could hear her strained voice, "Good afternoon,

Morgan Hall," and we muffled our giggles as Candy deftly grabbed a few extra cigarettes before Paddy returned.

Most of all, I was growing up, yes? I had responsibilities, relationships, a desire to succeed, and, oh, a guy who wanted me to be his wife, a guy who talked about college, having children, working and growing old together. He gave up drag racing and I gave up sucking my thumb. What a terrific pair we made, poised and ready for them all.

Well, not quite. A week before Christmas vacation, Pete got in trouble again, this time for drinking Aqua Velva and mouthing off to a North Hall housefather. "How could you stand the taste of it?" I asked during a class break. "Didn't you have to drink a lot before you felt anything?"

"The stuff definitely wasn't worth the high," he confided. "I guess I'm nervous about going home. I want to stay here with you. I have to clear it with my dad to take money from my savings account to buy you a ring, Judy. I want to buy you a wonderful ring, with lots of diamonds. I love you so much, Judy." Just as he leaned over to kiss me, a teacher walked down the hallway, cleared his throat, and then grabbed Pete around his biceps and walked him to the end of the hallway. Pete turned around and puckered his lips into a kiss. I smiled and went to class.

Christmas vacation came and, as always, most kids took the Greyhound bus to the Port Authority bus station in New York City. Pete and I sat together and planned our separate vacations: how we would write each other, how every night at nine o'clock we would look at the moon and think of each other, how we would tell our parents how much in love we were. Pete said he wanted to see his mom in the hospital and tell her about me, even though he knew his dad would try to stop him. He kissed me a long good-bye, while the chaperones unloaded the suitcases from under the bus. I dreamed of floating inside his body, staying there, here, deep in his arms, but I had a plane to catch for Albuquerque. Good-bye sweet prince, savior and stallion.

Christmas in Santa Fe made me sad. Store-bought ornaments hung perfectly spaced, properly facing out, on the synthetic evergreen (so no needles would fall on the rug). Just the right amount of tinsel hung carefully before we could toss our own haphazard wads onto the branches, as we had as children. A graceful taffy-colored angel, with a mournful gaze and a satin-layered skirt, nestled high up into the vigas of my father's perfect house.

This was the house that Dad built. At the end of a long graveled driveway (gravel delivered from his concrete plant, Colony Materials), the formidable home, surrounded by twenty-six acres of piñon trees, overlooked the Jemez Mountains to the west and Santa Fe Ski Basin to the east. At sunset, the eastern mountains flushed purple, and the western sky burned inside orange, pink, and yellow clouds. On a good day you could see the mountains of Colorado, almost one hundred miles to the north. The air was thin and dry and clear.

Inside, no crammed bookshelves or piles of erratic papers were evident as they were in my mom's house. Like a hotel, the house that Dad built was spotless. Toys and clothes were kept out of sight. Windows and mirrors never streaked. At dinner, crystal poised alongside pressed linen, hand-painted earthenware, two stainless wooden-handled forks, and a special glass salad plate. Original paintings adorned the walls: giant oil portraits of my dad as a boy; and my great-grandfathers, Ambassador Morgenthau and Elkan Naumburg, in gilded frames; a Velasquez; a Signac; a bronze Remington; and others. A completely stocked bomb shelter in the basement had supplies for a good long stay. Bed sheets were ironed percale. No shoes were allowed on the bedspread, the furniture, or the couch. Neatly folded towelettes were placed carefully in each bathroom to remind you to wash up after your visit. Expectations hid in every corner.

Essie still worked for Dad. She planned all the meals, perfected all the household duties, and even kept track of his social arrangements. Any hopes of ever enlisting her sworn friendship were kept in check as Essie simply called my dad "Boss." She always supported my dad. Dad wrote, "Putting Judy in a school where kids were not normal ... sick, or what have you, was a very tough thing for me to do. Essie was my power and strength on this deal. We were sure it was the only way out." I never really felt close to Essie, even though my dad maintained she was good with us kids.

I carried Pete home with me in a little wooden-framed photo. As I unpacked, my brothers nosed in and out of my room, curious as usual, making small talk, getting to know one another again, bantering and checking out boundaries. When I placed Pete's picture in front of the mirror on my built-in desk, Steve asked, "Who's that, the famous Pete?"

"Yup," I answered.

"What's all over his face?" I turned around quickly to see if anything had damaged the photo, or if he had.

"Nothing," I answered.

"The holes in his face," he gloated. "What's he got, acne?"

"No, he had smallpox as a boy, I guess." Yes, my handsome knight had a flaw—didn't we all? Especially at Anderson.

Sensing my mood change, my brother mellowed. "You're in love, huh?"

"We're going to get married after I graduate. I know you'd really like him." Then I went on to tell Steve all about Pete, all about love and the future. I told him nothing incriminating about school. I didn't know what he knew. I wanted him to think I was at a regular boarding school like Fountain Valley. He wouldn't have believed me anyway. Steve and I always seemed to be in competition, partially because my dad set the stage, comparing grades (mine were always better), letters, awards (I had more), anything. But Steve always got the rewards. He had lots of clothes and all the gear: new stereo equipment, top-of-the-line camping equipment, new skis, whatever. So, in most ways, competing with Steve was a lost cause from the start. He was the oldest boy in a Naumburg family, the one who would take over the business, carry on the genes, manage the money, and sit on a board of trustees. I was just a girl. No legacy there.

Flip had the only room that looked lived-in, because he had been living in Santa Fe since Dad won the third and last custody battle. Judge Montoya considered his the more stable family environment, because my mother remained unmarried. Mom thought money had a little to do with it. Flip was in fifth grade at Carlos Gilbert and very unhappy living with my dad. He loved sports, especially Little League, skied with the White Tornadoes racing team, and had sports pictures carefully put up on a pegboard behind his built-in desk. He knew all the names and positions and stats of the Philadelphia Phillies. Being with the boys felt good; a little bit of leftover family.

"You're too young to get married," my dad said when the subject came up at the dinner table.

"Dad, I know I'm only fourteen, but we are going to wait until I graduate."

"You need to spend some time together before you make that kind of commitment," he said, cutting the steak that he had cooked to a perfect medium-rare on the indoor grill with a hammered copper hood.

"We would if we could, but we never have time at school. When can we spend time together?"

"That's enough. I don't want to talk about or hear about this guy for the rest of the vacation, do you understand?"

Every day a letter from Pete came, and every day I wrote him back. It felt safe to stay locked inside his love, our world governed with warmth and kindness and hope. On the back of each envelope he wrote, "I love you" or "S.W.A.K." or "H.O.L.L.A.N.D." (hope our love lasts and never dies). The day the ring came, I ran to my room and opened the small brown package, savoring each second. When I saw the silver ring with seven tiny diamonds, I screamed with delight. My engagement was official. One day I would be a woman, live with this man, and have his children. We would have our own life, safe from the world.

But, of course, when my father saw the ring on my finger he wanted me to send it back immediately. He would not allow such a thing. Too young. Too young—just like the electric razor. When I wouldn't agree with him, he secretly wrote Pete's dad and convinced him our engagement was a terrible idea. I was in tears for the rest of the vacation. Nothing I seemed to do was okay with my father. Nothing I said to him seemed to sway his opinion, and fighting with him became the norm. All my father ever saw me do was cry, and I didn't understand why.

"We have to wait, Judy," Pete told me during afternoon canteen when we returned. I stared at him. He seemed different, more man than boy. I fumbled the bag of pretzels in my hands. *Oh God*, I thought to myself, *who needs a logical man at a time like this?*

"Why? I thought you didn't care about what they said. I thought our love was stronger than them," I argued.

"Well, it is, but maybe your dad's right. Maybe we'd better wait and try to spend more time together before we are formally engaged. Then we'll know. Don't you see, Judy? We'll win them all over eventually. We'll show them our love will never die. Time doesn't matter." We spent stolen moments talking and reassuring each other of our love, in spite of our fathers. He convinced me that waiting was the only way to prove our love would last. We focused on seeing each other over spring vacation, at my mother's house. This was the only vision of future we had, but it slowly blossomed into a hope.

Sometime in January, when the frozen ground seeped through the soles of our shoes and crystals formed on the windows at night, Dad flew to New York for some trustee meeting in the city and then drove up to see me. I was in English class when Mrs. Adams came in and reported in a cheerful tone that my father was here. The obvious conclusion might have been that I would rather go talk to him than stay in class. Nope. I knew better. I walked down the stairs, searching for answers to my anticipations, thinking the encounter might be more satisfactory with premeditation. *No such luck*, I thought, remembering the day at Buckingham Friends School. *He wouldn't kidnap me away from this school.* Still, my stomach churned like a Kennedy-Nixon debate.

When I saw my dad, I smiled a fake smile. He forced a strained and a determined smile also and gave me the obligatory hug. His energy felt strong, self-centered, and scary. I wanted to annihilate the moment, run back to my room or anywhere away from him, but we walked through the lobby, outside, and climbed into his immaculate rented town car, much too big for one person. The sun pressed through the cold January air; the world stilled in frozen animation.

"Judy, the people at school have a lot of concern about you and your boyfriend." Funny he couldn't say the name. Funny he probably wouldn't even want to meet him. Funny he's been talking to the school.

"Why?" I asked, knowing the explanation could fill the Pacific.

"I don't trust your boyfriend, Judy, and I don't think you should either." I waited for him to go on, waited for more of a reason to speak. I stared at the console, then to my hands turning over and over in my lap. I had an urge to suck my thumb or maybe twirl my hair like Lorraine. Instead, I half-heartedly chewed on my fingernails. How many bad habits could one person have?

"What do you mean?" I asked, dropping my hand.

"He's older than you and liable to do things you don't understand or don't want him to."

"Pete would never do anything I didn't want him to. He loves me."

After a long pause, he began the litany of details I was waiting for. "The school is concerned about your physical behavior with him. You know, your reputation is at stake here. You don't want to be known as a slut. You will never find a decent husband with these morals of yours."

The idea of screaming, "I have found my husband! I hate you!" into his face occurred to me, but I opted for a calmer approach. The intellectual argument seemed more appropriate. "Dad, they give you demerits every time you hold hands or kiss. They follow you, report on you, and eye you to death here. You have to know exactly everything I am doing."

"They say your dancing is not suitable for a lady and your boyfriend gets out of hand." Dad didn't look at me, of course. He rarely did even under the best of circumstances. As soon as we made accidental eye contact he looked away.

"When you dance your bodies are supposed to touch," I answered, knowing my logic wouldn't convince him, "and I am not responsible for what happens to Pete's body."

"On the contrary, I think you are, and I believe you have to be on guard." Victorian logic. After shifting in his seat and then taking both fists and wrapping them around the steering wheel, he asked, "Do you know what contraception is?" *Here it comes*, I thought to myself.

I didn't know whether to laugh or cry. "Dad, I have never done anything like that and don't plan to until we're married. Isn't that the way? Isn't that what you and Mom did?" I remembered the time when Steve and I sat on his lap while he read the long, detailed, heavy biology book by Kinsey or somebody. The diagram of two little fallopian tubes flashed in my mind. As my mind circled the years, I slowly focused on the monologue I wanted to block out: unrolling condoms, placing diaphragms, and spreading spermicidal gel. I felt sick. This man, who rarely hugged me, had never talked to me about my period, and was livid when my grandmother sent me an electric razor, was talking about sex as if we were choosing a book from the library. He had thought the whole thing in the elevator with the boy in Puerto Rico was my fault, and now he was condemning me again. His hands twisted around the steering wheel, and his eyes darted out the window the whole time he talked, which made the hour seem like a visit to the dentist. I hadn't done anything even close to what he was talking about, and he never mentioned the word love.

By the time I got out of the car, I felt nauseous. *God, if he thinks I'm doing all this stuff, maybe I should just go ahead.* Not that there was a lot of opportunity at school. I walked back into class and once again dove into the academic world. Boring or not, it was the only place to hide.

January 26, 1963, Candy left. She was the captain of the cheerleading team. Her parents just came and took her away. I was very sad, because I thought we were good friends. How could she leave? I felt deserted. I guess she managed to convince her parents about the school. Mostly, the school managed to convince my parents about me:

REPORT OF PERSONNEL AND GUIDANCE DEPT. SEPT-JAN 1963

HEALTH: Judy's health has been excellent. She received an influenza shot October 5th. Her menstrual periods have been regular. Her weight is 130 pounds.

DORMITORY AND RECREATION: Judy has utilized most of her activity this term in arts and crafts, cheerleading, dramatics, skating. In the evenings she has usually studied, knitted, or read. Each Friday evening she has attended the social-recreational affairs of the school which have included dorm-sponsored parties, two dances in the gym, a game night, the Freshman Class Dance, a special off-ground movie. Each Saturday evening she has attended the Forum meetings and, following these meetings, has joined her group in the monthly birthday parties and planned recreation. On Sunday mornings Judy has attended Chapel services where she contributed her efforts as a member of the choir. In the afternoon she has played co-ed volleyball, went roller-skating on three occasions, visited the Catskill Game Farm, attended a West Point football game and participated in the Christmas carol singing and dorm decorating. In addition she attended Thanksgiving and pre-Christmas dinners and programs. Her interest and enthusiasm in all of her activity program has been excellent. In her relationships with staff and students she has encountered some conflicts time to time. At times her outward manner has been sullen and defiant, while at other times she has been pleasant and cooperative. Her interest in one of the boys at the school has resulted in some show of negativistic behavior and at parties and dances her behavior with this boy has been subject to criticism. Her housemother reports that she has been cooperative in the care of her room, person, and possessions. In her evening study periods her effort and application have been excellent. Her record for punctuality has been only satisfactory, and in the dining room she has been able to improve her conduct. Her table manners and eating habits have been good.

ACADEMIC: Judy has completed English I, General Science, Algebra I, French I, and World History. She has encountered no difficulties with her subject material ... The California Study Methods Survey tests revealed Judy's lowest score was in attitudes ...

GENERAL BEHAVIOR: The overall picture of Judy's general behavior has continued to show much ambivalence in her day-to-day adjustments. At times she has been sullen and disagreeable, projecting dissatisfaction and criticism of the school. At the start of the term she received severe conduct penalty when she carved her boyfriend's name on the front of the piano. On several other occasions she received penalties for disregard of school rules of note passing and was involved in unbecoming conduct with her boyfriend in the school building. As the result of ten failing conduct grades and four weeks of excessive late demerits Judy has been ineligible for eleven weeks of this term ...

GUIDANCE DEPARTMENT CONTACTS: Judy has continued to be seen by her counselor in a daily review of her adjustments and in frequent office sessions. In addition, she has been seen by the school's psychiatrist and also by the psychologist in testing. In counseling we have directed most of our efforts this term to helping Judy gain confidence and security in her own achievements and abilities. In seeking security in her relationship with her boyfriend, Judy has tended to utilize this relationship as an escape from some of her conflicts and lack of security. In discussing with Judy her acting-out behavior on one occasion she was distant and protective, stating that she behaved as she did because she was forced to associate with students at this school. When we pointed out that her own choice of close friends was not from the more mature and better-adjusted students, she then said that this was the type she preferred. At this time we pointed out to Judy her lack of loyalty in her relationships at home and at school ... Constant support and encouragement have been utilized in helping Judy to alter her poor ego picture and to keep her focused on goals ... and escape her feelings of rejection. It will be sometime, however, before Judy is able to achieve the emotional and social growth that will permit her to function successfully outside a well structured environment.

My academic grade average was ninety-one, ten points above the school average. After my first-semester grade report, Mrs. Adams advised me that if I took one extra class next semester and an extra during the summer, I could possibly skip into the junior class in the fall. Wow! A radiant star glowed in the endless sky. Not only would I get out of this school, but also I could be married in less than three years.

As my academic average climbed, my conduct and demerits dove. Pete and I were continually targeted. All staff eyes were on us, hoping for a kiss or inappropriate closeness. Once, we were at a Friday night party. Green, yellow, and brown streamers and balloons gently swayed with the music. The theme was jungle night. We danced softly, slowly. Drums were beating. Construction paper cutouts of palm trees decorated the basketball court walls. Three couples were making out in various corners, sneaking kisses. Pete and I were content to just hold each other, dancing with the music, lost in a maze of couples, his strong arms around my waist, my head resting on his shoulder. Suddenly, two staff walked in. Of course, the couples immediately stopped making out, and we kept on dancing, "obscenely," we were told, and got the demerits. Dancing close felt so good, so warm, I found it hard to know why we were always being punished for it. I didn't care, really. I didn't care.

Most of our demerits were for notes. Pete wrote long, rambling notes about where our love would go, what he dreamt about, when we could be together: "I dream of waking up with you, some day, honey, and taking long walks on the beach. We would be free; our love could grow the way healthy couples grow. I dream of holding you in my arms until the world melts away. I have found the one girl in a million I was destined to meet. I look at you and my heart surges like a drum. I don't mean to sound ridiculous, honey, but this is how I feel. What we have is pretty big and powerful. Sometimes when I tell you I love you and you tell me that you love me too, it seems greater to hear you say that than any other important thing in life." Reading his notes was definitely worth a couple of demerits.

My mom became supportive of Pete, my needs, my new love, and me. Thinking back, she probably felt my relationship with Pete would and should take its own course and eventually die over time. She knew fighting us would only make us cling tighter. She agreed Pete could come visit us over spring vacation, if his father concurred. We spent weeks writing back and forth about the vacation, when Pete would come, who would drive where, what we would do with our days, Steve coming home, and being together as a family. I could hardly wait.

# CHAPTER 15

**New Hope**

I learned today the world is round
Like my big rubber ball,
With China on the other side,
Down there below us all.

And so I went and dug a hole
I started in at eight
And dug and dug and dug and dug,
Beside the garden gate.

**Olive Beaupre Miller**

During my freshman year, my mom moved from the farm into a small duplex in New Hope, just a fifteen-minute drive from the farm. New Hope was, and is still, a small town on the Delaware River, just east of Doylestown and our farm. In the summertime, madras-clad tourists strolled through hot bustling streets, wiping ice-cream drips from their shirts and babies' mouths, bobbing in and out of knickknack shops. In the evening, people came from miles around to visit the semi-famous Bucks County Playhouse for an off-Broadway show or the Lambertville Music Festival, where the Four Seasons, Benny Goodman, or Liberace performed under a giant tent. In the spring, fall, and winter, the pace slowed to that of a sleeping coiled octopus. The townspeople, light-years from the country farmers of Doylestown, became less involved with selling, serving, and soliciting, and grew introverted and temperamental as the weather cooled. Artists, gays, writers, and beatniks lived in New Hope. Everyone knew everyone else's business, name, and scandal.

New Hope was seasoned with scandals. One night a famous married newscaster got drunk and paraded uninvited in the early morning hours through my mother's house, chasing her from room to room in his boxer shorts. The whole town branded my mother with an affair, but my mother just laughed at the notoriety and said that, in reality, the whole thing had been terrifying. My brother and I also had a friend who shot a six-year-old girl with a loaded gun. I suppose you could call it an accident, but everyone in town talked about it for months.

I felt comfortable around my mother's new friends in New Hope. They spent hours sitting around the dining room, glasses of wine in hand, discussing politics and philosophy and literature. They were more intellectual and easygoing. There was freedom from dress codes, freedom from expectations, and freedom of self-expression. My father's friends had grown more conservative since he and my mother had separated. The two diverging personalities split like an earthquake, and I was beginning to wonder how the two of them could have ever produced three children.

Mom lived in a small three-story duplex on Mechanic Street, creatively remodeled with natural wood and heated brick floors, stained glass windows, white walls, and three tiny bedrooms, one for her, one for me, and an upstairs attic for my brothers to share. After living in our spacious farmhouse for thirteen years, I felt like the Jolly Green Giant in our teeny, tiny home. The walls were decorated with new mounted prints from famous artists: a bulbous court jester teetering on a horse, signing the name of Ben Shawn; a large-headed man floating upside down through the clouds, by Marc Chagall; a giraffe-necked woman by Modigliani; a Picasso blue harlequin. There were no carefully framed hunting hounds and thoroughbreds with their front legs tucked under in the midst of a jump; no hand-tooled, leather-bound books or mounted fox head—no signs of a past life at all. My bedroom, about one-third the size of my room at the farm, was so small that once the painted brass twin bed my mom bought and my old mustard Victrola found a space, only a sliver remained for me to walk through. Two tall windows brightened the room, so I began staring out onto the street, watching the cars drive by from the foot of my bed. No stuffed animals or rustling leaves of a giant walnut tree.

The tiny bathroom next to my room was the best room in the house. A large, opaque stained glass filled the whole west side, back-dropping the toilet and bidet—a fancy new contraption my brothers and I found more amusing than useful. Brass swans controlled the hot and cold sink water, and the tub was sunken, heated, and lighted. Only one person at a time could occupy the space, unless you were in the tub, but the ambiance was grand when you did.

Though the living room was on the first floor, most of our time was spent in the kitchen and dining area upstairs. Floor-to-ceiling sliding glass doors gave the feeling you were outside in a garden of rose bushes and poplars, or surrounded by snow without feeling the cold. A six-foot whitewashed wall encircled the house. This was my new life. There were no thoroughbreds in the stables, no dairy cows in the barn, no maids, lakes, farmhands, haylofts, or fresh milk—but it was home. Fifty-nine West Mechanic Street was a new start for us all, and home, now, for me, was where my mother was, wherever, whenever.

"Pete won't be coming to New Hope, honey," my mom told me once the car pulled out of the Port Authority station and headed toward the Holland Tunnel. "I'm sorry," she said flatly.

"You're kidding," I said, feeling my heartbeat quicken and my breath surging into the size of a letdown.

"I'm sorry. There's nothing I could do." She glanced over at me, but I didn't know what to say, what to do, how to act. Paralyzed once again, I wanted to scream. I wanted to burst inside and shatter into a million pieces, so no one could ever put me back together again.

"Why didn't anyone tell me before?" I asked.

"Honey, I didn't know, really," answered my mother. I didn't know whether to believe her or not, the way she answered; she wasn't giving me enough words to decipher. Suddenly, I saw another book being written without my authorization. I was the main character. My plots were predestined.

"Everything I had to look forward to is gone. Everything that helped me get through the days at Anderson—why I studied, why Pete and I tried to stay out of trouble. What's the point of trying? What's the point of even caring ... about anything?"

"I just found out about this myself," she continued slowly. "Your father thinks you are too young to be alone. He's afraid of what might happen." Finally, the *F* word comes out: "Father."

"He said we couldn't be engaged because we hadn't spent any time together, and, now that we planned to spend time together, he takes that away too. I hate him. *I hate him!* Why does everything he says have to happen? Why does he always decide? We weren't going to *do* anything; we just wanted to be together."

"Your father only does the things he does because he loves you," my mom said, one of many times in her life she attempted to rationalize him. "I know he has a different way of caring, but that doesn't mean he doesn't love you."

*I don't want to hear about how much he loves me or how much he cares. I hate him! How can you think he loves me? He tricked me and lied to me. He didn't tell me himself. He never talked to me or cared what I thought. I hate him.* "This can't be true," I said out loud, trying to breathe hope back into annihilation. I was trying to put all the facts in order so they made more sense, but my emotions kept jumbling things up. Facts in order couldn't cure. There was no cure for any of this. Shooting pains pierced my brain, as we drove through pointless New Jersey towns. I hated it all.

A few days later, a letter came in an envelope marked "I love you!!!" on the front and "I love you" on the back.

*Dear Judy,*

*I'm sorry this letter is so late but I forgot your mother's address at school and I had to hear from you first. My stepmother told me about the weekend when she picked me up Saturday night. It was quite a shock to me honey. From what she told me, your father called Gage (the headmaster) two weeks ago and told him your mother was irresponsible, and my being 18 and you being 14 wasn't good. So Gage called my father and told him this, so my father had no choice but to cancel the weekend. I hope we can work something out in the summer darling, but it's pretty doubtful. Your father seems to have made it clear that he doesn't like the idea of us ever being together. And this is what worries me. I'm sure he will try to stop every attempt on my part to see you next year. We can't fight him. We fell in love in the wrong school, honey.*

*There were so many things I had to talk to you about. I love you very much and I feel really depressed. I've really thought a lot about our future and how hard, in ways, it's going to be for us to see each other because of your father and of school. We might as well face the realities now. We have a lot on our side too Honey! These are some of the things I wanted to talk over with you because we are always going to do things and decide things together. Being in love is a great feeling, Judy, and I hope it is a feeling we both will always share together.*

*Take good care of yourself Judy, and always remember this; I truly love you very, very much!!!*

*All my love, Pete*

Almost every day I went through the wrought-iron gate to the red mailbox embedded in the whitewashed wall and pulled out a letter from Pete, covered with *XXX*s and *OOO*s, a blue five-cent stamp with an etching of President Monroe staring at me with raised eyebrows and stern mouth. In my mind I tracked Pete's days and watched a change come over him. In the beginning, he talked about his father being in a three-car crash that destroyed their Chevy convertible and two other cars, which his dad had to pay for. He told me how much he loved me and how much had longed for us to be together. But then he wrote about driving late one night with the top down in the pouring, freezing rain, laughing with the guys, and another where he stayed up until 4:00 am with his brother at his fraternity, and another all-night out with the guys bowling. This was the Pete I didn't know, couldn't picture—the Pete away from Anderson. Each letter swore undying love, respect, and passion, yet growing concern for what could happen in the years to come.

Then the letter came. "We're living in a dream world. There are many problems we are going to have to face the next three years … We depend on each other too much … I want to be able to date this vacation, and I want you to also, honey. The more we worry about the future and other people, the worse things get. I won't date until I hear from you, honey."

They were winning. They were knocking down the walls of the only thing I had cared about for a long, long time: a love

I could inhale, a future I could work for, a touch, strength. How could I live in a world where every feel-good thing was wrong? For years my heart had known only the feeling of bad. Now I wanted to feel good, and Pete was the only thing that felt good. Explaining to grownups was impossible, because they always knew another reality: the "right" one. I was only fourteen, after all.

I spent most of my vacation sitting on my bed writing long letters to Pete, listening to the Four Seasons sing "Big Girls Don't Cry" over and over, thinking about what I wanted to be and wondering if, in the end, I would just be what everybody wanted me to be. The strong will of expectations would wear me down.

My brother Steve was home for vacation, too. He was now a sophomore at Fountain Valley, an all-boys' school, which must have made him miserable, too, given his love of female nipples and such. Steve's relationship with Dad was different than mine, but he had his share of pain too, though he never talked about the hurt. He'd shrug his shoulders, laugh, and say, "You know how Dad is." When Steve got an F, Dad cut off his allowance and withdrew his permission slip to go to town. The headmaster, Lewis Perry, insisted the punishment was too cruel and suggested there might be a better way to achieve results. My dad, however, thought his punishment had worked, because my brother graduated with all Ds. If I tried to talk to Steve about being what we wanted to be instead of what Dad wanted us to be, he just looked at me as if I were crazy. He couldn't understand how anyone could be anything other than what they wanted to be. Or maybe he just thought what we were and what we wanted were the same. I didn't think so. He never seemed to engage in any questioning with me. The free-thinking style of New Hope gave me a little courage to believe I could live my own way, without being branded crazy, but I lost that courage as soon as I returned to school or visited my dad's house.

Steve and I palled around our new town, meeting new kids, exploring the canals and the riverfront. He kept me entertained. Johnny, still sort of my mom's boyfriend, business partner, and now landlord, made more of an effort to be with us as a family than he ever had before or after. Actually he hung out with Steve the most, because Steve thought Johnny was great, no matter what he did or how badly he treated my mom. Steve helped Johnny work on a new craft village he was developing, a mini-mall for artists before malls became the rage. I never cared about Johnny, because he made my mom cry and he looked sideways when you talked to him.

Johnny also owned a nightclub restaurant with a lounge and dining patio called the Canal House, which overlooked the New Hope canal. I remember watching slow, mule-pulled barges float past, Dixieland band playing, people drinking and gawking, sending a contagious level of energy into the restaurant. Some nights we had dinner at the Gaslight. Lots of performers from the Lambertville Music Festival hung out there. Bernie, the cook, made the best pecan pie you ever tasted, so she'd cut us a big piece, and we'd go sit at the tall mahogany bar in a room filled with red and black velvet wallpaper. The Gaslight stood until the Pennsylvania highway department came along and bought the site to widen the road between New Hope and Doylestown.

Mom also had a friend named Danny. Danny was gay. He used to be married, was the father of two girls, and worked as an understudy for Gene Kelly. After twenty years, he left his wife and kids and job and lived his life as a homosexual. New Hope was a good town to be homosexual in. Homosexuals weren't exactly considered first-class American citizens in 1963, but in New Hope, few could dare judge others. There were too many naked bodies in the closets.

Danny was one of the nicest men I had ever met. He and Mom spent hours cooking ratatouille, mussels marinara, or other new recipes from the *New York Times Cookbook*, drinking fine Italian Chianti, and talking into the wee hours of the night. She laughed full—bodied when she was with Danny. I knew he made her feel good about herself. He helped me feel good about myself. I loved Danny. I could talk to him about school, love, or anything—and I always felt he cared. He was the first grown-up man I ever loved. I wanted Mom to marry him, but she told me there were other things needed in a marriage. I guess I understood, but I wanted her to be happy.

Danny produced and directed a drag show. During spring vacation, I saw my first show. In the opening act, Danny came out and bid hello, dressed impeccably in a black tuxedo, shiny patent-leather shoes, and a velvet voice as finely tuned as Bing Crosby's. He acknowledged my mother, as I guessed he had done many times before, and even paid a special tribute to me. I felt nine feet tall. I don't remember how well I understood what a drag show was, but I never felt uncomfortable when Danny was around. I watched beautifully wigged ladies, dressed in glittering sequined full-length turquoise or magenta or silver gowns, strut and lip-synch through "Hello, Dolly" and "I'm Gonna Wash That Man Right Outta My Hair," dripping in diamonds, pearls, and feathered boas.

We sat in the front row. I knew some of the women were men dressed up, but I wasn't always sure. My favorite number was Danny doing "Singing in the Rain" dressed in an elegant tuxedo, balancing a big black umbrella. He sang and danced perfectly, as if Gene Kelly were dancing ten feet from my face. I loved the show.

In the end, the most radiant woman in the show came out, looking more ravishing than Ginger Rogers. She sat down at a dressing table center stage with her back to the audience, and sang "The Party's Over." She began slowly wiping off her lipstick, then her makeup, with a soft cotton ball. She brushed her long, pecan hair and seductively removed her jewelry. As she sat in her bra and panties after slipping her robe from her shoulders, she looked more seductive than ever. The contours of her back were stunning. I was still mesmerized by her face in the mirror as she took off her wig, but it was not until she finally took off her bra, stood up, and turned around, amid gasps from the audience, that you realized this woman was a man. She was Danny's man.

Toward the end of the vacation, a familiar panic swelled inside me. My head ached, my whole being ached. I didn't want to go back to Anderson. I knew, in spite of Pete, my trapped existence would return. I begged and pleaded with Mom to let me stay. I felt so good here in New Hope. I wanted to stay forever.

"I can't, honey. There is no way I can take care of you. Your father would find a way to blame me again, and who knows what the repercussions would be. You have to think of others beside yourself, Judy. But, I'll tell you what. Steve is going to an orthopedic surgeon for his knee on Tuesday. I'll call the school, tell them I think it would be a good idea if you stayed because Steve may need an operation, which is true, and maybe they'll let you stay a few extra days." I stayed three extra days. I loved her for that.

By vacation's end, Pete had written again about his dreams, his loneliness, the future we could never know for sure. I knew in my heart his rebellious battle had folded into the batter, his frustrations scattered into time. S.W.A.M.L. was written on the back of the envelope in his beautiful script. It was 2:30 in the morning. He'd been out drinking with his friends, listening to the jukebox when he wrote:

> *Well, it's late again and I'm writing my future wife again! And I mean the future wife bit Judy!!! I miss you so much and wish I could hold you in my arms and kiss you and tell you how much I love you!! My love for you has grown so much. I want to marry you and have a family and no one will ever be able to stop me! Not your father or anyone. I am tired of people saying we aren't really in*

*love. Hell, it's so wonderful to be in love with you Judy. I know our future is sure. I honestly can't take much more of being away from you Judy! I love you very much and mean that with all my heart.*

 *All my love forever,*
 *Pete*

My dad and I never talked about spring vacation. Silence between us became the cure.

# CHAPTER 16

### Going to the Chapel

Eenie, meenie, meinie, moe
Catch a tiger by the toe
If he hollers, let him go
Eenie, meenie, meinie, moe

I returned to the inner-city darkness of the Anderson School, where depressing moods quickly battled the good feelings I had sown during vacation. The distance between home and Anderson was as far away as Pluto, with no logic or road of understanding between.

Pete greeted me at the canteen with a somber face, which didn't help the electrical current between us. We walked over and sat on the rock wall without a word, me chewing a Baby Ruth, him turning a pack of Camels over and over in his agile fingers. He told me how his father had warned him not to see me anymore, because he never wanted to be mixed up with my father again.

"Your father is a real prick, Judy. He basically threatened to sue my father if we got together over break."

No one could deal with my father's control. I thought Pete would help me fight him, but all the energy he usually carried with ease drained from his heart as he spoke about our future. Our life, like the Kon-Tiki, drifted with a purpose and a focus, but no compass and too many storms. We both knew we had no input or sway with our fathers. I knew it didn't matter. My love for Pete would never go away, and I told him.

I wrote my mom, "Well it hurt pretty much because, if you will remember, when we first started going together all parents on both sides thought it was a good idea. Now the only person who hasn't acted against us has been you. We will make it, though. Please Mom, never think we are going to do anything stupid like elope or have a forced marriage. We may be stupid, but we're not that stupid. I could give a darn about this school anymore. I have no desire to please myself, Dad, or anybody else who hasn't given me anything."

My grades fell, and I received a cut for swearing during English class. I wondered if the school trend, getting thrown out, would seep into my core after Pete graduated. Would I flunk? Slit my wrists? Take an overdose of Aqua Velva, perhaps? Which poison would I inject? Pete went home. His mother had tried to kill herself, and the family felt he should return home. Every day was a day without definition.

A few weeks later, a day that began innocently enough took another cataclysmic detour. I was walking down the hall, arms full of books, chatting absently with Donna and Candy. Mrs. Adams trailed behind, dressed in a tight, straight-skirted suit. She wore her typical one-lip grin, and her two-toned matching high heels clattered on the concrete floor as she struggled to catch up with us. We all rounded the corner and headed down the steps. "Judy, your father's getting married," she blurted out—as if she were speaking of the weather. I turned up to face her, catching a last glimpse of those beady eyes. My mind began racing through a million conversations—when my foot missed the next step, and down I flew, books flying in all directions, arms flailing. I tumbled down a dozen concrete steps until the room stopped spinning and the floor felt firm beneath me. I looked around. Mrs. Adams stood motionless on the top step, her face turning into a faceless mask of the *Elephant Man*. A dull pain pierced my thigh and elbow. The girls were picking up my books. Someone was pulling me up by the arm, and it hurt.

"What do you mean?" I buzzed back, immediately linked into her madness. "How do you know? Who?"

Mrs. Adams started down the steps casually, eyes locked down on me. "He's marrying a French woman," she added, gleefully absorbing my reaction. She was my Francis Ford Coppola, always directing my life, calling the shots. After reaching the bottom step above me, she went on, "He's in New York now, but he said he would write you about the details." *Nice of him to write*, I thought. I stood up and took the armful of books from Sharon.

"Good—maybe now he'll be easier to get along with," I asserted, pretending to gain some control. Mrs. Adams led me into her office. Where did my mind go from there? Naturally, I wondered who "she" was, if anyone knew her, why I hadn't heard before, when all of this had happened. I wondered why he wasn't marrying the woman he had been dating since moving to Santa Fe. I wondered if this could be the end of all my parents' fighting. Mrs. Adams didn't know any answers, but then she never did.

The past October my parents had finally reached a divorce settlement after almost four years of fighting. Our custody had been awarded to the state, each visitation to be reviewed on a regular basis by Judge Montoya in Santa Fe until we reached the age of sixteen, an age when presumably we could make up our own minds. Our vacations were split equally. Steve and I were both at boarding schools. Dad now had full custody of Flip, because he had the money to take care of him, I guess, and my mom was now working late hours. I don't think my mom had enough money or power to keep Flip with her. During the years since my parents had separated, my father had spent thousands of dollars on detectives to reap pictures of two or three men my mother had dated (it didn't matter that he himself had girlfriends during the same time), and an unproved accusation that my mother was on dope and was irresponsible.

Thousands of dollars had been spent on psychiatric treatment for us kids, and hours and hours of arguments were brought before the judge who presided in an old adobe courthouse. For many years, their mutual anger kept lashing out in many arenas. Finally, one day a lawyer, who had been the attorney general for the State of Colorado and best friends with my mother's father, met with my father in Santa Fe and asked what was holding up the divorce. I think he did this as a favor to my mother. Several weeks later, he came back with my mother and her lawyer for what everyone hoped were the final arrangements. My father described the event in his memoirs:

> *"Dorothy was not there. [The lawyers] got down to money and somebody said something about Dorothy living in the manner to which she had become accustomed. I injected that in my opinion she had become accustomed to being a two-bit whore. [The lawyer] suggested I leave the room now! I did, but in the long run my comment set the stage for progress."*

So much money was spent by both sides for lawyers that both my parents were threatened with lawsuits over the final tallies. My mother couldn't afford her bill; my father, of course, could afford his.

Annette was her name. She had grown up in Monte Carlo and Paris, and I perceived that her big claim to fame was that she had nannied Grace Kelly's daughters, and her sister taught the children of Baron Elie de Rothschild how to ski after skiing for the French Olympic ski team. Fame through association impressed my dad. My grandfather arranged the matchup. He and his third wife, Cecile, now spent every winter in Monte Carlo at the Hotel de Paris in a twenty-room suite overlooking the Mediterranean. They became very good friends with

Annette's parents. After meeting Annette, my grandfather telegraphed my father immediately to fly to Monte Carlo. My Dad telegraphed back, "Does your matrimonial service include a round-trip ticket?" My grandfather was not amused but persisted in bringing Annette back to New York with him. He summoned my father for dinner. My dad explained we kids were in Santa Fe until Sunday (Christmas vacation). My grandfather ordered him to New York for dinner on Monday. He landed a few weeks later and stopped by Anderson to give me his lecture on contraception methods. Not a word about meeting Annette, of course, and five months later, they were getting married.

After a whirlwind courting period and pressure from my grandfather, the date was set. On June 22, a wedding would be held at Croton-on-Hudson; then it was changed to May 12, (Mother's Day, ugh) at Pound Ridge; then a final date was set for May 18, at the Carlyle Hotel on Madison Avenue where my grandmother lived. I would miss my first high-school prom for my father's second wedding.

My father's letter came a few days later, telling me that Annette spoke six languages, was very athletic, and the boys both liked her. "You will learn to like her, too." I wondered if liking my new stepmother would be as easy as flying to New York for dinner or as hard as understanding my father. Flip wrote about her visit to the house in Santa Fe but didn't say much about her. Steve wrote but didn't mention Annette or Dad or the wedding.

The wedding was a lavish affair held on the second floor of the Carlyle Hotel, where many celebrities lived and visited. My step-grandmother, Cecile, arranged each minute detail from the band to the champagne. The room was decorated in white gardenias and orchids. My father was livid when the bills arrived in the mail. My father's sister, Ellin, didn't talk to their stepmother, Cecile. My grandmother hadn't talked to my grandfather in twenty years and refused to be in the same room. My grandfather disapproved of Aunt Ellin's husband, so they didn't speak. When Dad went over to his Aunt Helen to thank her for coming, she answered, "I only came to keep my sister company." My stepmother-to-be had the flu, a 102-degree temperature, and, most unfortunately, wore the same Dior suit as my grandmother Ruth. My father couldn't smash the glass wrapped inside a white napkin, so the waiters had to find a more delicate, crystal glass. In spite of big diamonds, mink coats, and the most finely tailored clothing available in Europe and Manhattan, I felt not the faintest hint of sanity or love or passion in this room. Oh my God. It was as if Gene Kelly and Leslie Caron were dancing frantically through a dark surrealistic cloud, gigantic hands grabbing out at them as they tried to clear the crowd. Only Leslie had red hair and Gene was bald and wore glasses.

According to my father, "Annette never became a Santa Fean, an American, or a Naumburg. She always wore beautiful clothes and jewelry and tried to be at the right places, even if she was an hour or so late. Matters were bad from the beginning, when Annette insisted on telling the kids what to do." Actually, she physically told Flip what to do. Steve and I were never around long enough, but we got the gist. Essie soon got fed up and quit. Essie had been my father's household crutch since the day he walked out on my mom. She had cooked his meals, run his errands, disciplined his children, spied on his wife (wives?), and supported his opinions for five years. Though Dad was devastated by the loss of Essie, he didn't divorce Annette until after my grandfather died. My father never got easier to get along with.

After the wedding, for the first and last time ever, I actually relished returning to Anderson. My final days with Pete were precious. I couldn't imagine going to school without him. I tried to imagine the future, counting the years until we would be together always, because that was the only thing that would keep me alive. Pete's intensity for me increased, though he clearly focused on graduation now. He would soon be free. I wondered if I would ever be free, or if just at the point when I could reach it, someone would come along and blow the freedom off my fingertips like the white seeds of a dandelion.

Pete took even more risks, as if daring Anderson not to graduate him. One spring afternoon, dressed in my white cheerleader's blouse, tennies, and knee-length black skirt, I met him accidentally in the sun-streaked hallway. He wore his Anderson track uniform, a white sleeveless jersey with a winged foot flying across his chest. His eyes grew wide, and his mouth turned into a smile, as he quickly pulled me into the men's bathroom. Our eyes remained firmly locked as we escaped, or so we thought, from our oppressive life. Inside, leaning up against the closed door with one foot pressed against the door, he pulled me closer until my whole body pressed against him, his lips reaching mine, his strength molding armor around us. His tongue reached inside my mouth, and my body hollowed out, leaving room for a warm maple syrup to flow inside me. I grew weightless, expanded, transformed. This was a high that commanded me, addicted me like nothing before—a love beyond merry-go-rounds and ocean waves. This was a love with no rules, safe from criticism and expectations. A love I didn't have to clean up my room or stand up straight or cross my legs for.

A twinge of fear finally broke our embrace. How could this stolen moment have happened? Would we spend a thousand days in solitary confinement over one misdemeanor? Could they—would they—incarcerate the champion of the one-hundred-yard dash?

"I love you more than anything," he promised, kissing me again and again, deep and long. "When we are apart, I want you to promise to look up at every full moon and think of me. I'll be looking at the same moon, Judy, thinking of you." He put his hand on the curve of my butt and kissed me again.

"You feel so good to me, Judy." His chest was hot. Breathing was hard.

"I wish we could stay here forever," he said after a while.

"In the men's room?" I asked. We both laughed. Our mood relaxed, and the smile we felt just being together was forever.

"I better go out first and see if the coast is clear," he said after a few minutes. No one had ever loved me this much. My heart pounded, my breath stayed shallow, my knees weakened. I did not want to let go, but the Anderson fear factor held fast. Exit back into reality once again or face the gallows.

Again, at the Shakespeare Festival, a few weeks later, with his arm curled around my shoulders, caressing my neck and breast, he spoke through fingertips, leaving words behind, needing nothing more. Would he do this with another girl when I was gone? I never would. My body would be safe for him, I knew. Making the promise was easy.

# CHAPTER 17

### The Graduate

One potato, two potato,
Three potato, four,
Five potato, six potato,
Seven potato, more

Feeling loneliness before a departure is the same as knowing death during life. There is no preparation, no crash course. Graduation approached with the speed of an oncoming train. Bound and tied to the tracks, I tried to avoid imagining life without Pete, a life without love, a life without the warmth of another. Thinking about the past and the future brought pain, so my brain practiced the art of denial.

There wasn't much time for reflection or daydreaming. Hoards of weekend activities and impending exams kept our minutes filled, our minds focused. I think they wanted us to leave with the impression that school was great fun. Pete was so busy packing and planning, and I was so busy obsessing over exams, we hardly saw each other. Separation had already begun.

Each dormitory celebrated the year's end with a traditional forum banquet. This was my first forum, so I had no idea what to expect. Morgan Hall's forum was held at a restaurant called the Kitchen in Hyde Park. The menu consisted of Libby's canned fruit cup on top of a dollop of orange sherbet, roast beef with *Boulangere* potatoes, string beans, tossed salad, relishes and rolls, and chocolate parfait (vanilla ice cream with Hershey's chocolate sauce) for dessert. Each class president made a speech. I gave the freshman speech. Mrs. Adams and several others lied about what a great year it had been, poking fun at a few couples (me again) they kept having to pry apart during dances.

The big shocker was the result of the Morgan Hall poll. The results were printed in a little paper booklet with a pink ribbon on the top. The first page listed the speakers, the second page had the menu, and the third was a list of the winners of the Morgan Hall poll. I was elected "Best Figure." Not Most Popular or Most Athletic or Most Likely to Succeed. Not even Prettiest, just Best Figure. My peers voted to elect my body best body. Slash my wrists. Cut my throat. What are these crazy people doing to me? How dare they vote for the same body that betrayed my childhood—the same body where folds adorned the midriff, the thighs resembled a kangaroo's, and the waist was equally proportionate to a whale's? What were they thinking? I had spent my whole year staring down at French fries, pies, and any form of chocolate, with guilt-laden quivers in my stomach as I chewed each bite. How could I have the best figure? How could people see me so differently than I saw myself? Biggest breasts, maybe, they could have 'fessed up honestly, but there was no such category. What good fortune could "Best Figure" insure? Could it guarantee me a job, win me a contest, or make me sane? No, of course not. Best figure was good for sex, and I wasn't even allowed to be engaged or kiss or hold hands or dance too close. I remembered the elevator boy in Puerto Rico, the brown stranger who fondled this purported "Best Figure." I wanted to run and hide in the bathroom, but I knew an escape could bring even more unwanted attention. I sat erect in my seat, waiting for an end to the Machiavellian nightmare. They were crazy and they were winning.

My 1963 yearbook was signed, "Take always care of Pete," and "I want to be invited to yours and Pete's wedding" and "Go look at yourself in mirror and who do you see, Pete!!!" The councilors signed with a different fulcrum, "Let's settle down and live up to your potential," and "Makes good use of your potential it will take you a long way." The English was a bit sketchy. Luckily, a dorm parent and not a teacher wrote the latter.

Then came the Anderson School awards banquet, the gala finale to surviving nine months. Achievers received plaques or bronze medals for cum laude, alpha beta, house committees, scholarship awards, and committees I never heard of. The jocks received large orange $A$'s for outstanding participation in underachieving teams: soccer, basketball, track, tennis, cheerleading, and baseball. There were yellow paper certificates given to the stars of chess, checkers, swimming, field hockey, and even one for the best bowler. Fake certificates of self-esteem were desperately handed out in an attempt to erase the destructive forces of home and inject confidence where self-loathing festered.

My grade report related to my parents that my six-week grade average was 93, compared to the school's average of 81. My conduct was 76. My room inspection was 92, and, oh gee, I had received fifty-three demerits. More than fifteen demerits in one week represented an unsatisfactory standard. What did it all matter? I knew I had to return in July for another desperate summer. Everything was still out of control. Was I getting used to things that way?

Finally, graduation day came. Mothers and fathers smiled and swarmed around smiling and swarming teachers. Every smile and handshake was fake. No one talked about what crazy kids were going to do outside in the real world. No one talked about the suicides, the runaways, the dropouts, the seizures, the thefts, or the failures. Everyone acted as if graduating was something you celebrated. Every salute and speech was filled with words of an empty future. No one knew the pain I was feeling now, before he was even gone.

The graduation ceremony started with a procession; seniors dressed in black tasseled caps and gowns marched slowly, as if in a funeral. Mrs. Jones played the piano a little too slowly, occasionally catching up, groping the keys with her brittle eighty-year-old fingers. Her thin white hair frayed up under the neon lights. You could almost see through her celadon skin. After an invocation by the English teacher, moonlighting as a reverend, we rose and sang "The Star-Spangled Banner."

There were more awards: fellowship awards, citizenship keys, sportsmanship keys, athletic keys, choir keys, and activities keys. I had no idea what these were about, but it seemed only a few selected brown-nosers and dorks were winning all the keys. I didn't care.

The king of the dorks gave the salutatory address, and the queen of the brown-nosers gave the valedictory address. He had thick, black plastic glasses (yes, plastic had invaded our culture, permeated our lifestyles); she had perfect hair, even in the morning. She wore a hair net to bed. I kept looking over at Pete. He wore his glasses, which he usually didn't do during a social event. He seemed so studious and grown-up. I tried to remember the man I loved; freeze him into my heart so he could not escape. The quasi reverend gave another benediction, and then down the aisle walked my first year at the Anderson School.

The crowd congregated on the lawns for a buffet. Little rolled-up slices of ham, roast beef, and turkey were piled high on silver platters decorated with orange slices and radishes. Soft white rolls, pickles, potato salad, and Jell-O were presented as if they were Lobster Thermidor or freshly shucked oysters. I picked at my food. Pete and his dad sat talking about people and things I knew nothing about. I couldn't even pretend to know what was happening today.

Pete and I said good-bye in front of the bus to New York City. The moment was so surreal I couldn't think. Never seeing this person again would ruin my life. I had to believe we would be married if and when I graduated this nut house. Suddenly we discovered a window. "How are you going to your aunt and uncle's?" Pete asked, knowing I would be spending the night there before I took a plane to Santa Fe the next day. We moved away from the crowd.

"I have money for a cab," I told him. He was driving to New York with a friend and going to a seniors' party. I couldn't go. Wasn't allowed.

"Why don't I take you?"

"What do you mean?" I asked absently, still in a daze from the day. Quick thinking wasn't on my agenda.

"I mean," he said, leaning close to me, that big, wonderful smile crossing his lips, "Rick and I will drive to Port Authority and pick you up." After a pause, he added, "That way we can say good-bye with a little more feeling." I looked into his green eyes again and sensed the strength inside him. "They don't own me anymore, Judy. I'm free. Out. Finished. I never have to go back." He gave me a hug and sent me onto the bus with a wink.

The trip on the bus was not easy, even with the plan to see Pete in New York. My thoughts traveled to life without him, denying promises of a future together; the days between now and then seemed unbearable. The further away from Anderson I got, the more the same overwhelming sadness overtook me. My life, my family, and soon my love would be gone. Would the promise of marriage in three years be enough to get me out of bed in the morning? The sun settled lower in the sky.

New York's Port Authority Terminal, an Ellis Island of the sixties, overloaded your senses if you didn't recoil into a tight reality of purpose. People brushed by at obsessive paces. They all seemed to know exactly where they were going. As I waited for my bags, the dean of women checked each one of us out individually, obtaining signatures from parents on hand and meticulously collecting letters of release. I waited to hand over my letter, collected my cab fare, and then headed off into the crowd.

"Judy, where are you going?" Mrs. Adams bellowed. "The cabs are right here on the street." What a pain this woman was. She pissed me off. There was something about her that just made you want to get back at her, outsmart her, or even bash her stupid face in.

"I know, I'm going to the bathroom first," I added with mock enthusiasm. This plot could fail as easily as it had been planned and driving fifty blocks to my aunt and uncle's was not exactly a honeymoon walk on the beach. My palms grew sweaty in anticipation of another failure. I wandered into the bathroom, sat on the toilet and stroked my lips for a few minutes, then headed slowly back toward the street. I didn't know how to look for Pete and the milling crowd blurred my vision. I watched as people climbed into square yellow cabs and drove off.

"Let's call your aunt and uncle and ask them if you can stop for a bite to eat." I turned around and saw the big, boyish grin I knew so well and forever dreamt about. I didn't dare speak. We quickly headed off in the other direction, so the staff would not spot us. A sense of freedom brought a smile to my face, a warm dampness under my arms.

My aunt and uncle lived at 1136 Fifth Avenue. My grandfather had an apartment on Park Avenue, and my grandmother lived on Madison at the Carlyle Hotel, though I never stayed with either of them. I remembered a small Italian restaurant downtown in the Village that I had been to with my mom, so we looked up the address in the phone book and headed downtown. The setting sun showered the tall, serried buildings with a rusty hue. The humid air slowed movements through space. Pete and Rick ordered beers with fake IDs and I drank a Coke.

When time could stretch no further, we headed uptown. Pete and I crawled into the back seat, kissing and exploring each other without fear, from the moment the door closed behind us, first talking between kisses, then totally unaware of the passing streets. His hand caressed my breasts, my stomach, and then slowly down along the insides of my thighs. The memory of this would help me brave the empty years at Anderson. His love would give me strength to endure the madness.

"I'll walk you up," he said when the car had been stopped too long in front of the apartment. I put my clothes back in order and said good-bye to Rick. Pete took the bags from the trunk and walked me toward the door. I announced my name to the doorman, who told me the floor, and we walked to the elevator. We rode silently. Pete held my hand. I watched the elevator operator. My lips throbbed; my body pulsed from his touch. I never knew a good-bye could feel so good.

"There's still no one here," I said after waiting for an answer. I reached for the large brass knob, and the door opened. "Hello," I yelled into a dimly lit entryway. "Uncle George? Michelle?"

"I guess they're not home yet," I felt myself say from my stomach.

Pete closed the door behind him and grabbed me quickly into his arms. "I love you; I will always love you. I want to marry you, and I'm going to wait for you." His wet, soft lips covered my swollen mouth, my face, my neck, and, suddenly, my breast. I heaved air into my lungs, trying to still the pounding of my heart. All this was new to me, and suddenly I wasn't sure how far he was going to go. There was an urgency I had never felt before. "Oh, Pete, no," I said weakly when he put his hand in between my thighs. He didn't stop, and I didn't want him to. He led me into the living room, dimly lit by the city lights. "What if they come back?" I whispered. He pulled me down onto the rug, kissing me again.

"I love you," he said in a coarse, heavy breath, undoing his belt. "Hold me here." He took my hand and put it down inside his pants. He was warm and hard. He unzipped his pants, pulled them away, and began moving my hand up and down. I lost perspective, and the night began to spin around and around. I enjoyed the feeling of him, the smell and the movements, but suddenly he pulled my hand away and began stroking himself with faster, harder hand movements. I flattened my hand into my chest and watched motionlessly as he moved back and forth until he released a long steady groan. His body quieted, his breath deepened, and I felt like a failure.

"I'm sorry," I muttered. Did we have to part like this? We had no time for learning, no time for slow exploration. He lay still on his back on the floor. I was afraid to speak again.

"I better go," he said, flat as film. "Rick is waiting in the car." I watched him pull his clothes back on, then stand, zip, and tuck. He pulled me up from the floor, and we walked through the silence.

"I love you. Don't let them break you down," he whispered, cupping his hand around my cheek. "Write me every day." I watched him turn and leave, caught between confusion, ecstasy, and a creeping loneliness. I stood at the door until I realized I had stayed too long. I ran over to the window and looked down at the street. I watched his tiny figure walk out of the apartment building, open the car door, then disappear. He didn't look up and wave. I wanted him to.

As the car moved away into the darkness, I noticed the outlines of the night. There was nothing inside of things, only a thin, glowing line *around* every car, every person, every building. The trees in Central Park faded from sharp bronze outlines to a thick black obscurity in the distance.

# CHAPTER 18

### Living Up Your Potential

I slit the sheet
The sheet I slit
Upon the slitted sheet I sit

The July heat of the New York summer sapped my energy and drained my heart; a 75-rpm record played at 33 rpm. I hated Anderson's snooping, recording, following, assessing, and reassessing. I couldn't visualize even one more day at Anderson; the madness was dripping through my bloodstream like an IV, and I knew I would never extract it from my soul if I stayed. I asked my mother to write away for a transfer to the George School, where many classmates from Buckingham Friends were, without telling Dad—but she never did. She avoided talk about transfers or coming home. I knew there was no use even trying Dad. Facing the reality of the inevitable became too painful. I lost my reason to get up in the morning. I planned weekends and transfers every chance I found, but nothing helped. I lay in bed after the 6:00 am wakeup, staring into the darkness of my mind, trying to re-enter my dream or make sense of the looming reality. My purpose was trapped inside a giant spider web wrapped around my bed. My want was gone. Everything good had been erased.

"Get up, get up!" Mrs. Longo blurted, after I failed to rise with the bell. "You'll be late, get moving," she persisted, trying to put motivation where there was none. I longed to turn back the clock to my days at the farm. Only now could I understand the freedom there: long summer days bareback astride Dinky, my pinto pony; washing off the salty sweat of summer in a lawn sprinkler or frog-infested pond; tracking a box turtle through the woods; or running with Steve and Flip through rows of corn. I remembered taking pitchers of sweet lemonade to my father and the farm workers as they worked, baling hay under the sun or hauling irrigation pipes. Mom would be planting flowers, planning dinner, or driving a tractor in the fresh air. Parents were there to Band-Aid wounds or put us to bed, but summer meant three hundred acres of freedom.

Now there was no time to nap under a tree or run off to a hiding place near the peonies. Not a moment, a morsel of food, or a maudlin mood went unrecorded. "You're doing very well academically, and, now that your boyfriend is not there, you should do even better," Dad wrote after receiving a ten-page report on everything from my menstrual cycle to my fewer failing conduct grades.

If I was as great as my school report had said, why couldn't I go home or go to another school? Out of twenty-four freshmen, nine didn't come back. Out of thirty sophomores, eighteen didn't come back. Of the twenty-five juniors, only nineteen went on to graduate. Of the total seventy-nine undergraduates, thirty-three didn't come back. We had new students, but the total student body dropped from one hundred eight to ninety-three students. Why couldn't I have been a lucky one? I envisioned sympathetic parents listening to Anderson tales and deciding their child could escape maximum sentencing.

"I think I'm going to make you a monitor," said Mrs. Adams, locking me up with her eyes. She sat sideways behind her desk, legs slightly parted, showing her stocking hooked by a garter at mid-thigh. The skin under her eyes drooped a faint inky color. I couldn't decide if there was any possible reason to like this woman. I saw her daily whether I wanted to or not. In her cramped office, we talked about kids, boys, school, health, anything. I wanted to trust her with my secrets, though she often betrayed me or—beyond tolerable—teased me in a group later on. But she kept sympathizing and prodding and challenging, and I couldn't craft my words well enough to keep her out of my life. Basically she brainwashed me.

"I don't want to be a monitor," I answered flatly.

"Why not?"

"I just don't," was all I dared. *Don't take the bait,* I warned myself. *Stay away.*

"You have great leadership potential, Judy. The girls like you. The students like you. You've been elected president of your class twice now. I think it's about time you showed some responsibility." *Flattery will get you everywhere.*

"I won't be very good at it," I fished. Being a monitor meant more responsibilities around the dorm but also a bit more privacy. Monitors checked rooms in the morning and night, organized lineups, handed out cigarettes, and were asked to do errands, which meant more freedom. God, freedom, even just a slice, would be wonderful. I started thinking about being a nice monitor, not strict and bossy like Diane and the others. The vision of redefining the role began tempting me—just as she came up with her next brilliant idea.

"I want you to be a monitor and a member of the house committee," continued Mrs. Adams.

"Ohhhh no," I said, sobering in a moment. "You're not going to put me on any tattle-tale committee. If you think you're going to turn me into a rat, you're wrong."

"A role is as good as you make it. You don't tell on anyone. Your job is to help keep order in the dorm. All monitors are house committee members, Judy." After a pause, she added, "If you want to quit either one, you can quit. I just think now that Pete is gone it will be good for you to have more to do, and I think you can be a real leader someday. You have the qualities. You are not a follower, and you will never be." I hadn't heard from Pete in a week. I knew he was working; maybe he even got the summer job he wanted so badly. I envisioned him sailing off into the ocean on a giant freighter. I supposed taking on more responsibilities could help my loneliness. I could be a nice monitor. A leader, after all, was a president, a dean, an executive, a den mother, a grownup. A leader was free.

"Okay, but if I don't like it, I'm going to quit," I compromised. What the heck. She pulled her half-smile at me, wrote something down on paper, and then explained my new jobs.

We had one new roommate my sophomore year. I moved my bed and belongings closer to the window, closer to a world Anderson could not filter out. I taped all my pictures of Pete to the wall above my bed. On my desk, I placed a sepia portrait of my brothers and me, taken our first Christmas in Santa Fe, in front of a stone fireplace in a rented adobe house on Camino Pequeno. The picture was taken my first Christmas away from Mom, long before my dad remarried. We were under custody of the State of New Mexico, because of a landmark decision where the court refused to award custody to either parent. The court basically retained legal custody of us itself, deciding where we would spend holidays and, in Flip's case, where he would live. My parents still fought too much to decide anything. In the picture, we were sitting on a flagstone floor, me with my signature mohair sweater accented by a string of add-on pearls, from Mom Knight, and a straight wool skirt carefully pulled over my knees; the boys were dressed in button-down collars and mainstream ties. Our German shepherd, Mr. Lucky, provided the main distraction. The photographer forgot to say, "Smile" or "Cheese." The result is three kids pretending, far from a smile, staring blankly into the camera, with too much on our minds. Mr. Lucky looked away.

Betsy Wolf was my new roommate. She was the happiest sad person I had ever known in my life. Kind of sloppy, very goofy, and a bit squishy like vanilla pudding, Betsy endeared herself to me almost immediately. Her usually uncombed hair, librarian circa 1930s, cut rudely across her forehead, puffed out on the sides, accenting her large ears. Her body looked more neglected than a basement and her clothes as if they had been stored there for a generation. Loud and exuberant as a new puppy, Betsy made me laugh.

Her father was vice president of Noxzema Chemical Company. He and his wife had adopted Betsy after years of frustrating attempts to become pregnant. When Betsy was a baby, her mother miraculously became pregnant and Betsy moved to a remote corner of the family. The more the biological baby blossomed, the more her mother ignored Betsy. Her father, an elegant white-haired man, tried to be a good father, but, because he was not often home, he could not soften the rejections of motherhood.

Betsy never cried. She never cried when the mail came and she got none. She showed no emotion when she flunked a test or when kids made fun of her. She talked about her younger sister, a perfect role model, the greatest thing since sliced bread, the apple of everyone's eye. She met every disappointment with a shrug of the shoulders and pursed lips. She reminded me of my older brother. He never cried. I always cried. I cried myself to sleep thinking of Pete. I cried when another mail call went by and he still hadn't written. I cried when Dad wrote me one of his typical critical letters, warning, scolding, and degrading me. Maybe I was a bit melodramatic. Betsy was a kleptomaniac.

As the year progressed and Mrs. Adams prodded, I became Betsy's mentor, friend, and big sister. I could understand her needs. I felt I could actually help her by listening. Other kids liked me, too, when I took time to hear their long stories and then threw out advice of my own. With every response, "Yeah, I never thought of that," or "I feel better just talking to you," I gained power within myself. I didn't want to be better than anyone. I just wanted to be better than crazy.

I wasn't, though. I started sucking my thumb again. When I went to bed, the only thing that helped was my thumb slipping back into my mouth, my possum in a pouch. As my tongue caressed my thumb and my forefinger stroked my lip, the sadness dulled, and my thoughts softened until I lost the battle and fell sleep.

# CHAPTER 19

### Growing Up

Life—the longest distance between two points.

**Dorothy Parker**

Growing up. Where did *grow up* come from? The cornfields? The forests? The pediatrician's office? Growing up is more than sprouting tall. You grow out. You grow in. Your mind grows wider, your feet get bigger. Your understanding is supposed to grow deeper, your senses keener, your intentions clearer, or maybe not. You get a bra and you're expected to fill it. You get an allowance and you're expected to budget. You're expected to speak when spoken to, in the proper tone, with the proper response. Wash your hands before dinner, cross your legs when you sit, understand without challenging, obey the rules, play the game, or get out.

Growing up meant changing myself; learning to live in a world designed by grownups. No warm baby chicks to cradle in my hands. No barns to build hay forts. There were people everywhere, yet I was lonely for the cows with the looking-glass eyes, for Lily with the starched flower dresses, and the box turtles in the woods. I was lonely for a home, a hug, a hope. Now my home consisted of a world where the touch of love was forbidden, and freedom was just a word in the classroom for riders escaping racism. Cast out into a sea without gills, the only thing I could grab onto was Mrs. Adams' hook.

Growing up meant life became easier living by the rules, learning them, mastering them, breaking them gently, without comment or challenge. Life became living with a hundred students, sharing their weaknesses and learning their methods of deceit, emulating their successes, and stepping over those who fell. Existing in this ant colony of constant movement slowly stifled my yearning to escape, my quest for peace, my innate desire for independence. Whatever my course, it included others. Now that Pete was gone, I became more involved in too many lives, no longer sequestered on my island of love. I lost my protective shell. A new boy had a crush on me. He held his left hand close to his chest, wrist limp like a dead eel, his large lips contorted sideways. He tried to put his hand down when he talked, but it kept coming back up spastically. He followed me down the halls, shuffling his heels. He asked me to dance and watched me with a creepy intent whenever I was near. I couldn't understand why he even wanted to be near me. I hated him. He knew I hated him. I could no longer screen out the crazies.

As monitor, I touched all the girls' lives daily, checking their rooms, calling roll, and rounding up the herd. I had difficulty with the public life of a monitor, standing guard over each student as we boarded the bus before the sun rose above the trees. Too many kids believed they had access to me. Over time I learned to separate, to stand back, but in the beginning I became too involved in so many lives—and I hadn't yet learned to master my own.

I became friendlier with the girls on the cheerleading squad. Aileen, a full-bosomed senior with Kilroy legs, taught me the merits of bleaching your hair, which she did with regularity. We talked while she painted foul-smelling bleach on a swatch of hair held straight in the air. We played cards on the bathroom floor while she waited for the color to set, then I helped rinse her new locks in a small wall sink, removing traces of a scent so painful it was a miracle the inside of my nose remained intact. I awkwardly cupped the water over her neck. Her long bony fingers urgently laced through her bleached strands flowing down the drain, as if one extra minute could turn them a threatening shade of mango. Those same fingers taught me how to vomit, or tried. "Just take your two fingers," she instructed, me holding her two long, defiant digits up in the air, "and shove them down your throat. You'll throw up."

"What? You just throw up what you eat?" I grilled.

"Do it right after you eat; then it's easy," she finished nonchalantly. "Anybody can do it," she added impatiently. The lesson followed a time I had actually heard her throw up after declaring at the table she had eaten too much. Too often I had felt I ate too much: one too many helpings, five too many bites, one more dessert, ten too many pounds. *What a great way to eat all you want without having to gain weight,* I mused. A whole piece of chocolate cream pie a la whipped cream, without guilt. Fill up but not out. I had discovered the holy grail. Self-confidence, here I come.

Heeding her instructions, more important to me than a homework assignment, I took off after my next apple pie and stuffed my two fingers down my throat. Gag. Cough. Choke. Spit. Nothing. *How could anyone not throw up?* I thought to myself and tried again. Maybe I didn't eat enough, I rationalized when still nothing came out. The next meal: gag, cough, choke—nothing. "Anybody can do it," she had taunted.

I tried unsuccessfully once or twice more to rid myself of freshly chewed beef stroganoff or chicken a la king, changing the time between meals and throw-up or reaching deeper down my throat. Nothing worked. Over the next few months I occasionally visualized streams of vomit down a toilet, testing my fingers down my throat to see if I had miraculously mastered this art, but I never succeeded at purging, not once.

I think the idea actually grossed me out. I decided it wasn't so bad being a little pudgy and soon forgot about the whole failure. Each morsel of food I ever put in my mouth went straight to the scales. Aileen, meanwhile, lost more and more weight till she looked deformed. Her skin looked pasty, and her jaw bones stuck out weird-like. By the time she graduated, her legs and arms had become sticks. Her cheekbones pushed through her skin. Her bleached hair grew stringy and thin, and her teeth turned yellow and pocked. Her arrogance faded into a shadowy reclusiveness. Rumor had it that she died during her freshman year at college.

Growing up meant living in a fishbowl, feeling communal disappointments, and revealing pasts. Marylee told me about her father, who used to lock the door behind him and play with the inside of her. She was glad to be at Anderson, but she missed him, too. She hated her mother. I couldn't imagine a father loving you in any way but a formal, perfunctory way, lined with more conditions and expectations than you could meet.

I wondered if having your father put his fist up inside you felt better or worse than always being criticized and degraded. I guessed that, for a lot of kids, life was easier here at Anderson than at home.

Pete eventually stopped writing. The time came for me to grow up alone. I had lost my champion. One more carved face on the totem pole transformed me back into the girl no one loved. I still sometimes cried myself to sleep. My sadness was the night, ever-present and void. I spent the summer of 1963 playing coed softball, swimming, and practicing with the cheerleaders. I sang in the choir for Sunday-morning chapel services in the gymnasium. Though my grades weren't as good, my parents received a glowing report for my summer term:

Judy's outward manner and behavior this term has shown much improvement. In counseling, Judy has discussed plans for her future, and her relationship with her boyfriend. Freed from the excessive demands of this boy, Judy has been able to project a more positive and wholesome attitude toward her environment. She has talked about the possibility of being permitted to remain with her mother next summer and work, stating that many of her friends at home were doing so and she felt she would like to do this also. We discussed this with Judy and discouraged her from making plans of this sort. She feels that she would like to continue at Anderson, where she is becoming more fully aware of the progress she has made. Judy has been praised and encouraged in her efforts to gain leadership status in her group. She has shown a more positive attitude toward planning for college. Judy's progress during this term has been excellent.

Growing up is learning to accept that the world sees you differently than you see yourself, even if you don't understand why.

# CHAPTER 20

### David

Listen to the rhythm of the falling rain
Telling me just what a fool I've been
I wish that it would go and let me cry in vain
And let me be alone again.

**Sung by the Chordettes**

All bruises, backstrokes, tantrums, and temperaments were recorded, analyzed, and sent home to our parents. Lots of kids never questioned as much as I did. My whole life, I questioned. Whenever my brothers received preferential treatment, or whenever my parents passed down a word of law I disagreed with, I questioned. My dad's favorite retorts: "Because I said so," or, only half jokingly, "Children should be seen and not heard," put walls up inside me. I grew up with, "Look it up," and "Figure it out yourself." Maybe I was disagreeable. Maybe I wanted too much. Some kids just accepted life at Anderson, graduated thinking we were all normal. I questioned all the unacceptable roads.

The boys, in my mind, had it easier because their rules clearly differed from the girls'. They carried their cigarettes with them and were not subjected to fat Paddy slowly puffing her way from the kitchen with a tray full of Marlboros, Camels, and Chesterfields, then handing one little cigarette to each girl with a permission slip. (In 1963 I knew of no public information concerning the hazards of smoking.) The guys could go back to their rooms, because they lived on campus; they could earn freedom of the grounds, and they occasionally went to town with a teacher. Nothing big, just enough to bother me again. I knew I should have stashed away the scales, but I didn't.

David was one of those kids who never seemed to question life at Anderson. He never needed to consult his soul for guidance; as if destiny had drawn him a simple diagram in his heart; he just followed it without scraping, erasing, or evaluating. I liked David. Or maybe David liked me enough for both of us. Hair the color of a lion, eyes the color of the shallow waters off Barbados, he wore his package of Marlboros rolled up in the right sleeve of his shirt: plain white T-shirts in the summer and classic button-downs in the winter. David was unique, funny. He wore his baby-fine hair greased straight back on the sides and squared off flat on top, with a little puffy square of curly frizz just above his forehead. He pranced defiantly about, reminiscent of young Bambi in a spring meadow, when anyone reached for his frizzy pom-pom, which happened regularly. His skinny legs bowed in and wobbled like a young buck struggling to drink from a stream for the first time. About five feet eight inches, one hundred fifteen pounds, clouded with the scent of Canoe, David moved with the soul of Al Jolson. Every step, every motion had rhythm. So we danced.

If you didn't have a boyfriend—with the three-to-one ratio of boys to girls—you were considered a wallflower or a dork. Besides, I desperately needed protection from the retard. There were so many functions, a proper debutante would have been envious: dances, plays, movies, bowling, and roller-skating, for God's sake, and, of course, Sunday afternoon volleyball. Having a guy around was a requirement. Not that David was terrible; I just happened to still be in love with another guy. But, what the heck. Three years was a long time, and

I really loved to dance. I practiced for so many years with the doorknob and suffered through tortuous cotillions, why should I let such talent go to waste? I laughed when David broke off into an African mambo to Chubby Checker's "It's Pony Time," bobbing up and down chicken style. We slow danced with enough room to set up housekeeping. The prying hen chaperones pointed their talons the other way. He smiled when we danced, living in his own world and happy to be a part of mine.

Thin and angular, David had been adopted at birth by a short, chubby doctor and his wife from Silver Springs who planned their life around Jewish holidays. Their bodies looked as if they ate Passover Seder every night. I don't think they were taller than five feet. Their thick European features bore no likeness to David's narrow, chiseled face, but I don't think David was at Anderson because he was adopted. I wasn't sure why David was there. Maybe he kept too much company with trouble at home. David was cocky. A few of his schoolmates thought he took being a monitor too seriously, bullying them around. Once or twice I watched a well-toned anger boil inside him, exploding out at a teacher or another student, but David made *me* feel special, so we joined together much like a brother and sister.

Maybe David was at Anderson because a large delivery truck had crushed his eleven year-old body outside their suburban home, concaving his entire chest, breaking over one hundred bones in his body, demolishing his bicycle, and leaving him lying in a hospital bed for almost a year. At Anderson, everyone had a story.

In late September, David had permission to go to a temple in Poughkeepsie for Rosh Hashanah, a celebration of the Jewish New Year. Actually, with a school full of Nathans, Goldbergs, Kaplans, Wolfs, and Rosens, a large Greyhound bus pulled up for the excursion. Having been baptized and raised Episcopalian, then Unitarian, I had no working knowledge of the Jewish religion. I knew there were Jews in my heritage, but I didn't really understand or care for any religion. No miracle on either side, as far as I could figure out, but another outing was not about to leave me stuck in the dorm. The more I could escape Anderson, even for a minute, the more of the "real" world I could pretend to be a part of.

As far as I knew, this was the first time I had ever been inside a temple. We were ushered upstairs to the second-floor balcony, overlooking the synagogue where only men congregated. "Why are only men in front?" I whispered to David, as the men below began their service.

"That's just the way it is," he answered. The answer sounded too familiar. Some of the men had beautiful embroidered floor-length sashes around their necks. Most wore white robes and little caps on the back of their heads. They carried prayer books, often bowing their heads into the pages. Sunlight jumped off the fine gold thread of their sashes and the ornate decorations in the room. When their prayers grew audible, the room filled with foreign words. Had I traveled further than Poughkeepsie? I noticed David's finger following symbols backward across the page, his lips in perfect sync with the din of the room below. I wanted to know so many things.

"Why are you reading backward?" I asked, discovering a new talent in David.

"Hebrew."

"Where is it from?" I continued my basketful of questions.

"Israel." He smiled. I wondered if I had asked something stupid and kept quiet for a while.

"Why do the men wear those caps and sashes around their necks and not the women?" I wanted to know. It seemed the women were just along for the ride in this religion.

"Tradition," he answered. I had an innate knowledge of this tradition, where women came along for the ride. I never understood any segregation, but something about the Hebrew and the songs held me captive. After much sitting down and standing up, two men slid open giant doors in the back of the altar and pulled out cumbersome scrolls, which they carefully laid on a table, then unrolled. One man placed a silver pointer down on the scroll and droned a chant or prayer with the words. The sound echoed beautifully through the room.

"What is he reading?" I whispered my next question.

"The Torah. All Jewish history and law is written in the Torah. The Jews worship the Torah."

"Why?"

"It's what they believe, their Bible. Judaism is a religion, but it's a heritage, too. Jewish people think their history is as important as their belief in God." He sounded so impressive. I saw an extraordinary part of him in this temple. I watched intently as he read again in Hebrew. "You are a good Jew, aren't you?" I thought out loud.

"Yeah, a good Jew who only goes to temple once a year," he said, admonishing himself for not living up to someone else's expectations, something I could easily relate to.

"What about Jesus?" I asked.

"What about him?" he answered, as a smile curled over his thin lips. His confidence grew around us.

"They don't talk about Jesus. In the Episcopalian church, they talk about Jesus more than anything else," I remembered. Jesus saves. Jesus Christ is born. Little Lord Jesus, lay down your sweet head.

"The Jews don't believe in Jesus as the Christians do. They believe he was a prophet but not that he was the son of God or that he rose up after he died."

*Wow*, I thought to myself, remembering coloring Christ images during Sunday school, frustrated because I never could keep the worn crayon tip inside the lines. I remembered the last time I went to an Episcopal church with my parents, the movie of Christ hanging from a cross while people shouted and pushed and reached for his naked body. His hands and feet, stained with blood, were staked to the wood. His eyes looked upward, while the people wailed at his feet. Someone in the audience marveled because the movie was in color. I had screamed and screamed because I couldn't take the yelling, and they asked us to leave. My mom said later she didn't care, but her anger at the church was difficult to conceal. *Wow,* I said to myself again.

"You mean this religion doesn't believe in Christ?" I wanted to hear the answer again. David nodded his head. My legs felt tight, so I sat down.

"You have to stay standing until they put the Torah back," he warned me. I was intrigued with this religion without Jesus but disturbed by all the rules and the blatant inequality between men and women. Something inside me felt familiar. I felt as though I had been somewhere like this before, but I couldn't remember.

That Sunday, I wrote my mom my normal lifeline letter. In between reports of cheerleading, *The Great Escape* starring Steve McQueen, getting elected president of the sophomore class, roller-skating "again!" and standardized testing, I threw in my trip to the temple. "Next Saturday, I'm going to temple again. Just to see what more they have to tell me. It's very interesting—but not my religion," I wrote. I was totally confused when my mom wrote back telling me that well, actually, I really was Jewish—so if this religion interested me, it made sense, because my heritage was Jewish. Oh great, another thing to sort out. I knew my grandfather had been an ambassador and my great-uncle had been Secretary of the Treasury under Roosevelt, but I hadn't known anything about being Jewish. I hadn't known Mom Knight and Grandpop were Jews. I thought they were Episcopalians like us. I didn't know my mother's father was Jewish. I didn't know anything about the Jews except for the history of World War II. As far as I knew, nobody Jewish came from Doylestown, Pennsylvania. Certainly not me.

The first of October, my mom forwarded a letter from an Anderson friend who used to sing and play the piano with me:

> *Dear Judy,*
>
> *I don't know if you've written me lately or not, but I have to write you and tell you to write the same place Carol does, in the same way, too. My mom is on another one of her kicks about me being sick, and she reads and keeps or throws away all the letters I get from my 'neurotic friends,' as she says!*
>
> *I'm still the same, so be good and pray for snow. I love snow, you know, and I want it real bad, 'cause it's so pretty and I think it would be beautiful with the colored trees especially up there cause it's so pretty up there now.*
>
> *Loving you always,*
> *Candy*

There were always reminders. I tried to pretend. I tried to forget, but there were always reminders. Even my mother never really said I was *not* crazy.

The trees bathed us in blood-red and golden showers. The discarded leaves reminded me of happier times: my brothers and me diving into raked piles with the resolve of kamikaze pilots, in those years of living with little consequence. Life was just a series of explosions.

Like the army, we moved with preordained cadence: all rising, eating, studying, and sleeping in the same circadian rhythm. Mail call followed lunch. Every day Mrs. Adams walked in with a crooked arm full of letters for the girls. She usually handed them out two or three at a time. You knew she had screened them all and read some, too. Today, after handing out a few letters to others, she stood in front of me, arm's length away, and held out a box to me, which I knew from the label was a food "care package" filled with cheese crackers and chocolate wafer cookies from Mom Knight. She then held a letter over to me, simultaneously challenging my stare. I glanced at the envelope marked from my brother. A brief instant flashed, and she handed me another letter. As my eyes darted from the letter, I realized she was holding her hand out again with another letter, her face determined, lips pursed much like my grandmother's. This letter came from my father. I wondered if his letter had anything to do with the display she was choreographing on the spot. Had she read the letter? She held her hand out again, then again. Before I had time to realize—five letters was more than I had ever gotten in one day—she held her hand out again for the final time. Her eyes had been transfixed on me so long they'd lost their meaning. I looked down and saw the letter from Pete.

My brain, my heart, my body exploded into the unopened envelope. I felt my chair shoot behind with me in it and a scream resonate from my lungs. The letters on my lap dropped, as I clutched the final letter in my shaking hand. I could feel the entire school staring at me, but I couldn't abandon the letter. Mrs. Adams grabbed my arm fiercely and ushered me out of the dining hall. Once outside, she began reprimanding me, "Judy, stop this behavior. This is ridiculous." I was crying, shaking, possessed by a demon. I didn't care what she said or did. As we walked toward the main building, she held onto my arm tightly. Her words could not penetrate my rampaging thoughts or my chaotic feelings. She shoved me into her office and yelled, "You stay in here until you calm down! You're foolish."

I looked down at the letter still clutched in my fingers. Why did he have to come back? Why did he abandon me? Didn't he know how it felt to live without him? I couldn't open my hand. Why did I scream out loud, and why couldn't I stop screaming inside? This was nuts. I could feel it now. Crazy. Yes.

Out of control. They got me. I began laughing out loud, still shaking, salty tears wetting my mouth. "See, they made me crazy," I said to Pete, somewhere inside the letter. "I'm really crazy now. They won, you know. You didn't write, and I lost my strength." I remembered his arms around me and feeling secure in the defiance we fought the world with. I felt the madness inside me take a life of its own.

"Are you ready to come out now?" harped Mrs. Adams. I knew a long time had gone by, but I still had not read the letter.

"No," I snapped.

"We'll take you to the infirmary then. You can lie down there," she told me, visibly unhappy with the circumstances. "I can't believe you are so worked up over this guy. He hasn't written you in five months. He doesn't care about you. You are better off without him."

The nurse, actually the Health teacher, came in after Adams left, muttering about "something to relax you." She laid her cigarette on the left side of her mouth. As the smoke rose up into her face, she squinted with one smoke-irritated eye. Just as the ashes fell to the floor, she placed the burning cigarette on a small tin ashtray. I lay down on a cot covered with starched white sheets. I rolled over, watched the red burning ashes, and then slowly slid my finger under the flap. His handsome handwriting hadn't changed. He wrote as if the months had been minutes and not one tear-filled night had passed. He hadn't written because he was busy with work, school, etc. He wanted me to come for homecoming weekend at Northwestern University. For a moment, I harbored a hope I could go. He loved me, longed for the days we would see each other again, shot me up with butterflies, and signed off. I tried to fight off a heavy, siphoning sleep, wondering what had changed for him while so much had changed for me. I wanted answers, I wanted clarity, but the little pill finally pulled me into a deep, drugged sleep.

About a week later, I wrote my mother about losing another soccer game and Lorraine getting "bounced." Many kids were upset over another unjustified expulsion. Our collective mood turned sour. Her boyfriend tried to put his fist through a brick wall. I wrote about transfers again. "I don't care about much anymore. Things haven't gone well for me since I have come back, and, as usual, I don't want to fight, but I want to quit. My grades have been pretty good, and I haven't the energy to get into trouble." I focused again about going to the George School. I needed more than ever to leave, go somewhere else, and redefine myself before so much time passed that I disincarnated.

She never wrote back about going to another school and, afraid of becoming tapped again, I never wrote Pete—but I would see him again.

# CHAPTER 21

**Eating Worms**

Nobody loves me,
Everybody hates me,
Guess I'll go eat worms.
Long, skinny, slimy worms,
Big, fat, juicy worms,
Oh, how I love worms

First one was easy,
Second one was greasy,
Third and fourth went down easy,
Fifth got stuck, and sixth came up,
Oh, how I hate worms.

House committee, more reminiscent of Nazi-appointed Jewish councils than a court of law, frustrated my personal sense of morality. Every Sunday evening, I sat in the dark, wooden study lined floor to ceiling with empty bookshelves, listening to value judgments and varied punishments passed down on virtually every infraction heard. Old Mrs. James slouched in her chair at the head of the table, shirtwaist dress hanging loosely over her skeletal shoulders and knees. One arm dangled over the chair onto her basset hounds heaped next to each other on the oak floor. Mrs. Longo, dark and determined, generally voted without discussion. Fat Paddy was the only one who engaged in mindless conversation, as if her career depended on each outcome. She reveled in each bit of gossip, every fact she knew. In spite of her attempts to investigate circumstances, she didn't show much flexibility; the verdict yielded healthy doses of demerits and groundings.

Whenever a girl stood in front of the house committee to argue a case, inevitably her case was lost from the start. I cringed during these hearings. There was no avenue for change here, no Rosa Parks in sight. This was a kangaroo court of law, bound up in rules and regulations and outcomes that had existed long before my coming and would continue long after my departure—if, indeed, I ever did depart. I would never instigate my own investigation of a fellow student, unless it was another house committee member. Listening to stupid, minor infractions being punished with the resolve of a German warlord made me crazy. But I had committed myself personally to gaining more freedom, more space for myself. The more you sucked up to the school, the more privileges you earned. As a result of my house committee participation, I now occasionally spent Sunday afternoons alone in my room, savoring every moment of my earned solitude.

This only worked for a short time, however, because, even without Pete, trouble followed me like a little brother. I failed another test of life. One Saturday, while reading in the afternoon sun on the porch of Morgan Hall, I watched a girl walk out of the dorm and head down the dirt road traveled only by the yellow school bus and sporadic visitors. I looked around quickly to see if anyone was following her, but she was alone. I shouted her name as softly as I could. When she turned around, I saw her face was streaked with tears. I rose and walked to where she had stopped.

"What's wrong?" I asked softly

"Nothing. I gotta get out of here," she answered plainly.

"Yeah, it would be nice, wouldn't it?" I said, but when she started walking away, I persisted. "Wait. Where are you going?" I could see in her eyes she needed to talk and was tempted to trust me.

"None of your business."

"Yeah, hmmm, I know. I was just wondering." I moved closer.

Her red eyes seemed lost in the battle. "My mother was in a car accident, and they won't let me call her. They told me she's okay, but I just have to find out. I just want to talk to her. This place is the worst." She stared down the road again, waiting for me to make up my mind. I knew she was heading for the drugstore in Staatsburg.

"You'll be expelled," I warned her, looking toward town, wondering too. I was afraid for her but confused by this self-governing court of law. Now was my chance to either be a true house committee member or defect.

"I don't give a shit. You're gonna tell, aren't you?"

"No," I told her after a pause. She collapsed into my arms. I could feel her sadness come through my skin and fought back my own tears. I really didn't want to be known as a tattletale; I needed to shed myself of this classification. We all needed help here, and the house committee was not the way. She pulled away, and I walked back toward the porch. I didn't watch her go.

I sat back in the warm sun, closed my eyes, and listened for barking dogs hot on the scent, chasing her through the thick forest, but heard only a soft rustling of dry leaves. I thought of all the things I should have said. Secretly, I hoped she could resurface safely back into Anderson without expulsion. Who draws all the unfair lines? The rules at Anderson were etched too deep. We needed new ones. Maybe they would send me on to a Culver Military Academy for girls or even worse, jail for juvenile delinquents. My judgment on right and wrong wasn't exactly mainstream around here.

After a while, Jean Crissy walked onto the porch and asked, "Have you seen Shana?" Jean was a senior, one step away from becoming a dorm mother herself. I think over the years she must have set her sights on Paddy and Mrs. Longo as role models and eventually evolved into a future candidate. Jean was chunky, to put it mildly, with skin the color of Elmer's glue and the simpering voice of Marilyn Monroe, though the resemblance stopped there. She often wore her frizzy hair in a thin net to preserve her curls and moved around in bobby socks and saddle shoes, arms straight down along her sides, never swaying with her step. Her fists clenched, like a crying baby left in a crib too long. She didn't have a boyfriend, though I saw her occasionally engaged in sporadic discussions with Porky Pig at dances (they made a great match); she was on the late committee, the entertainment committee, the citizenship committee, and, most unfortunately, the house committee.

"No," I answered, but, when curiosity overcame me, I added, "Why?"

"Well," she began in her high-pitched singsong voice, "she signed out to be in her room, but she's not there." This girl wanted me to join the posse and I wanted her to take a powder.

"Oh, what a disaster."

"No, really."

"Maybe she just went to the bathroom," I told her, trying to come up with something more original.

"I don't think so. She's been gone for about fifteen minutes," she sang.

*Who appointed you keeper of the clock?* "Well, maybe she's down with Mrs. James," I continued.

"She's supposed to sign out for that," she said, stressing the word *supposed*.

"I'll look for her in a few minutes," I said, trying to mastermind an alternative plan—when, when out of the corner of my eye, I saw Shana walking up the sun-soaked road. Jean's eyes caught mine.

"Where have you been?" squealed the wide-mouthed girl from house committee over my disappointment. "You were out of bounds, weren't you?"

"None of your business, Jean Prissy Sissy," Shana answered, walking past us, up the steps, and into the dorm without missing a heartbeat.

A special house committee session was called once the ruling powers gathered all their preliminary data, the judge and jury, and their star witnesses, me and Marilyn Monroe. Mrs. Adams made a special guest appearance. I knew I was in trouble for not reporting Shana, but what concerned me the most was her fate in the hands of this impending kangaroo court. I sat in my regular seat at the dark mahogany table honestly believing any person with a milligram of compassion could find Shana in due stress or justified by reason of temporary insanity. I rehearsed my testimony over and over in my mind; I would never actually *tell* them I saw her leave, but how could I argue in her defense?

Of course, nothing I said made any difference in the way these people thought, and the longer I talked, the more apparent this became. The jury had deliberated before the court had been called to order, and I was useless in the game of plea-bargaining, as helpless as when I was arguing with my father. When the verdict was reached, the decision to recommend expulsion was final. I hadn't felt this much anger since my older brother tried to smother me with my own pillow. I stood up with everyone else, turned, and watched Jean rise from her seat. "You stupid *jerk*!" I screamed.

I ran up to my room, paced back and forth until my whole body exploded. I put on my coat, walked down the polished stairs, and out the door. I walked down the same sun-soaked path that Shana had chosen, then detoured through the crisp fallen leaves. Maybe if *I* left too they wouldn't expel us both, I rationalized. It wasn't as if she had really done anything bad. She hadn't sneaked out to drink or meet a boy or run away.

She hadn't hurt anyone. God, how could people be so stupid? What was the purpose of all these rules and no exceptions? I couldn't live in a world with no compassion. I dug my shoes into the blanket of leaves, kicking them apart as I walked. I couldn't stop the anger. I finally reached the thin wire fence I knew by now to be the property border of Morgan Hall. The fence wasn't barbed, so slipping through was easy, but once I got there I didn't know what to do. I had no place to go. I had no desire to go to town; not even a phone call appealed to me. I wanted them to expel me. I wanted them to crucify me. Hang me up and drive nails into my palms, till blood dripped onto the forest floor. I walked along the fence.

I burst into sudden laughter in the cool, fresh air. Out, out, out, damn spot. I was never going back. I was free. I walked until I found a place on the ground and decided to wait for a turtle to whiz by or Thumper to come and show me the way deeper into the woods. I sucked my right thumb and stroked the leaves on the ground with my left. I thought about playing sardines in the woods on the farm with the boys from my brother's eighth-grade class, praying dark-eyed Randy found me first so we could be alone before the others discovered us. I think the boys actually arranged the game so Randy found me.

When the damp ground soaked through my skirt, I looked up into the canopy until I spied two thick limbs cradling a seat just right for me. I wrapped my arms around the rough bark of the lowest branch, then swung my Keds up into the sky and took a koala bear view. The world was all upside down. I knew that. When I reached the crook that cradled me for the next several hours, I felt happier than I had in months. I was going home. I would see my brothers. We would laugh again like last summer, driving to the Port Authority station in New York City to meet the bus to Anderson. I remembered hearing a song on the car radio called "I Want to Hold Your Hand." My brothers and I sang loudly, in a mocking nasal twang.

We sounded so bad inside the tiny Karman Ghia that Mom cringed. When the song was over, the disc jockey told us some beetles sang the song, and I told my brothers I'd eat my hat if it ever made the top ten. I never actually ate a hat.

I hoped my mom would think this whole episode really stupid and understand my defending this girl. Maybe she would secretly whisper how proud she was of me standing up for what I thought was right. Maybe I could live at home and go to Central Bucks High School, try out for the cheerleading squad. I could go to a real football game where the home team actually won and cover the walls in my room with pictures of Frankie Avalon and Annette Funicello. No, I thought, I probably couldn't make a cheerleading squad anywhere but Anderson School. At a public high school, I would have to compete, and I would lose.

As the hours passed, my uplifted mood began eroding. What if I couldn't go home and live with my mother? My mother was already trying to win back custody of Flip, because my French stepmother thought discipline was a form of physical exercise. My father had declared Mom "irresponsible" and an unfit mother, citing her boyfriend and her restaurant as bad examples. He did everything to keep me from her, even though he didn't really want me. I would probably have to go back to court in Santa Fe—Judge Montoya, adobe walls, creepy kids, and cactus. Could reform school or an insane asylum be worse than Anderson? Living in Santa Fe, the city of dirt roads, certainly was.

I remembered an old black-and-white movie called *The Snake Pit*, starring Olivia De Havilland, about a woman whose husband committed her to an insane asylum because she had a nervous breakdown and tainted his image. She tried to hide inside the insane asylum. There isn't any place insane people can hide. We don't fit into little spaces.

I imagined falling out of the tree and landing on the ground with a dull thump. I imagined lying paralyzed on the bed of leaves below until nightfall, then being transferred by ambulance to a safe, neutral hospital. Mom stood by my bed, stroking my hand, tears pouring down her cheeks. "*Oh, honey,*" I could hear her say, "*I'm just so glad you're all right.*" My father was there, and they were actually talking to each other again, my father no longer brimming with anger.

"*The most important thing is that you are going to be okay,*" my father assured me, moving closer to the bed. It felt so good to hear my father say these words, even in a daydream. I couldn't feel the white sheets or the tubes in my arm, but I could feel how wonderful it felt to have both your parents care about you.

"*You were right,*" said my mom, "*They had no right to keep that little girl from calling home. You were very brave standing up for her.*" The room filled with friends and family. I was the hero.

"That's a stupid place to be," I heard suddenly from a pit below. "Do you think you're a monkey?" I broke from my dream and stared at the voice coming from the familiar, misshapen mouth. "I told them you wouldn't run away," she snickered. "You'll be punished anyway."

"I don't care," I documented for the thousandth time in my life.

"Perhaps you plan on spending the night in that tree?" she taunted. She always taunted. I looked out at the fading sky.

"You just had to prove something didn't you, Judy?" she asked, looking even funnier from up in a tree, her duck feet sticking out sideways from her oversized head. For a second I had the urge to hug her, but I stayed firmly perched in the branches.

"If you climb down from there now, I won't report you for overstepping the boundary," continued Mrs. Adams when I said nothing. "It will make the difference between expulsion and grounding, you understand." I watched her in her stillness, trying to decide if she was telling me the truth. "You've worked hard Judy; don't ruin it for yourself now. You're all worked up over nothing."

"I don't want to be in your stupid house committee," I blurted out. "I hate them. They're rats."

"No, I know you don't. I made a mistake in thinking you belonged there. I see now you have talents better used somewhere else. Your grades are good. If you work hard you can make cum laude again after this blows over," she tempted me. I knew you had to have conduct and grades over ninety each week to make cum laude. "You are a leader, Judy; the girls look up to you and trust you. Don't throw it all away because you're trying to prove a point." I thought about my Sunday afternoons alone. I didn't dare ask her again if she was going to report me when she read my mind, "I'll tell them you were in a tree on this side of the fence. It will be our secret. You'll just get demerits for unauthorized freedom of the grounds." I wondered how she managed to bend the rules. Would she lie for me? I wondered if I could believe her. This was the first time I felt anyone had done anything special for me since I'd arrived at Anderson. I knew I would be punished, but if I left school, the punishment would be death. Reform school. Mental hospital with IV drips. Electric shock therapy. Grow up, Judy. You can't win without playing, and you have to play their game.

I slid down the branch, feeling the bark scratch against my bare thigh. My stomach rumbled quietly, and my legs tingled as I wrapped my arms around the lowest branch and dropped to the ground. We started back toward the dorm in the failing light. Mrs. Adams placed her arm on my shoulder. I wasn't sure if she did this because she liked me or because she was afraid I would run away. I had enough running away for one day. I guessed she knew that.

# CHAPTER 22

### Interpreting Freedom

If wishes were horses,
Beggars would ride;
If turnips were watches,
I'd wear one by my side. '

**Mother Goose**

When the leaves lost their stronghold, and the cold winds sequestered us indoors, we were sent home from school one day to watch TV reruns of the only Catholic president America had ever elected being gunned down on the streets of Dallas, Texas. In black and white, over and over again, the girls in Morgan Hall watched a smiling, waving Kennedy suddenly slump into Jackie's lap, splattering blood, as their motorcar sped out of camera range.

We watched David Brinkley and John Chancellor fight tears as they reported each event: the hole in his neck, the bullet in his brain, the slim chances, and then the doctors, the death, the search for the killer, and the rusty stains on Jackie's suit as Lyndon Johnson took the oath as president less than two hours later. The shock of a nation was mirrored in the face of a young widow. *The guy who shot Kennedy certainly must be crazy,* I thought to myself, fighting back sympathy tears.

The days of winter, like rooms in a barrio boarding house, each held an event, an aneurysm of their own. The Beatles made their grand debut on the *Ed Sullivan Show*. The girls on my cheerleading squad, every single one, quickly deserted Sunday-night practice and gathered around the television set in the den. The light inside the dorm reflected off the gently falling snowflakes outside. Leaning up against the doorway, I watched my friends huddle intimately close to four guys desperately reaching for the high notes: "I wanna hold your hay-ay-and." (*I'll eat my hat,* I had promised my brothers.) The camera panned several screaming teenagers in the audience, wiping tears or sweat from their faces, bodies collapsing against their writhing friends. Why weren't these girls locked up, I mused? Girls gawking over guys they didn't know, screaming in public, twisted out of control. If my father saw me acting that way, I'd have shackles for sure. And I couldn't believe Ed Sullivan, with his crooked smile, the king of circus acts and conservative comedians. Had he been struck by a bolt of insanity? Watching from light-years away, I now suspected these four British crooners, long hair flopping with the beat, were bigger than Ringling Brothers and the Mormon Tabernacle Choir put together. Ringo Starr commented, after witnessing so many screaming fans, "So, this is America. They all seem to be out of their heads." I knew that.

The world continued on its own path. We watched some on TV Sunday nights, but mostly our world existed planets away. We had our own rules, our own traumas and sequence of events. We had daily scams and seizures, riots and ridicules under a thick ceiling of depression. What happened in the real world rarely penetrated our days.

In late winter, I collapsed in the hallway on my way to class, so they sent me home. I had my period for about six weeks and had lied to Mrs. Adams about my secret. I had lost too much blood and fainted. Of course, I loved any excuse to go home, even for a few days. Mom took me to her gynecologist, who put his hand up in my vagina and told me I had a cyst on my right ovary, one of those weird round things I had learned about in Dad's diagrams. The doctor prescribed birth control pills. Since they had some complicated medical name, I had no idea what they were really used for.

In the spring, David handed me his gold tiger's-eye ring and asked me to go steady. "Me?" I giggled and squirmed. He looked at me like a monk seal. I could tell he took going steady seriously, much more than I—I who had known the ecstasy of true love. "Sure," I replied. The pain and the drama I could anticipate if I said no would be much worse than a simple yes. Later, I dripped hot candle wax under the stone setting, so I could display the opalescent showpiece on my ring finger, knowing how imperative going steady with a jock was for good social standing and protection. My friends usually had boyfriends, so we palled around: David and Judy, Bill and Marianne, Sharon and Lee, Ellyn and Mike, and Gerry and Jane. But then Gerry and Jane ran away to New York City. They sort of eloped, only just lived together. Gerry was a very cool and talented guy. We used to talk for hours about how good our souls felt when we were loved. He talked about having lots of kids and taking them to the circus every Saturday and the zoo on Sundays. I knew I could never be a good parent, but he knew just how he was going to be a better parent than his were. He thought leaving Anderson with Jane meant living in a small Greenwich Village apartment happily ever after. I cried when they left. Then I cried again when Jane left Gerry high and dry in New York. He was so sad. He wanted so much to be loved. His dreams were too big for real life.

Then our headmaster, Mr. Gage, died suddenly of a heart attack. He was fifty-three and had worked at Anderson for thirty-two years, first as a teacher. Everyone at school was pretty shook up. Because we had less contact with him than our regular rotating psychiatrists, I thought we had basically just lost a figurehead. I remembered the first day I interviewed and the spell he had cast over me on that warm autumn day. The school lost their seducer.

Every week a story, event, or soap opera unfolded somewhere on campus. The school expelled someone for drinking; other kids went home for spring break or a weekend and never came back. Unexplained departures were common. The only part of normal life to me was my studies. Funny, my brain made me crazy, and yet it was the one thing affording me sanity. I became obsessed with scholars' worlds, poets' words, fantasies, languages, and faraway lifetimes. I mastered 97s and 98s in geometry and algebra, so my other grades averaged up. I read every book, finished every assignment, and had no trouble earning As and Bs. I soon figured out that because every one else was either crazy or lazy, all I had to do was finish all my work. I joined the yearbook and the newspaper staffs. I did anything to keep me away from the inside of my heart. I explored the deeper sides of my friends, those who had them, and I pretty much wanted it all. I wanted popularity. I wanted to be smart. I wanted a cool boyfriend. I still wanted out, but I decided to live in their world now, because no one wanted to hear about my world or my birthright.

Then the day came I had often wondered about. Mrs. Cartmell came to my room one Saturday morning. "Pete is here," she told me calmly, without fanfare.

"Who?" I heard myself ask, feeling a rush of sweat swarming through my veins. She stared at me with little expression. She knew and I knew. What did she know and what did I know? Nothing, without a crystal ball. Life kept piling more on my plate than I wanted to eat. What was I going to say? Would I feel the same? Would he look the same? I stared outside into the sunshine, feeling the heat meld into me and sensing, but not acknowledging, Mrs. Cartmell's exit. My mind swirled into a whirlpool, reversing thoughts and then reversing them once again. Could I dare to hope our love could ever return? All of a sudden, I was the soap opera of the day. The *Days of Our Lives* was now the day of my life. The drama would unfold no matter what I felt or did; all eyes would be watching. Would he steal me away so we could make love in the woods? My thoughts scattered when I heard Betsy's voice, "You're not going to hurt David, are you?"

I turned around and saw her nestling onto her bed, crossing her ankles and curling them into her crotch. She pulled a pillow onto her lap and stared at me like a puppy at the pound. Her words became entangled in the whirlpool but eventually grabbed my full attention. "I don't know."

"Everybody in school is gonna be mad if you do," she went on. I couldn't feel Pete's arms around me. I could only feel the heat of my heart.

"Like I care," I replied, reworking my adolescent retort with updated cynicism.

Whatever decision I made probably wouldn't go unassisted. Friends and counselors and parents would no doubt have way too much input. "David will be crushed if you let on that you still love Pete. You don't," she paused. "Do you?" I wondered if Betsy made sense.

"I don't know. This is all too weird." Was this a defining moment for my personal insanity?

My first glimpse of Pete was across the crowded dining room, where I had watched for him daily during my first year at Anderson. Friends and teachers took turns patting him on the back or shaking his hand like he was some kind of Mick Jagger. There were so many eyes darting back and forth between David, Pete, and me. I slowly focused on my lunch and kept my eyes down. I couldn't make anything work.

When Pete and I finally spoke during canteen, I had lost all concern for anyone else and found every word between us a struggle. "So, how are you?" he wanted to know.

*What do you mean? I don't know how I am! You left. You never wrote. You said you would love me forever. You gave me reason to live, to fight this place. You were the only reason I got up every day. We were supposed to get married, and you didn't even write! You left, and now you're back. I hate you, but I love you. I am still at Anderson, and you are living in the real world. We are a thousand miles apart. Why did you come back? How could you come back? Please take me away from here.*

"Fine, I guess."

"How are you?"

"I'm okay."

We talked about teachers and kids and scandals. We had the length of canteen, one half hour to put our life back.

"How's college?" College was great. Life was great. Actually, life was pretty big out there, and we are at opposite ends now, which is just as well, because we don't want to hurt David, who stayed back at the dorm chain-smoking. Do we?

"It was great to see you."

"Yeah."

Then he was gone.

At the end of my sophomore year, I learned that all I had to do was take two extra classes during the summer, maintain good grades through the winter, take another extra course next summer, and I could graduate next year. I was going to skip my junior year! I could buy a year of my life as easily as shopping for a dress with a pocketful of cash. How much time had passed since I could celebrate? How long it had been since my laughter came from deep inside. I bounced around like a kitten after a ball of string, ignoring Mrs. Adams' cautions. I would, some day, walk away from the Anderson School.

Once again I won the award for Best Figure at the Morgan Hall banquet. I also eked out Most Popular. Betsy won Wittiest, and my first lumberjack roommate, Ann, whom I had managed to avoid since my first summer at Anderson School, swept Most Athletic, Best Housekeeper, and Done Most for the Dorm. I think they made up Best Housekeeper just so she could win, because I never saw the category before or after. Well, she was graduating this year. She needed these important, distinguishing titles to carry with her into the real world. Maybe someday she would be the First Lady of housekeeping.

# CHAPTER 23

### Seniors and Scenarios

Hey, hey
You, you
Get off of my cloud.

**Mick Jagger and the Rolling Stones**

In the fall of 1964, I miraculously entered my senior year at Anderson School—miraculous because I skipped a grade and miraculous because I survived two years in a prison with no bars. Not only had I skipped a grade, but I was also elected president of my new class, president of the Alpha Beta Society, captain of the cheerleading team, editor of the yearbook, the *Andersonian*, and the newspaper, the *Ander-Sun*. Add all this vapid prestige to "Best Body" and "Most Popular," and anyone would have thought I was the Rock of Gibraltar. Actually, I felt more like the leaning Tower of Pisa, a slapdash monument poised for imminent collapse.

All the insecurities I had packaged in my youth remained intact. I checked my self-esteem regularly with the reminder that all the adulation had come from retarded kids, crazy kids. I knew I shouldn't be lulled into thinking my successes transferred to the real world—should I? Wouldn't I be just another maniac at large after I graduated? Where would I fit in? Who would ever want me? At Anderson I lived by someone else's life formula. What if I freaked out in a grocery store or something? The rules of the real world were different. Who would teach me the new rules?

I wondered if my father would love me now that I was smart and president or whether he saw my peers as just a bunch of crazy kids too.

My senior year meant hope: two-thirds down, one-third to go. Yet, Anderson School had become my family now, the cytoplasm for the new me. All my learning processes had come from a life I had not chosen and could not escape. I couldn't be sure the lessons I had learned would serve me where I was going. So I tried not to think of graduating or life beyond. I concentrated on the little things.

On the third floor of Morgan Hall, two single rooms tucked back in a corner next to the bathrooms were reserved for senior monitors or girls with severe social problems—phobias and stuff. If I had been David in *David and Lisa,* where he couldn't stand to be touched, they would have put me there. I dreamed of having one of these rooms from the minute I arrived at Morgan Hall, from the day I wandered through the halls looking for a more suitable roommate than the gorilla. I wanted to live by myself more than anything. In a room with four girls, the conversations consisted of constant complaints, hysterical boy problems, chatty talk of shitty teachers and crappy parents, and on-going amorphous depressions. I wanted silence.

The greatest reward of my senior year was, finally, the gift of the tiny sliver of a single room, on the third floor, facing the gravel driveway. From here I could watch the setting sun turn the trees rust, and the rising moon dust the night sky. I still cleaned toilets and took out the garbage, but at night I wrapped myself up in a blanket of privacy, safely warding off the chill of total assimilation.

Once again, I placed the black-and-white photo of my brothers and me on the desk. I taped pictures of David on the wall, but kept pictures of Pete in the top drawer of my desk. Lulled into a false security, I believed the room was mine to keep until I went home. I guessed wrong about a lot of things that fall.

Betsy comfortably took up housekeeping in the neighboring single, presumably so I could continue to keep her kleptomaniac tendencies in check. Though her room met morning inspection regulations, she still lived in the most junk-concentrated room I had ever seen, a pack rat's denizen in disguise. I imagined Paddy or Mrs. Longo, garbed in gas masks and astronauts' mittens, searching among vast mountains of clutter for stolen bracelets or cotton panties. The girl across the hall had some condition which caused her to scream out of control every so often, but otherwise the living situation was as good as I could hope for.

"Judy and David, sittin' in a tree, k-i-s-s-i-n-g," I heard Betsy singing through the thin wall. I think she got as much thrill from my going steady with David as I did. Maybe more.

"Cut it out!" I yelled. Everything Betsy did and said begged for laughter, and I was a very obliging audience. She plopped herself onto my doorway, legs stretched up the door jamb. I watched my mind replace her with myself and go back suddenly in time. I was at the farm, in the den, and my father caught me with my feet up on the curtain, sucking my thumb absently. My thigh stung from his slap. His anger swarmed into me, like venom from a bee. I shook my head to clear the thoughts. Why couldn't I control my memories? The past was addictive.

"What did David think about you getting elected president of the senior class?" She handed me a box from home. Thanks to her dad, I had a lifetime supply of Noxzema.

"Thanks. I think he is pretty upset, because he's two years older than me, and I'm a year ahead of him now. He'll get over it."

"He loves you so much; it doesn't matter what you do."
Yeah, maybe that was David. I loved sharing stories with Betsy,
looking through the clouds toward clearer skies. Occasionally
the advice I handed out sunk into my own brain.

In the beginning, Betsy presented me with various
baubles to show her friendship. Never trusting exactly where
the trinkets came from, I continually tried to convince her
I didn't want "things" from her; I just wanted to be friends.
I also didn't want to get pegged with her stealing. Soon she
began writing me poems. Her happiness grew as our friendship
grew. Her first poem, written carefully on soft, lined pink
paper made me smile:

> If I told you all my good thoughts
> It would take a long, long time
> I will only think of Judy
> And her pretty smile.
>
> I will think of all the good times
> That she would spend with me
> And think of her in college
> And how lonely I will be.
>
> I will think of only Judy
> And how I like her so,
> And then when she was happy
> I could see her brown eyes glow
>
> Oh, I will remember Judy
> Until the day I die,
> And how when she was sad,
> She'd sit there with a sigh.

Oh, I will always remember
I never will forget,
To see me pass in conduct
Weekly her heart was set.

But most of all I always heard
A certain little chime
Yes, and I remember Judy
For a long, long time.

In October 1964 the Rolling Stones appeared on the *Ed Sullivan Show*, and the fans rioted. Sullivan swore they would never come back, but they did—six times. By December, the floppy-haired Beatles had five number-one hits. America, the beautiful. Home of the brave.

My brother Steve was in his senior year at Fountain Valley and sibling rivalry kept us from writing. He wasn't happy about his little sister being in the same grade, and he hated being compared to me academically. I thought because Steve was a boy and the oldest, all he had to do was tread water and he would have gotten the world: cars, clothes, and golden doubloons of love. But all three of us had the same problem of existing right below the line of acceptable, wherever the line fell. We weren't old enough to realize unconditional love wasn't in our makeup case.

My father's business had evolved into a monopolistic success, and, for the first time in his life, my dad was kind of a big shot around town. My father decided he didn't want Flip around anymore, because he insulted lots of Dad's friends and became uncooperative with Annette and the hired help. Flip was floundering at Santa Fe Prep, a new school my dad helped get started with a small donation. When he told me at Christmastime about possibly sending Flip to Anderson School, I lost every ounce of self-control I had gained. The same feeling of hopelessness I had felt many times before began spinning around me like cotton candy.

"Anderson did a great job with you," he spoke seriously at the dinner table during Christmas. "Maybe it can do something for Flip." What had I done? I had succeeded just so I could get out, and now he thought this school was the answer to every problem child. I loved Flip. I never loved anyone as much as I loved my little brother. I loved him from the day he came home from the hospital. I taught him how to play canasta and Monopoly. I had to protect him now.

"Dad, he's not as bad as I was," I reasoned, trying a different approach than attack. "He just needs to go to a good school away from home, and he'll be fine." I carefully considered every word I spoke. I knew all too well how these conversations could turn out. If I said too much, everything would backfire. If I showed feeling, he would react.

"He needs help," he singsonged. He said this about all three of us, as if we had wandered into quarantined quarters and contracted a case of failure to survive. I knew I had to stop before everything I had worked for lost its meaning. I backed away, into my dark world, and prayed to God, any god, that Flip wouldn't follow in my footsteps.

Dad also talked about my becoming a debutante. He wanted my shoes in the closet arranged in neat rows like my grandmother's and my stepmother's, but he had the wrong girl. There would be no Dior suits in my future. I could just see myself sharing at the Debutante Ball. "Hi where do you go to school?" they would ask.

"Oh, I go to a school for crazy kids. Where do you go?" Talk about a conversation stopper.

I spent my Christmas vacation in the adobe house with no dirt, the perfect house on the hill, never asking for more than the butter.

The Anderson basketball team ended with a three-win and thirteen-loss record, losing the last game by sixty points.

David, my sweet, skinny, determined steady, high-scored the game by darting under the armpits of bulky and awkward opponents. He reminded me of David and Goliath, sort of, but he never slew the giant of the real world. The only schools we ever beat were smaller and probably more dysfunctional than Anderson. The other cheerleaders and I shouted on, worrying about scuffing our white Keds or landing in the splits with our skirts flared properly around our thighs. Defeat was a way of life.

David started growing on me—not the same as Pete; I loved him differently. His unwavering partnership with the world was a welcome contrast to my constant battle. He had a harder life than most but survived with less drama. No hint of humiliation showed on his face when he lined up with the rest of the team, shrunken arms jutting out of the thin-strapped uniform hanging loosely over his concaved chest. He smiled when he had his picture taken, like a circus sideshow phenomenon, with the six-hundred-pound organ player at the roller-skating rink. He looked at me for reassuring smiles. In a way, I loved him like a brother, and that was something I knew well.

During the winter of my senior year, Ted Kennedy survived a plane crash, Winston Churchill did not survive his life, Beatlemania had become pandemic, and Joe Namath signed a three-year contract with the New York Jets for a staggering four hundred thousand dollars. It didn't matter to me that a crop failure forced the USSR to buy wheat from Australia and Canada, and I thought little about the slowly escalating Vietnam War.

Every Sunday, we were required to put on our church-goin' best and attend the temporarily transformed gym for compulsory chapel. Mrs. James played "Rock of Ages" on the pine upright piano on wheels. Everyone sat on gray metal folding chairs. I sat with the choir in the front row and watched as Mrs. James's long, ancient fingers fumbled awkwardly over the keyboard. We had everything at Anderson: education, religion, therapy, guidance, rewards. We had it all.

During spring break, I miraculously had permission to visit David and his parents in Silver Spring, Maryland. They lived in the suburbs: short, fat people in a short, fat house with plush, peach-colored wall-to-wall carpeting. We went to Passover Seder at the country club and ate miles and miles of food that I had never seen before: gefilte fish, smoked salmon, white fish, bagels, mushy salads, and hills of rolled chocolate things.

I slept in the guest room for three days and learned about David's world, met his friends, saw his grade school and the streets where he grew up. We stole a few kisses, but Emily Post herself couldn't have planned a more proper vacation, until the night he drove me home to New Hope in his red Ford Falcon. Because we both came from Anderson, this was one of those special "normal" experiences most teenagers took for granted. We talked about school and listened to the radio. My parents weren't as concerned with David as they had been with Pete, maybe because I was older, or maybe because they thought David more acceptable. I never knew. They never said.

We got home around ten and parked in the public parking lot next to my mom's house. Under the street lamp, we spent the next few hours making out in his little red Falcon, navigating over gear shifts, under steering wheels, between closed doors, around buttons, zippers, and fabrics. While Elvis crooned, "I … can't … help … falling in love … with … you," my emotions intensified, and we explored each other's mouths, caressed breasts, and rubbed each other below. Then, when we both were running out of breath and the day was running out of night, he asked me, "Have you ever gone all the way?"

I realized suddenly how little we knew of each other; there were mountain ranges we had never climbed. Though we had dated almost two years, we never penetrated the intensity of each other. We danced and we laughed, we sat side by side in movies, we had become friends, we kissed, but I never thought this would be the man. Would this be the night?

"No, have you?"

"Well, yes," he stated shyly, after a cloud of silence moved between the two of us. This could not possibly be a man of the world, I thought to myself.

"Thanks a lot," I said, sitting up, beginning my natural state of jealous pouting.

"No, no," he interrupted, visibly pleased at the least sign of jealousy. Why did boys always think jealousy meant a pledge of undying love? "Before I met you," he clarified, pulling me back next to him, "a long time ago." I had to admit my jealousy gave him a boost, and I loved the intrigue of him being experienced, braver than I.

"How old were you?" I asked, challenging his story.

"Fourteen," he said. I was in love with Pete at fourteen. I wanted to marry him and have kids. I remembered I would have done anything for Pete and how much I had needed him, how he could drive a passion deep inside me with his eyes. "Freddy set me up with some girl in Washington." The thought of Freddy brought a smile to my lips. I could just see David's young, dark-haired friend, the Italian stud with smiles as big as the night and his overt manipulation of the freedom I longed for. Freddy knew no fear. Freddy set no boundaries. The four of us: David, Betsy, Freddy, and I had explored the streets of Freddy's world in his black 1957 Chevy convertible with the silver stripe.

"Freddy's bad," I joked. "What was it like?"

"Okay."

"Just okay?"

"I think it would be better with someone you really love," he answered.

"You're kidding?" I said, straightening up, wishing to explore this further. Here truly was a man of experience, a man of the world. "What was her name?"

225

"Well, I don't know. I don't remember, Andria or Adrian or some-thing like that," he answered, becoming increasingly annoyed with my line of questioning.

"Geeze. You slept with someone you didn't even know?" Now I knew I was crazy. First, girls screaming and fainting over some singers they didn't know, now David sleeping with someone he didn't know. God, I really boarded the wrong plane. "Do you remember what she looked like?"

"Sure," he said, but I wasn't convinced. I knew he didn't want to talk anymore about this girl with no name, so I reconciled a return to the original discussion. My heart's pounding left tightness in my chest.

"I don't think I'm ready yet," I said, rubbing my arm.

"Judy, I really love you," he said. "I won't ask again. Just know I want you, and when you're ready, you tell me." I looked down, as he took my hand into a bathtub of down feathers. I kissed him gently on the lips and reached for the door. "You're not mad, are you?" he asked.

"No," I said truthfully.

"I'll see you at school."

"Thanks, it was fun."

I climbed out of the car and watched him disappear into the darkness. The still, low cloud cover reflected the few remaining lights of night into a false ceiling. When I walked through the gate, I saw my mother through the sliding glass doors. She was sitting at the round oak table with lion feet, head bent down over a paperback, reading under the Tiffany shade. I wondered if she was upset and wondered why she was still up. I took a deep breath, ran my hand through my hair, and, scrambling to clear my mind and body, I opened the door.

"Hi," I stammered.

"How was your trip?" she asked, laying the open paperback upside down on the table and placing her reading glasses on top. Her eyes looked tired.

"Good."

"Well then, we'll talk about it tomorrow," she said. "It's pretty late."

"Mom, I need to talk to you about something. Can we talk now?" I asked.

"No, I'm tired. It will have to wait till the morning."

Filled with the emergency of the moment and a tremendous amount of courage, I knew I could never brave the subject of sex after the sobriety of a full night's sleep. "Please?"

The one thing I truly believed about my mother was her love. "Good to remember," she once wrote, "not just the balloons and the pony rides, but the temperamental bouts and baseball mitts taken away—all part of the wonderful deal—mothers and daughters." We had exchanged years of letters, both in search of a painless landing strip. Some days she was the only reason I went on. Her tired eyes closed, as she sunk back into her Mexican leather-back chair. "All right," she said, as a smile came over me.

"How important is it to be a virgin when you get married?" I quickly dropped the bomb, as I sat down at the table. She sat motionless. She didn't laugh, or grumble or react. She just sat quietly looking at me, her fifteen-year-old crazy daughter, who still sucked her thumb. I could tell her mind and her heart were preparing a statement.

"Well, I don't think it is important at all," she answered after a time.

"It's not?" I asked a bit confused. The simple answer came from a personal reflection of a lifetime I knew nothing about.

"I was a virgin when I married your father," she began. "I believe that was one of the biggest mistakes of my life and ultimately why our life together did not work. Your father and I were both virgins when we got married. I assumed he had some kind of experience while he was in France during the war, but I was wrong."

"Didn't you ask him?" I probed.

"No, we married soon after the war, and most of our courtship was long-distance. We were still getting to know each other." She went on, recalling memories of her honeymoon and her subsequent struggle with loving my father both physically and emotionally. I listened as she unfolded into a real, honest, woman, capable of knowing life's confusions and unafraid to share what she had learned with her daughter. As she spoke, her words gave her new strength, as if saying them out loud in front of me underlined her own acceptance of the truth. For the first time in my life, I understood why my parents divorced, and I don't believe I ever loved my mother more.

"Now, this is not a license to sleep with every Tom, Dick, and Harry," she clarified. "Sex should be the by-product of love, a researched, thoughtful love, not just an infatuation of the moment. You have to decide if you are old enough to make the distinction for yourself." I stared out into the night through the picture window. I had no sense of age. Was I young, old, or caught in between? Sometimes I felt I had lived longer lifetimes than other kids. I knew the innocence of my childhood no longer existed; every expectation placed upon me had erased the child within.

"Are you ready to go to bed now?" she asked, breaking my spell.

"I love you, Mom," was all I could say. We stood up, and she folded her arms around me, stroking my hair with her fingertips. I was taller than her now, and it felt strange. There was no way I could ever look down on my mother.

She held me until all the world's pressing matters melted away.

"I love you, too," she said gently, "more than you'll ever know."

# CHAPTER 24

**Morgan Hall**

Ring around the rosy
Pocket full of posies
Ashes, ashes, we all fall down

Two years of repetition turned morning monitor duties into a robotic performance. I stumbled daily through the routine without fully surfacing from the residue of nighttime. Ever since the mornings on the farm, when I woke to a black depthless sky and a cold bathroom floor, I rebelled against morning darkness. At Anderson there were also beds to make, floors to scrub, banisters to dust, and garbage to take out, along with showering, dressing, combing, primping, then lining up, signing out, and filing onto the bus. I could perform morning without experiencing any cognitive thinking whatsoever.

My head monitor duties included checking each room on the third floor after the girls had gone downstairs to line up. I remember one morning in late March vividly. As I walked through the halls in my habitual stupor, I stopped in the doorway of my own room and stared at the streak of sun bursting through the window, blazing to the floor. The sunlight radiated warmth, hurling my gaze into a hypnotic trance. Tiny particles of dust danced in concentric circles inside a beam of sunlight like ballerinas at Lincoln Center. I had difficulty breaking my eyes from their spell. Finally, I went to check the other rooms. Odd how fast the dust moved, I thought to myself. I walked down three flights of stairs to the hallway, where Paddy was signing out the girls. "Everything's fine," I told her absently, believing myself. We climbed onto the bus and headed for school.

Just as we were finishing breakfast, I heard sirens in the distance. The faint sound filtered through the chatter of students, the rattling of dishes and trays. "Do you hear that?" I asked Mrs. Cartmell, the new dean of women, who was sitting across the table. "What do you think is wrong?" I asked. All through the morning I heard sirens in the distance. I suspected some sad, strange event was unfolding somewhere.

During lunch we were told Morgan Hall was burning down. The fire, burning out of control, was a five-alarm fire. Fire trucks from as far away as Poughkeepsie had been called in to contain the blaze. The dorm had exploded into flames shortly after we had arrived at school. The fire department thought it might be days before the fire would die completely. Attempts were being made to contact parents and arrange for a place to stay. A sense of urgency took over the campus.

Finding it impossible to concentrate on studies, everyone whispered all afternoon. Where would we sleep? What happened to our things? Would we have to go home? The hub of excitement overwhelmed any school order, more than the usual epileptic fit or runaway student. The fire didn't mean much to me. I welcomed the distraction. We all welcomed what we thought would be an adventure. We thought a little Godzilla on campus could be fun. Each classroom discussed the latest developments and projections instead of given subjects. Girls were being called in and out for telephone calls and meetings. As the reality of the fire oozed forth, I thought of the photograph of my brothers and me with Mr. Lucky and the pictures of Pete I knew could never be replaced. I remembered the new silver and pearl ring my mother bought for me when she was in Mexico and a swift sadness overcame me. If only I hadn't taken the ring off last night for my shower.

When the school day ended, all the students met in the gymnasium. I sat next to David, wanting to hold his hand. The new headmaster, Dr. Bartlett Chappell, related to us in detail what we already knew: Morgan Hall was burning out of control. It now was an eight-alarm fire; trucks from all the neighboring towns had been called in to fight the blaze. Because of possible danger to Mrs. James's cottage and the surrounding woods, none of the girls were allowed to return. While he spoke, I felt a permanence of separation from my material things. I didn't really care, for real this time. I looked down. I was wearing a blue-jean wraparound skirt with red and white checkered lining and a matching red and white checkered shirt, a pair of blue-jean Keds, and white bobby socks. Annette had sent me the outfit from The Guarantee, a store on the plaza in Santa Fe. I wished I had chosen something else to wear.

"I don't know where you will sleep tonight. We are still working on possibilities. Everyone will stay on campus until dinnertime," said the silver-haired clone of the deceased Mr. Gage amid snickering and cheering. "If you don't have a sport activity, you will remain upstairs in the study hall. At six, we will all go to dinner as usual, and then we will tell you where you will stay."

Questions flew. "How did the fire start?" No one knew at this time. "Is the fire out?" Not completely. "What will we do about clothes?"

During dinner, Dr. Chappell again addressed the students. We were told we would sleep at a boys' camp next door. There were plenty of bunks, and they were looking for sheets and blankets. In the meantime, homework was excused, and we would all watch a movie until bedtime. More cheers erupted.

After the movie, we rode our little yellow bus out through the entrance of Anderson School and turned right instead of left, into the summer camp. I had no idea there was a boys' camp next door. We drove down a long, bumpy dirt drive, far less maintained than ours. The deserted, unfamiliar setting looked like an army boot camp under the single floodlight. We filed into the whitewashed building made of wooden slats and concrete. There were no windows. We stood on the bare floor silently perusing our new home. About twenty bunks lined the large, otherwise barren room lit by three uncovered light bulbs. Several cardboard boxes sat off in the corner.

"The girls from Vassar College have very generously donated some clothes for you girls," said Mrs. Cartmell, breaking the abnormal silence. "I want you to go through the boxes over there and pick out what you need. You'll have to figure out a way to share. I am not getting into that." Her face became startled when a flock of giggling girls thrust past her and started sorting through the large cardboard boxes. For a moment I sat still, feeling too old to be silly. The surrealism of my life moved beyond anything I could have made up. I watched a few girls retreat with armloads of clothes, their level of chatter deafening. They chattered and giggled and tried things on. I helped Mrs. C. get blankets out of the closet and put them on each bed. Then I slowly nudged in and began rummaging through the remnants of rich girls. I needed something to sleep in, didn't I? I reached into the cardboard box, and lifted out a Victorian-style full-length pink cotton nightgown with neck and cuffs of lace. It could have been Edna St. Vincent Millay's. The cotton had been washed so much it felt soft as the ears of a newborn kitten. I touched the nightgown to my cheek, then over the top of my lips, wondering why no one had chosen it. I had gone from a room of my own to a summer camp in the cold with way too many girls. This bad movie was getting worse.

In spite of—or maybe because of—my attitude, I became a leader. With the grownups scampering around attending to details, lots of girls started asking me for advice, and Mrs.

Cartmell often gave me information to share with the rest. I helped organize, clarify, and solve simple problems. That, and my melancholy, set me apart. I didn't seem to care as much as everyone else. Never did. Never would. I had been homeless for a long time.

Each girl received one grey wool blanket. Because there were no pillows, I suggested we roll up our clothes. I showed them how to roll to minimize the wrinkles. The dorm had a hollow sound. As we talked, the words bounced off the slatted walls, echoing on top of words still resonating. Then, when the girls had climbed into their bunks, I made my way to the deserted communal bathroom. I stood before a tiny wood-trimmed mirror and changed into my secondhand nightgown. Watching my dim distorted reflection, I ran my fingers along the translucent yoke of the nightgown, wondering how it felt to be the Vassar girl who had donated her clothing: tall, pretty, but not *really* pretty. Maybe I had wheat-colored curls falling softly down my shoulders. I was rich, and smart, and my parents bragged about me to their friends at the country club back home. Maybe I studied literature and Edna St. Vincent Millay.

I washed my hands and face in the icy tap water. *I probably won't get into college at all*, I thought. My father had decided I would go to a finishing school in Gstaad, Switzerland, because, in his mind, at seventeen, I would still be too immature for college. One of the Morgenthau girls, a daughter of Barbara Tuchman's, had attended the school, called Montessano. Barbara Tuchman was yet another overachieving family member I would never live up to. Though I had applied to Radcliffe, Middlebury, and Colorado College, I knew I wouldn't get in. No, I would never go to college. Grades transferable only to finishing schools and asylums.

I crawled into a single makeshift cot next to the bathroom after everyone had settled in. I inhaled the silence, pulled the hairy wool blanket around my shoulders and scanned the room. The outside floodlight squeezed though cracks in the walls, casting stripes on the rows of bunks, flickering urgently as the pine branches blew in the breeze. I shivered off the cool night and wandered into a thin sleep.

Somewhere through time, a distant rumble of a train came from nowhere and grew larger and larger until I startled awake in unavoidable awareness. I clutched my blanket and felt the room begin to tremble, my cot actually vibrating on the concrete floor. First the giant locomotive passed. Then each individual car sped by for what seemed an eternity, clicking over each track, gasping in between cars, louder than if I had been on the train itself. I was certain everyone else was awake, but no one stirred. I lay alone in my own terror. Then, as the train faded off into the distance, my body claimed my thoughts. The cold March night dug deeper inside, my thin scratchy blanket no longer kept out the night. I lay tense and shivering, while my mind raced through the meaningless hours of early morning. My body trembled until the pale ochre distance gradually mutated into another day with alien answers.

I slipped off my nightgown and put on my blue-jean skirt and red checkered short-sleeved shirt. The hair spiked up on my arms. I stood purposefully in a sliver of sunlight coming in through the slats. Everyone, it seemed, had heard the train and felt the cold, though most were able to sleep on. I listened to the headmaster brief us again before breakfast. The fire had been contained, though it was still smoldering. Two fire departments were still at the site. The eight girls who lived in the cottage would return and pack up their clothes by nightfall, though they were prohibited from moving back in. Those of us who lived in Morgan Hall would each receive two thousand dollars in insurance money and go on a shopping trip with Mrs. Cartmell this afternoon after classes. I was called up to the headmaster's office for a meeting with the insurance agents.

"I understand you were the last person to check the dorm before you left yesterday morning," said the man in the oyster suit. Another man sat behind him, diligently taking notes on a yellow legal pad.

"Yes, I'm the house monitor, and I check all the rooms in the morning," I told him.

"Did you notice anything different during your rounds?" he asked. My tired mind wandered back to the swirling dust dancing in the sunlight. I thought about why I had stopped and stared. I slowly described in detail how I stood yesterday watching the dust, how I became mesmerized by the sun, and then had moved on through the halls.

"Do you think that had anything to do with the fire?" I asked, coming back to the present.

"Quite possibly," answered the man, after turning to look at the other. "We suspect the fire started from the wires in the wall between your room and your neighbor's."

"Wow, how can you tell so soon?" I wondered.

"By where the flames were when the firemen arrived and how hot the fire was burning at that time. The fire has the characteristics of an electrical fire."

"You're kidding," I projected. "You think the fire was already burning while we were there?"

"We can't tell for sure, but it's quite probable. The fire went out of control quickly. The fire may have been smoldering for some time," he went on. "Our guess is you girls are lucky to be alive." He watched as I tried to register his statement.

"Maybe I should have said something."

"It wouldn't have made a big difference. We would still be looking at a major fire." He quickly shot down my attempts for self-blame.

"Well, you have been a big help to us, Miss Naumburg. Thank you."

"Sure, if there's anything else, just let me know," I told him, feeling very special and more important than the others.

My mom called, and I felt special again being called out of class to hear her voice tremble over the phone. "Oh, sweetheart, I'm so glad you're okay," she went on and on. "I can't believe how lucky I am you got out of there alive." I wondered how much she knew. It didn't really matter. She was just glad I was alive and worried about me. All my aches and confusion basked in warmth until my dad called. King Kong. For his call, I was strangely summoned to the headmaster's office. I picked up the receiver of a phone on a small table across from his desk.

"Judy, I am not releasing any insurance money to you," I heard the familiar voice come through the wire. For a second I couldn't figure out what he was talking about. I guess he forgot the line about "How are you?"

"But Dad, all the girls are going shopping this afternoon," I said, jumping immediately into the argument.

"You will not go shopping with the other girls this afternoon," he snapped. I kept my sarcastic mouth shut. I knew I would eventually hear the rest of the story. I had been called to the headmaster's office for the second time in one day. This time I sat in a stuffed chair lined with carefully spaced brass tacks, running my fingers along the spiraled umbilical cord of the black receiver. Dr. Chappell sat behind his desk, across the room. "You and your mother had no right to go to Bloomingdale's and charge clothes to my account without asking," he went on when I didn't answer.

"What do you mean?" I asked, filling in the blanks and feeling my pulse rise.

"You know very well what I mean."

"No, I don't know what you mean."

"During your spring vacation you and your mother bought clothes and didn't pay for them. I have the bill right here on my desk from Bloomingdale's." I instantly remembered the beautiful new white dress and matching hat my mom had just bought me for graduation and felt a new sense of loss. I had forgotten all about the sleek white patent-leather flats I had bought even though they were too tight, because they were so beautiful and grown-up. Now they were ashen dust.

"I didn't know she didn't pay for them. I needed something to wear for graduation. I'm graduating valedictorian," I added carefully.

"You don't need a new dress to wear under a cap and gown. What about the dress we sent you? Why couldn't you wear that dress?" he asked, clinging to his point.

"I don't know," I answered, feeling the tears slide down my cheeks. I thought about the box of clothes he had sent me. The five outfits I had been wearing every day since then, along with the denim skirt with the checkered lining.

"Your mother is always doing these things. She is breaking the law, you know. I could have her arrested. I should have you both arrested. Neither one of you know when to stop. You are a real pain in the ass." I couldn't tell which was greater, his hatred for her or his anger at me. I realized no matter how long I stayed at Anderson, my relationship with my dad would never change.

*I'm already in jail*, I thought to myself. I said nothing. I was really tired. I pushed my knuckles hard into my closed eye until the pain distracted my need to lash back.

"Mr. Naumburg," interrupted the headmaster, picking up the extension on his desk. "As you know, your daughter has been through a terrible ordeal in the last twenty-four hours. We have had a major fire, and there are many things to work out. She has been invaluable to us. Her leadership qualities are very important right now. I need her to continue to help with the other girls, and I don't believe your problem will be objectively resolved at this time. You and I will speak further about arranging for Judy's clothing and necessities. If you don't mind, I'll have to ask you to hang up now," he said bluntly. I turned around toward his desk. I heard a click and sat motionless.

I placed the receiver down lightly and looked over to Dr. Chappell. I hardly knew this man. "Thank you," I said, wiping my face dry. I couldn't remember anyone standing up for me to my father. I couldn't ever remember *anyone* standing up for me.

"You can go back to your classroom now," he said, giving me a sideways hug, hip to hip. I walked slowly down the hallway, thinking about the conversation with my dad. He didn't ask if I was okay. He never said anything about the fire. He only cared about the money and hating my mother.

The girls went shopping and came back with new outfits, new panties, socks, shoes, curlers, hairbrushes, toothpaste, and other things I now remembered we had stuffed our drawers with. The school decided to put us up in a motel for a while, so mercifully we never returned to the icebox by the tracks. Mrs. Cartmell handed me a toothbrush, a new tube of Colgate, a hairbrush, and a towel. I wore the same blue-jean skirt, red and white checkered shirt, washed-out undies, and Vassar nightgown to bed for about a week until a box of clothes came in the mail from Santa Fe. Overnight mail hadn't been discovered yet. Everything in the box was a size thirteen, two sizes too big, but I took out the least ugly skirt, pinned the back with a safety pin so it wouldn't fall off, and threw the blue-jean skirt in the wash. As I took out each item, I could picture my stepmother, the same stepmother who could go to Paris and buy five Dior suits in five different colors, down at the Guarantee Shop on the plaza, grabbing outfits off the rack for her stepdaughter. In the box was a plain navy dress with a powder blue collar. She had scribbled "for your graduation" on a piece of paper pinned to the lapel. I wondered if I would have to wear my blue-jean Keds, but it didn't matter—they would be hidden under the gown.

Many days later, after the ashes cooled, the girls who had lived in Morgan Hall were given permission, four or five at a time, to return and sift through the rubble. I secretly held a hope that the pearl ring my mother had bought me would be hidden under a pillow or appear sparkling through the piles of soot. At my first glimpse of the dorm, resting amid the wreckage, I realized how foolish such a hope had been. The walls around Betsy's and my third-floor rooms had totally collapsed into a black pile of timbers and ashes. Glass and mirrors were shattered, almost everything indistinguishable. Only the bottom stairwell, two chimneys, and the northwest side of Morgan Hall were standing, though charred and ruined.

I poked through three floors' worth of wet ashes, until I grew tired and my lungs burned. I laughed at my earlier hope of finding the ring, or anything. I turned and saw Paddy bent over a heap of charred belongings and walked over to her. I saw a single tear had cleared a path down her gray cheek, and for the first time in three years I actually felt a twinge of compassion. So much time had passed, so much fun had been made, and I had never stopped to see her as a human being. I stroked my hand softly down her back and walked on.

Danielle, whose father was some big Hollywood producer, they said, had lived in a second-floor room on the opposite end of the dorm from mine. She seemed to have what looked like a garage sale at her disposal.

"Gosh, you didn't lose much at all," I said with a predominantly jealous tone. All her clothes, and she always looked wonderful, were just as she had left them. "You're lucky."

"Yeah," she said absently, paying absolutely no attention to the piles of cashmere sweaters or her matching lambswool skirts. I picked up a fur-lined winter parka. "This still looks great!" I said, shaking off a few ashes.

"It stinks. Everything smells like shit. Help me look for my Kleenex box," she insisted. I quickly looked around at the others in the distance sifting through the ruins. The place looked like Hiroshima.

"The what?"

"I have a blue tissue box I have to find. Just a regular Kleenex tissue box," she said, stretching out every word. I started absently pushing things around, wondering why the hell she wanted a tissue box. "You are really lucky having so many nice things," I told her, as I helped with her search. "Your parents must really care about you."

"My stepmother's a bitch. She hates my guts, and my father buys all these things so I don't look like a slob and embarrass him. He figures it's easier than being a father." Her search never let up, and I watched as she grew almost fanatic, tossing perfectly good clothes into heaps.

"What about your mother?" I asked.

"She's a drunk," she volunteered curtly. Things were never the way they appeared.

"Is this it?" I asked, turning around, holding out a heavy blue tissue box in my right hand. Her beautifully lined eyes widened. "It's pretty wet," I told her, lifting the box up and down, forcing streams of water into the air. Danielle had a bewitching smile.

She quickly stumbled up next to me and took the box carefully in her two hands. "It's okay, they'll dry out."

"What'll dry out?" She knew I was a part of the game now, and there was no escaping. She actually didn't even care much. She just seemed so happy to have the box. I watched as she sat down and gingerly peeled off layers of tissue, dropping them absently to the ground, one, then another, and another. She uncovered little hand-rolled cigarettes arranged neatly in rows. "All that for cigarettes?" I couldn't believe it.

"They're marijuana joints. I rolled them myself."

"Oh," I said, trying to stifle the magnitude of my surprise. I glared at the tiny mummies lying in the sun until she wrapped them up again in dry pieces of paper.

"Aren't you worried about getting caught?" I asked, realizing too late how dumb the question sounded.

"The worst that could happen would be they'd send me where I can get it a lot easier. Home." Good point. Danielle started going through another box of jewelry and makeup with less enthusiasm.

"I've thought going home would be a lot better than being here, but I never knew if that was where I would actually end up. My dad didn't seem to imply home was my next stop," I told her, reflecting back on my early decisions.

"My dad's not that smart," she said, reducing her famous Hollywood father to the size of a tiny mouse scampering through the woods.

# CHAPTER 25

### Passing in the Night

The Owl and the Pussy-Cat went to sea
In a beautiful pea-green boat:
They took some honey, and plenty of money
Wrapped in a five-pound note

**Edward Lear**

A churning sensation seeped into my sleep, and, as I became more aware of the night, my grip on sleep faded. I squinted through the darkness and seized the room faster than my brain could assimilate the details. I had forgotten where I was. Yes. Anderson School. The dorm had burned down and, after sleeping in a boys' camp and then a motel, I now lived in Delinwood Mansion, the smaller of the two white mansions on the hill overlooking the main campus. I remembered feeling mildly annoyed at once again having a roommate, Patricia. Patricia, with the beautiful face, silky jet-black hair, and beautiful green eyes, reminded me of the hills of Ireland my father had described about his annual fox hunting with the Craigies. Patricia had high cheekbones and perfect lips. Her beauty ended at her neck, however, as the curves of her body immediately headed off into opposite directions and remained on opposing courses until about knee level, when the lines smashed back together, banging into each other like two Stooges, resulting in the worst case of knock-knees I had ever witnessed in my life. I wondered if my knees would have ended up in such turmoil if my mother hadn't sentenced me to years of ugly corrective Buster Brown shoes.

A tiny ray of light came in from the window, and I lay facing Patricia's silhouette on the single bed next to mine. *She must be dreaming*, I thought, as I watched the motion of her bed. A nightmare perhaps. Then something urged me to peer deeper, and I watched her more carefully. She and her bed were thrusting, back and forth, back and forth. A slow sense of disgust seeped into my body when I heard the sounds that grew into slurping and moaning. Patricia was not dreaming. She was not on a boat in the ocean. She was masturbating. Right here, in my room, less than four feet from my bed she was going at it loud and clear. As the pulsing and probing and sucking of her fingers grew louder, I strained to absorb exactly what she was doing, but I became so disgusted that my brain rebelled at the concentrated effort. Christ, how could I shut her off? What could I do to escape? I wanted her to stop. My foot itched, hair irritated my eyes, and there was no end in sight. I wanted to turn over. I plotted pretending to be asleep as I rolled over, but I couldn't move.

Then I heard a final series of disconnected groans swelling into a satisfactory crescendo. Night, once again, claimed supremacy over the heavy breathing. I wondered how I could ever look into her face. Humiliation burned me throughout. Why did I have to live with this? I wanted out of this stupid school, and, somehow, graduating didn't matter as much anymore. What was this weird and twisted life I belonged to? I lay awake most of the night wondering if I would ever get out of Anderson School or if Anderson School would ever get out of me.

The room reminded me of my grandmother's guest room at Blue Herons. The smell of pressed linens, everything about the decor was perfect: perfect paintings, lamps, and end tables. Unsoiled wall-to-wall carpeting. A rich and perfect life—except I didn't feel at home here. I belonged nowhere. I could sleep nowhere.

The next night, sometime between bedtime and morning, I woke again and couldn't go back to sleep, in spite of the lack of sleep the night before. I tossed around, fearful of the return of last night's escapade. Maybe Patricia had surmised from my moodiness that I didn't want to be a part of her self-gratification anymore. I pulled a pair of pants up under my nightgown and tiptoed out into the night. The moon beamed from a distant place in the sky, far from the earth's complexity.

I walked up the hill toward Manswood Mansion, recalling that first October day, almost three years ago, when I arrived for my interview, thinking how wonderful life would be living amongst the mansions on the hill. The moonlight dusted the hills rolling off into the distance. I imagined walking up through the clouds until the arms of safety encircled me and I would no longer be afraid.

I walked barefoot through the wet grass, just as I had as a child. My feet felt damp and cold. I approached the mansion and thought about what Ellyn told me had been going on since we had moved on campus.

"Mike and I meet almost every weekend," Ellyn had told me.

"No! You're nuts. Where do you go?" I had quizzed her.

"In the shed behind Manswood. There's a utility shed right there, just in the trees." She spoke about sneaking out at night as if it were no big deal. "Lots of the girls do. Ask Donna." So I did.

Donna didn't seem quite so thrilled about sharing her secret with me, a monitor, even though I had denounced my house-committee status and was not a squealer. Donna was a good friend, but I gathered the shed was getting a little crowded.

"There are too many couples now," she told me. "If you want to do anything serious, you have to go out into the woods." I gathered *serious* meant going all the way.

Unable to face more pulsing bodies in the shed and a possible court martial, I decided just to walk through Manswood instead. "*Just making the late-night rounds,*" I rehearsed silently in case the housemothers caught me, or "*I thought I heard a terrible noise, and I came up to see what it was,*" I would lie. If I crafted the story just right, Paddy would begin creeping around with me, looking for the imaginary disturbance. I would never tell her the truth: I couldn't sleep because my roommate masturbates and I want to see my friends sneaking out at night. I wondered what time it was. If it were four o'clock in the morning, she'd be too tired to care. I didn't care; I probably wouldn't get in trouble, anyway. Was I beyond expulsion?

I walked upstairs through the long hallway. Moonbeams raced in from the open bedroom doors. Ten demerits if you didn't sleep with the door open. My vision, acclimated to the night's light, didn't need a switch or a candle. The hallway looked regal, with the long Oriental runner and the dark polished wainscot. Living in these mansions somehow lost the flare, however, knowing what I knew.

I reached the first room and looked in. There were two empty beds on either side of the window. Empty? No, it couldn't be. I wrinkled my nose and squinted hard at the disheveled sheets on the twin beds. They were definitely empty.

I continued down the hall and repeated similar gyrations in each room and surmised, by the end of my journey, that almost half the girls were plum gone, out of bed, out of sight, balancing on some tightrope in the night. How could all this be going on? Should I turn on all the lights and start screaming, "*Where is everybody? What's going on here?*" Paddy would wake up, waddle down the hall brushing back her silver hair, and I would win the Congressional Medal of Honor for my discovery. Jesus. Something different had to happen in my life, now, before it all became too predictable.

I felt a quick urge to go traipsing through the woods, looking for the infamous shed, pouncing in on pulsing bodies. *"Hey, what's going on here? How dare you all get away with this without me?"* I would say. My mind swarmed with negative results. There had to be a better, more logical conclusion to these nights. I headed back to my room in a semi-numb state. Maybe all these kids felt there was safety in numbers. They wouldn't expel half the school, would they? The kids had figured out the new scheme of living on campus faster than the adults had. The teachers were probably still trying to figure out why the dorm burned down, how to make up for lost time, planning the upcoming graduation, and planning where the girls would live next year. Important logistics were clogging their minds, while couples were grinding in the grass. I wondered if they were going all the way. I wondered how I had missed out.

The next day I began planning with David. "Did you know all these kids sneak out at night?" I asked, as we walked to our first class. David was a South Hall monitor.

"Yeah, I had a pretty good idea," he told me with a serious look. I had a momentary flash on why we hadn't discussed this, but I went on.

"So, what do you think?" I asked. David's long suit wasn't creative ideas or picking up innuendos. He was funny, sweet, and star of the basketball team in spite of his size, but insightful wasn't one of his strongest qualities. He was kind of normal, I guess. I hoped the normal would rub off. I wanted to talk him into sneaking out.

"What do I think about what?" he asked.

"About everybody sneaking out?" I asked. His blue eyes darted in and out of mine. "Why don't we?"

"Oh, now wait a minute. Judy, you are going to graduate in less than two months. Why do you want to risk getting thrown out?"

"You asked me in New Hope to tell you if I was ready to go all the way, and now I'm ready." I watched his face grow older. "After this summer, we may never see each other again."

"Don't say that, Judy. I want to be with you always, you know that. I just want you when the time is right." When the bell shattered our thought pattern, we both knew we were late for our next class, and we both knew the discussion would continue in bits and pieces through the day. I couldn't decide why I was ready to go all the way with David—maybe because I thought everyone else did. I'd been with David for almost two years. He was my friend. He was safe, and he was now. It was possible I would never find someone to love me in the real world. I was almost sixteen, a senior in high school; next year I was going to an all-girls' finishing school in Switzerland. I didn't even need a diploma. Wanting David now seemed more important than graduating, more important than some future you couldn't see or touch or feel inside. Consequences didn't register in my immature brain; only my personal rationale had meaning

When I saw David during canteen, I knew he had spent most of the morning thinking about my proposition. I also knew he wouldn't want to risk his position at school just to sneak out at night with me, even if it meant going all the way.

"Okay," he said when we sequestered ourselves as far away from the others as possible. Some of the kids were reading their mail, and others were standing in line buying candy bars. David snapped a Marlboro from the red and white pack, flipping the filtered end into his mouth.

"Okay, what?" I asked, feeling my pulse quicken and a smile surface.

"If you want." He brought the match to his lips and I watched as his cheeks sunk in further. "Let's try meeting and see how it feels. We don't have to do anything right away, but we'll figure out where we want to be," he explained. "I don't think we want to go with everyone else in the shed."

"Aren't you worried about getting caught?" I asked.

He slowly blew a steady stream of smoke through his nose and teeth simultaneously. "Of course. I think we have to be careful, but from what I hear the risk level is pretty low. Bill's been going out for a while and never sees anybody."

"If you knew all this was going on, how come you never asked me to meet you before?" I envisioned Bill and Danielle smoking pot and making love in the moonlight.

This was one of those moments when Pete would have brazenly held my hand or slipped his hand under my shirt and caressed my skin, but David hated to break rules. David didn't live dangerously like Pete, the master of the edge. Right now David showed me in his eyes that he wanted me every bit as much as Pete. "Judy, I would never want to get you in trouble. You're graduating with honors. You tell me how much you want to get out of here. I don't want to ruin that for you. Besides, I know we'll be together in the future. There's lots of time for us." I wasn't so sure.

"So why do you want to meet me now?" I asked.

"Because you want to," he paused, then added, "and because I want to be with you, and I don't care if I get caught. Nah, we won't get caught." I thought of Patricia writhing and groaning and wondered if I could ever blot the image from my mind. Making love with David would be different. I knew how soft and safe it felt to crawl in his arms, to feel his lips, to touch his body.

The bell rang again, and we both knew we had five minutes till our afternoon class. "Look," he began, without backing down, "I'll figure out where we want to meet and if you change your mind, that's okay. I mean it."

"What about a, you know, a rubber?" I was surprised how calculated I sounded and wished I could take it back.

"Don't worry about that. There are plenty of those around," he smiled. "Plenty." I wondered why there were plenty around, and how many were being used, and who bought them. Maybe the boys carried them around in their wallets for status. I didn't have time to ask. "We don't have to do anything, and we don't have to do something now," he finished.

"Tonight," I told him, "if it doesn't rain." I glanced up at the clouds and laughed.

"I'll see you down at the softball field," he said, as I headed into Citizen Education class. During class I imagined making love, trying to keep thoughts about being expelled in the background, but somehow I couldn't. I knew how angry my dad would be and how downtrodden my mom would be. They'd probably send me to reform school, but before my final sentencing, I would have experienced love in the truest form.

Mr. Fusels stood in front of the class with an armload of final reports. He went around the room dropping them one at a time on the wooden desks. "Delinquency of Young Girls" I had written on the front cover. I leafed through the pages, looking for red marks or corrections. There were none. As in all my work, I mainly wanted to see the grade, so I skipped to the back page. Mr. Fusels had scribbled in red ink, "Interesting—well put together," then circled a 95.

I was going to graduate valedictorian, with the best grades in my class, if I graduated. Somehow, nothing mattered. A high-school diploma wouldn't guarantee college. No one had ever heard of Anderson School probably, or if they had, the conclusion would be worse. I could hear the college admissions board members whisper, "The school is a special school, you know. We can't really ..."

The chapter I had written in my report on sexual behavior caught my attention: "We have seen that sexual behavior of the young female is the largest factor entering into their delinquent patterns of behavior."

Then I quoted from the *Encyclopedia of Social Sciences*:

Sexuality denotes the complex of drives, attitudes, habits, and actions of an organism organized around coition. No animal's sexual behavior is ever guided by any form of degree of incest, taboo, or by normal beliefs.... Human nature naturally is selective in choosing mates so frustration upon this results in looser morals.

... Such is the sexuality of man and woman. A little girl feels unloved, pushed around, frightened, grows up searching for love the only way she knows--promiscuity leading to prostitution and problems. Helen Parkhurst, author of *Growing Pains* talks with some wayward girls who innocently admitted, "When you are lonely, you do just about anything."

# CHAPTER 26

## The Night Out

Here comes the bride,
All dressed in white,
Stepped on a turtle,
Down fell her girdle.

I slid out from under the covers. Nocturnal navigation was now second nature. I was an owl unruffled in night. David and I had agreed to meet in the field across the road from Delinwood Mansion, my new and not-so-novel home. As I moved toward our rendezvous, images about making love darted in and out of my mind: the hot desperation of Natalie Wood as she lay prone in *Splendor in the Grass*; the scintillating love of Troy Donahue and Sandra Dee as they gazed into each other's eyes on screen. Could we reel breathlessly like them? Could we grow lost inside a full-bodied lust? I realistically suspected perhaps this would be a bit more like a scientific experiment, a biological treatise to be used for future reference. Nonetheless, my yearnings would be consummated. We would join the ranks and move on, fully accepted by our peers.

I settled underneath a tree and leaned against the bark. Crickets chatted away, while a soft breeze played with infant leaves. Ultimately, I was alone. The feeling of freedom brought a smile to my lips. Mutiny. Exhilaration. Fear extracted from oppression. I thought of the farm, the smell of dirt and cow manure and moist grass, the feeling of Primrose between my thighs, the pillow on my twin bed. At Anderson, there was little room for past memories. Everything was now. Everything was survival in the moment. Time had little meaning, either forward or back. Perceptions were constantly challenged, constantly flipped upside down into new forms with new meanings, mostly in directions I could never foresee. You didn't dare count or dream, because the rug could be pulled out in a second; the future had no definition, not even a feigned outline for me. So if I got thrown out, I wouldn't ever know where I could have gone. "If you don't know where you are going," wrote Lewis Carroll, "any road will take you there." I would tell them something, make up an excuse. What would it be now? What could I possibly be doing here, at this time of night, under this tree, that was within the rules? Everything about me was cocked, loaded, and illegal.

I waited in the night's stillness until my energy slowly faded. Nothing more than the breeze came my way. A chill had long ago moved into me, with less than titillating sensations. I waited for about half an hour, then snuck back to the dorm and climbed into bed.

The next day, "Don't give me any shit," said David, strutting toward me, both palms in the air. An explosive smile covered his face, and his feet moved in a jiving motion, Cassius Clay on the defense, with a touch of Captain Kangaroo. He looked so funny I couldn't help but laugh.

"Thanks a lot!" I said, pushing my palms against his collapsed chest. He darted back, and then took a stance with his fists bobbing in front of his face. "You don't know what it's like hanging around in the night—it's cold!" I whispered.

He approached me slowly and lowered his arms. "Brown caught me just as I was heading out the door. I told him I was going out for a smoke, and he believed me because I had a cigarette in my mouth." David was respected by most of the staff. The con story was plausible.

"You're such a genius," I said, going after him again.

"No, really, honest. Cross my heart and hope to die," he said in a mocking voice, crossing his nonexistent chest. "So then, he decided to come outside and have a smoke with me. We talked about some babe back home he's got the hots for. She doesn't want to live at Anderson, can you believe that?"

I wondered where the conversation would go. He knew I still thought he had chickened out.

"We'll try again in a few days, when things settle down. It ain't my fault, really," he stressed, "but I guess I'll have to be smarter next time."

"Yeah, no shit, Sherlock." I gave him a smile.

On Thursday, a letter from my long-gone friend came inside my mother's weekly letter. The fear of leaving Anderson began choking me. At a time when things were supposed to become clearer, absolutes were becoming clouded with the unknown. Gerry's letter helped me see more clearly just how confusing and ridiculous life was, inside and out:

dear judy,

boy am i depressed ... i am so depressed that if you look in my navel you can see daylight. first off the theater up in maine is not I repeat ... the door to the stage was slammed and they didn't give me a chance to take my foot out.

and do you remember jane? you do? well how about that! now heres why i asked. ever since i came home my mother, being the **!+//?#% that she is, has been harping on the fact that it was i that wanted to come home and not them that wanted to have me. now lets (you and i) look at why this whole mess is happening.

1.) i was thrown out of school.

a) for calling mr. greene, mr. horne, mr. fuessle, mr. whitcome every name in the book.

b) why?

1. because they all said that over vacation I had sex with jane.

2. they had it coming to them for a long time.

3. i can't stand any of them. i was thrown out while defending jane ... right. so if i never met jane then this wouldn't have happened, right?)

2.) jane was thrown out of school for telling the committee off.

a) why? they told her i was:

a homosexual

cheap

I used all my friends

stupid

and out of my mind

(so jane would have been better off if she had never met me)

3.) jane was thrown out of the house.

4.) she called me for help.

5.) i gave her help

a) money

b) love

c) sex

d) me

e) the shirt off my back (which happened to be a brooks brothers pinstripe that I wish she would send me back)

6.) she up and left me.

a)$10.00 ticket to boston

b)$25.00 spending money so she wouldn't starve

7.) i got lonely

a) no money

b) no love

c) no sex

d) no brooks brothers shirt

total assets lost:$248.00 spending (just on her)

$35.00 to get to boston

$23.00 for phone calls to try and find her

$18.00 to get to newport folk festival to meet her, she wasn't there. $13.00 to get to boston, where she told me she hated me and always had.

.05 for a stamp to send her a nasty letter.

total          $337.05

now here's my problem. i still very much love her. we were going to get married. i wanted her to have my children. to be with me when i licked the world. i have every reason to hate her. but i can't.

judy ... help me. much love,

Gerry

Life wasn't going to be easier when I got out. I was fooling myself. I had lived so long at Anderson and had become such an integral part of everyone's life that I would have no idea how to leave. At Anderson they taught us how to exist amid their rules. They couldn't teach you how to survive in the real world because they didn't live there either. They offered no courses in mastering life. Or did they?

I found another poem on my bed, which I knew right away to be from Betsy. She wasn't allowed in my room—or anyone's—but she managed to move through life like a bobcat, without being seen, choosing the moment. I picked up the scribbled poem and wondered what would become of Betsy after I graduated. I had no way of knowing she would be thrown out of school just months after I graduated, then would spend most of her life in a mental institution.

Why

Oh why is the sky so dark today?
And why is the sun so sad?

And how come at night the stars are not out?
And the moon is hidden away.
Oh how come the flowers are not happy today
And why are the trees so sad.
Why aren't the birds singing loud like they did
And why is my heart not gay.
Is it because it's the end of May,
And the flowers are faded and gone
And the birds will no longer sing their song
And the sun will never be gay

The second time I snuck out at night, I focused more on my sweating palms and racing heart. I knew the inevitability of our meeting. Tonight would yield my rite of passage. Under the cloudless sky, in the vastness of space, my growing up would be complete. As I walked toward the meeting place once again, I saw David walking confidently across the empty field, hands tucked inside his hip pockets. I watched the moonlight radiating off his slicked-back hair, as he moved with the same goofy stride I knew so well. When we reached each other, he looked around quickly, then gave me a stiff hug. My heartbeat dominated my thinking. "I see you made it this time," I said with a managed smile.

"Piece of cake. Where shall we go?"

"I guess we should go in the woods somewhere," I told him, trying to grapple with the image of where I wanted to lose my virginity.

"You're okay with this, right?"

"Why do you keep asking me?" I couldn't decide if I wanted to talk more, talk less, or what I wanted.

"Just wanted to make sure. Well?"

"Yeah, I think so," I answered.

"Then let's go," he said.

A sudden pain ripped through my heart. I quickly glanced at David. Together we saw the car lights coming through the woods in the distance. In equal time we registered the situation: we were next to the road, no trees, no shack, nothing to hide behind, under a bright, moonlit sky. We had approximately twelve seconds before we would be expelled from Anderson School. There would be no graduation, no valedictorian. No cap and gown. I saw myself with a one-way ticket in hand and heard Dr. Chappell reprimanding me, "We gave you such support," and my dad, boiling inside: "After all I've done for you, this is how you repay me." Maybe I did care, after all. But now it was too late.

"Quick, lie flat and still," David ordered, tugging my arm to the ground. *This truly is bizarre*, I thought to myself. How can we possibly hide from car lights about to pass five feet from us? I went flat as a quarter, though feeling quite a bit less worthy, and prayed to some god, any god listening, for a miracle along the magnitude of a second coming. I couldn't believe I had been stupid enough to end up back where I started, crazy enough to do anything where I had to face my father, and dumb enough to be caught. I felt David's body, lean and hard against mine. I held my breath and then blew it all out trying to make myself thinner.

When the lights came closer, I realized the road had dropped off a little and we were actually lying in a small ditch. Dirt from the road irritated my eyes while the night's dew dribbled down my cheek. I wasn't sure if there was any air at all making it into my lungs.

As methodically as it came, the car passed us by and headed toward the main campus. We were below the headlights, and the bend of the road had forced the beams away from us as the car approached on the curve. The night grew still. I listened as the sound of the car faded. I had a macabre vision of jumping up into the air and yelling, "Hey, you missed us! After all this, you missed us! Send me to an insane asylum or juvenile detention, but don't make me go out into the real world!"

"Jesus Christ," whispered David.

"Yeah, I know."

"I think maybe I better find a better line of work," he added after a splash of silence.

"That," I stressed, "was a miracle."

"No shit, Sherlock."

# CHAPTER 27

**Dropped in Heart's Deep Well**

The hand that made you fair hath made you good.

**Shakespeare,** *Measure for Measure*
**Quote under my senior yearbook picture**

Since Morgan Hall no longer existed, the forum committee (which included myself, three other senior girls, and Mrs. Cartmell) renamed the Morgan Hall Forum the Lewis Gage Forum. Lewis Gage no longer existed either, so I didn't quite understand the reasoning. Once again I won Best Body and Most Popular when the ballots were counted. Then, as a farewell token, my peers voted me Most Successful. Really, there was no getting around the fact: I had medals for volleyball, bowling, swimming, choir, and tennis (all competitions within the school, because the girls had no sports teams at all). I had been elected May Queen and president, editor, and friend. I wore a bright orange A with three black stripes on my sweater for cheerleading. I had alpha beta keys and cum laude keys and citizenship keys and activities keys. I served on the bus committee, food committee, late committee, and entertainment committee. Now I was valedictorian. I had more keys (that couldn't open a single door) than Carter had little liver pills. Betsy won awards for the Biggest Flop and the Noisiest.

I wondered what I would do with all these awards and the knowledge from my past sixteen years. In public school, I had learned about Groundhog Day, Abraham Lincoln, and how to pledge allegiance to the flag. At Buckingham Friends School I joined Quaker meetings, read *The Good Earth*, and learned firsthand about kidnapping. I knew how to ride in a foxhunt, drive a tractor, bale hay, milk cows, and chop heads off chickens, but the farm was gone. I was a good swimmer, though I had almost drowned, and I played great coed volleyball. I could hand in homework, but wasn't very good at sneaking out at night, and I was still a thumb-sucking virgin. I still had no idea if I was a success or a failure. Would I be Episcopalian or Jew, crazy or sane? I had gone in so many directions in my life, I wasn't sure in which direction I would be heading. And how could I judge myself in relation to the world, when I was graduating from a school whose basketball team lost games by scores of thirty-nine to one hundred and nine? If I took my Most Successful certificate with me, would I get a job at a bank? Or perhaps I could take my Best Body award to *Playboy* and apply there. Previous experience: lots of making out. In spite of my wealthy grandparents, ambassadors, and cabinet secretaries in the background, somehow I didn't think riding in limousines was in my future. Well, I didn't have to make any career decisions until they finished me off at finishing school. After I was "finished" being molded and scolded, fluffed and buffed, I could decide about the rest of my life. So, on with the show.

On graduation day I knew I would give the valedictorian speech and participate in the ceremony. I also knew I would walk up to the stage when my name was called, shake the headmaster's hand, and receive a blank piece of rolled-up paper, while everyone else would have a signed diploma. The entire senior class (except me) would lift their tassels from right to left during the final procession, as they had rehearsed fourteen times. I wouldn't technically graduate. Only my father would notice. I needed to complete three more classes during the summer before I would earn a signed diploma, but now all I cared about was leaving in the fall. There was no way I was throwing this brass ring back into the bin.

The day was a perfect, warm, June New York one. The sky mirrored the blue of a young girl's eyes, not yet discolored by toxic French fries, whipped cream, mistrust, or anger. I wore the navy blue dress with the powder blue collar, safety-pinned in the back, and a pair of borrowed white pumps. I didn't mind. After the ceremony, I knew I would take off the gown and become aware again that the sweet white Bloomingdale dress fitting for a Valedictorian had burned. The continual dichotomy of my dad's position on wealth would hang most apparent there on my body, today and ongoing for the rest of my life. Today I would hold my head above the fray, believing in the transparency of the day, taking away only what I needed. Kids all across the nation were moving on today, poised for success after years of careful grooming. I knew my best hope for the future was simply to survive.

I had rehearsed my speech a hundred times: in front of Betsy, in front of the mirror, and in front of the headmaster. I rewrote the words almost as many times, never reaching a point of satisfaction. I wondered if I would be rendered speechless from fear and need an understudy at the last minute.

I knew my parents would both be there, and I was not surprised to see them sitting at opposite sides of the room, well padded with unfamiliar bodies. My brothers were both there, basically oblivious to what I had been through the past three years. Separately we were struggling in our own little worlds, far apart from each other and the Pennsylvania farm. The auditorium hummed with seemingly meaningless energy. I had spent time in this gym for over what seemed a lifetime: dances, basketball games, sermons, assemblies, plays, volleyball, and two graduations. This would be my third and last. I wondered who I should spend more time with during the picnic after the ceremony, my mom or my dad. I knew I would stay very close to David either way. (We had secret plans to put an end to my relentless virginity in New York City.)

As I began my speech, I felt the stage shimmy interminably. Whatever foundation I had depended upon was thoughtlessly eroding. When I opened my mouth, my throat rattled like the train from Poughkeepsie to Grand Central. "Yakety Yak … Don't Look Back." It was all I could do to keep my body from going into a spastic fit, but I knew I was done battling crazy. I wouldn't let the impulse to run away ever again overtake me. Not again. I would do nothing that would bring me down. I inhaled deeply the sanity of life. I tried diligently to keep my focus on the words I had written down:

When we were children, getting an education meant going to school every day and learning all the facts that were placed before us. Soon we began to see how one fact led to another, forming a somewhat balanced picture. Today, however, we begin to see that education is not just the accumulation of facts, but also the gaining of a perspective, the understanding of human and factual relations.

If we were each to turn back the clock a few minutes, we could clearly see how education has brought us closer to maturity in every way. We are not so quick to resist a helping hand, nor do we fail to extend one. Despite our previous rebellion we see now that our teachers, guidance counselors, and parents were actually trying to mold our points of view the way they felt would be most beneficial to us. We begin to realize that truly educated people can speak together comfortably, even though there are differences of opinion, social standing, or personalities.

Of course, I cannot expect the underclassmen to fully share my points of view. You are not faced with the same abrupt realizations today as we are. You are not yet faced with a sense of guilt that you perhaps did not accomplish as much as you would have liked to in your high-school years. You are not sad because you are leaving wonderful friends or perhaps earned too many enemies. You have time to finish; we must be going on.

A long time ago, my father gave me a poem that his grandfather had given him, which somehow says everything I've tried to say here today, and I'd like to leave you with the same lasting impression.

Speak gently; 'tis better far to rule by love than fear.
Speak gently; let no harsh word mar the good we might do here.
Teach it in accents soft and mild; from evil do refrain.
Speak gently to the little child; its love be sure to gain.

Speak gently to the young, for they will have enough to bear;
Pass through this life as best they may; 'tis full of anxious care.
Speak gently to the aged one; grieve not the care-worn heart;
The sands of life are nearly run; let such in peace depart.
Speak gently, kindly to the poor; let no harsh tone be heard;
They have enough they must endure, without an unkind word.
Speak gently; 'tis a little thing dropped in the heart's deep well;
The good, the joy which it may bring, eternity shall tell.

The poem, written by David Bates (1809-1870), was not quoted perfectly in the version my father gave me.

I had no premonition that I would receive a standing ovation when I finished my speech, or that it would be the first

263

and last time my little brother remembered seeing my father cry. I didn't know about life without the people of Anderson, without all the rules and reins—whether I would survive or if my friends would survive. In spite of my speech, I didn't know how to live in the real world. I was someone's robot now. Inside was a young girl still uncertain of all the trains she missed, resentful of the paths chosen for her, defeated by a thousand mixed messages. Though elated with the prospect of walking away from Anderson School, I knew they were letting me out without the proper tools.

For now, though, my time was up. I knew that in a few months I would have a real, live world to learn again. Perhaps I would survive.

# EPILOGUE

## Not Quite a Reunion

No we're never gonna survive, unless,
We are a little crazy.

**Seal**

There wasn't a cloud in the Westchester sky, in spite of afternoon thundershower warnings. I hoped the weatherman's prediction of heavy afternoon showers was wrong, as I climbed into my aunt Ellin's tan Mercedes SL. The elegant old car reminded me of the one my grandmother, Ruth M. Knight, had in the same garage at Blue Herons thirty years ago: polished mahogany paneling, soft leather seats, spotless floor mats and windows. My aunt insisted I drive the little sports car, because she rarely drove it, and she wanted me to take it for a spin. I gladly agreed.

"I could get Bo to take the top off, if you want," she offered, in the sometimes-meddlesome way in which she sought control, much like my father and grandmother had, and which I prefer now to interpret as awkward love.

"No," I answered, slightly annoyed for no immediate reason. "It's too cold, and, besides, it's supposed to rain. I don't want to be all the way up in Poughkeepsie without a top if it starts to rain." It was the last day of April 1992.

For lots of people, digging up old high-school memories is a pretty exciting endeavor. I felt no excitement. I had no reason to believe that the school still existed, so my reasons for traveling sixty miles north on a day when I could be playing tennis, canoeing, or walking in the garden with my aunt were purely for personal reflection. I was writing a book.

My book was about me, even more ridiculous, because, who was *me*? Not Katherine Hepburn or Armand Hammer, not Carl Sandberg, Deborah Norville, or even Charlie Manson. Never famous, never known, *me*.

So, why was I writing a book? Well, I felt that somewhere in my burdened heart there was something to say about children of divorce, adolescent loneliness, and this crazy school I had gone to. Too crazy to be true, really, but maybe if I went back to Staatsburg-on-Hudson and walked through the old grounds, memories and feelings would resurface and substantiate what I had been trying to write about for the past few years: this book about me, this book about my school.

I pulled the car out onto Highway 684 and had miles to think before my next turn. I tried to envision what could possibly be there in place of the school. The grounds had covered probably over a hundred acres, with two magnificent hilltop mansions and beautiful ivy-covered-brick school buildings; dormitories; a swimming pool; tennis courts; a lake; and a cafeteria with a huge rock fireplace, used for cooking long before the Vietnamese chefs I remembered had been hired. Hundreds of trees over forty feet tall created a dense haven for chipmunk and squirrel and raven. Probably condominiums now, I mused. The best scenario would be a new school, where all the buildings were still intact, and I could walk through the halls of the past. I doubted whether anyone would be rich enough to turn the place back into another magnificent Hudson River estate.

I exited onto 9N and headed north to Poughkeepsie. Would I recognize anything? Yes, a striking old bridge, a few churches with steeples jutting high into the sky as if reaching for God's touch and substantiation. I tried to figure out which buildings were over twenty-five years old. Many had been built since 1965.

When I reached the town of Hyde Park, familiar buildings caught my eye at a more rapid rate: the library, the general store, and the corner buildings all looked just as I had known them. No MacDonald's or Jiffy Lubes, no shopping malls or Cinema Eights. Everything looked fixed in time, safe from the expansive grasp of growth. Historical Area a small sign designated, confirming my sense of hindsight. I drove past the Roosevelt Museum and the Vanderbilt Estate with its glorious tree-lined entrance. I recalled the view of the Hudson River from their front porch. I looked for the house across the road where the girls had lived after the fire. I couldn't recall the exact location, but I remembered tales of secret tunnels and clandestine Vanderbilt lovers.

I drove until I saw an old sign secured into a pillar made of stone. The small brass plaque rippled in the daylight as if someone had madly hammered at it in desperation, trying to rip the name from the stone. I slowed down, searching for another sign, a new sign of existence. There was none. The little rock wall had not changed.

I turned the little car around, stopped, and read the words *Anderson School*. My emotions mutated with long-ago memories, as I edged slowly between the stone pillars and drove down the softly wooded lane shaded from the sun by tall pine trees. Everything looked the same. I recalled very clearly the first day I drove down this lane in the fall of 1961: my first and only high-school interview.

I continued through the campus, searching for signs of new life, objectionable condominiums, golf courses—any hint of a new existence. Every bend I turned increased my fear and anticipation as if I were winding through for the first time. My mother and I had driven here in *her* Mercedes SL. I drove along the softball field and saw the two mansions still on the hill: Manswood and Delinwood.

I parked the car in what seemed to be the first detour from vivid memories, a parking lot where a flowerbed once had thrived. The temperature of my soul fell to a depth I had forgotten. I became disoriented and feared that maybe I could be trapped again. I gazed toward the main school building, freezing a present into a past, a memory into now.

I walked up the exact cement pathway I had walked every Monday through Friday thirty years ago, day after day, with an armful of books, chatting on and on with Donna or Candy or Sharon. I listened and heard nothing, just as before. A sordid quiet remained. As I spied a kid in a classroom, feet propped up on the seat in front of him, gazing out the window, an abysmal fear overwhelmed me. Must be a new school, I rationalized with myself. It can't still be here. I looked around for more changes to this crazy little school, but there weren't enough of them to soothe me.

I pulled open the metal front door that still looked and weighed the same. Once in the hall, I searched the gym on the left, the stairs up ahead, the bathrooms on the right where Pete and I had kissed, and the sunlight still piercing from above. Oh my God, everything was exactly the same. My blood grew clammy and cold as I stared at the timeworn bulletin board, covered with notes about recycling and this month's honor students, reading each name as if I were expecting to know one or see my own. I couldn't move. Was I in the past or was it the present? How could I enter this world on my own? I wanted to run. *Don't do this to yourself,* I cautioned. *You are grown up, married with two joyful children, and you are happy.* Slowly, I turned through the two doors I now knew would be the administration area, and a secretary greeted me immediately.

"Can I help you?" she queried.

"Uh, yes," I answered, sensing that much was the same here, yet not daring to believe the appearance of such a horror.

"I would have called, but, uh, I was told the school no longer existed. I was actually just driving around. Is this still the Anderson School?" I finally blurted out, heart thumping too hard to be silent.

"Yes," she answered, growing cautious, shifting her massive weight in the chair. She was no longer eager to offer enlightenment, and we exchanged several glances. I was waiting for my heart to settle down. She was waiting for guidance.

"I graduated here over twenty-five years ago." As if I were being swept back through a vacuum into a hose of indeterminate time, the following events unfolded as if I had never graduated and gone on to another life. The jolly secretary hoisted herself from behind a small, cluttered desk in the dim yellowish room. I guessed she weighed over three hundred pounds.

"I'm Margaret," she toasted, as her right hand jutted out toward me. "When were you here?" A big smile spread across her face, and her breath was short, I guessed, from standing up. She was totally thrilled I had come.

"Well, I graduated in 1965. I mean, I came in 1962, but I graduated in three years after skipping my junior year," I began the long detailed explanation I had no preconception I would ever have to do. Here I was, standing in this office, and, except for the rearranged walls and furniture, I felt as if I had never left. She listened attentively; then Margaret shuffled off to find yearbooks.

When she returned, a stern, puzzled-looking "principal" accompanied her and reluctantly extended a hand out for me to shake. The updated mini-Mrs. Longo uttered, "How do you do?"

*My God*, I thought to myself, *this can't be the same school*. As if reading my mind, Margaret handed me a pile of old yearbooks and said, "The school is probably a little different now. There are only about fifty students, and they've separated out autistic students, who live in North Hall and have classes

269

over in the old Staatsburg Elementary building." *Great*, I thought. *A real change.*

The principal left without saying another word, and then Margaret began asking me too many questions, excited about the possibly of me shedding historical light onto the present day. "What kind of school is this?" I finally interrupted, looking straight into her eyes. I wanted to catch her if she lied.

"Well," the word rolled cautiously but sounded well rehearsed: "the kids come here because they have emotional and social problems. We have kids that need special care, kids that can't make it in their own school or at home, for one reason or the other. Polly Anderson sold the school in 1976, and now we are state-subsidized, though Miss Polly is still on the board."

"Miss Peggy," I thought out loud, recalling the headmistress in 1962. Now the daughter-in-law is Miss Polly—how quaint.

"It would be great if you would talk to the senior graduating class," she suggested, unaffected by my reactions. "It would be great for the kids to see how well you turned out. Let me go ask if it's okay." I was stunned. There was even a graduating class. How did they know how I had turned out, just because I was brave enough or stupid enough or *insane* enough to come back? I wondered whether today would be a dream come true or an unchartered nightmare. My head began spinning with what I might say and the questions I still had unanswered myself. I took the yearbooks and began pointing out some of my pictures to the other women in the office who had gathered around. I had looked at these yearbooks so often I knew exactly where I was in each one. Christ, I *made* these yearbooks.

After the bell rang, I followed the principal into the library. The room was small and probably had two hundred books, at the most, stacked aimlessly. I introduced myself to a lovely young teacher with short, clay-colored hair. Five kids sat haphazardly on window ledges, tables, and chairs. I sat down cautiously to tell my story. The boy to my right had irregularly shaped hair, as if he'd cut it himself: long down his back but pulled off the left side of his head, where it had been shaved. Wisps of hair from the long side fell over his eyes. I had never seen a hairdo quite like it. He gazed at the floor, and only rarely during our discussions did he lift his eyes to look at those in the room. When he did, his eyes seemed to focus on nothing, as if he were staring through the room into some other space.

I didn't feel one minute older than the kids in the room. Another boy sat in an almost-reclining position but seemed interested mostly in what job I had—if I were normally employed. The girl sitting next to him reminded me of my friend Donna.

Today her name was Laurie. She looked at me through the dark eyes of a panther while slouching into a bookshelf. I watched as she chewed gum with an open mouth and turned a pack of menthol cigarettes over and over in her hands. Next to Laurie sat Diane. Diane had blond hair curled over her shoulders. Her features were soft and flowing as a mermaid's, and her light blue eyes looked at me fearlessly. "This place wasn't as bad when you were here," she taunted.

"Actually, in some ways, I think it seems better, much less strict." Several kids shifted positions, mumbling denials in their throats. I had them. "You see the boys more informally, you carry your own cigarettes, you have doors on your rooms with locks, no dress code—you even have coed dorms, and you can sit on tables." I pointed at one of them sitting on a table. "We didn't have any of that."

"I *hate* it here," Diane retorted, her sentiment penetrating the small room. All of a sudden I flashed back: looking at myself, listening to myself as if no time had passed, and I was back at Anderson School, and everything was the same. Could I believe she put as much feeling into the word *hate* as I had so many years ago? These kids were the same. The system wasn't a day older. I became so incredulous I could barely speak. "I don't really belong here," she went on. "They told me there would be a beautiful campus and horses to ride. All I've seen is one broken-down nag that nobody rides because it would fall apart if you got on the fuckin' thing." A few chuckles and a group discussion followed about the pathetic state and lure of "the horse." *I didn't belong here either,* I thought to myself. How could this day be so predictable and yet so distant from my farthest-reaching premonitions?

"We're locked up here. It's like being in prison; they never let you out," said Laurie, smacking her gum.

"You're free to go anytime," interjected the teacher quickly, with a smile. "There are no chains on you." I remembered thinking I had been locked up too, but actually we, too, could have run away, gone away anytime. Why is there such a sense of being locked up? These kids were not here by choice.

"Why are kids sent here?" I asked, turning toward the teacher for an answer.

"For many of them, it's their last chance. They couldn't make it in their own school, often because of their home situation, but every kid is different." God, if only we could control our home situation, no one would ever come here. Did I just figure this out? "Some kids we help; some we don't even scratch the surface," added the teacher. I looked at the boy staring at the floor. She continued as if reading a manual, "Some kids are depressed, hyperactive, bipolar, or ADHD, the usual. Some have Tourette's, OCDs, or other anxiety disorders. Most are on psychotropic and antipsychotic meds, Thorazine, Lithium, all kinds of antidepressants, though they don't like to admit it."

"Kids try to kill themselves a lot. Did they when you were here?" asked a girl named Bridget. Her skin absorbed the neon light overhead.

"Yeah," I told her, then recounted an event that had happened my first summer.

"They never really die; they just want attention—slit their wrists or swallow too many pills or something," finished Laurie.

"Do girls ever get pregnant?" I asked, thinking about the coed dorms. Countless "Oh yeahs," and "Sures" answered me in unison.

"When they do, we just send them home, and their parents usually take care of it, you know, and sometimes they come back," the teacher explained. I guessed they weren't given demerits anymore for holding hands, dancing too close, passing notes, or kissing.

After a discussion on sex, the kids wanted to know about getting out. What was "out" like? They each had a sense of being crazy and not being able to make it in the real world—a simple fear of graduating, which I could recall as if it were again happening to me. I wanted to stay in this room for hours and hours. I had more questions than they did, and maybe I could help.

"The town thinks we're all retarded," said Diane. Conversation flowed easily now.

"I remember. Our dorm used to be off-campus, and I cringed when the school bus drove through Staatsburg and everyone would stop and stare, or so I thought." The difference between retarded and crazy remained elusive.

"The kids hated to go anywhere in the bus with The Anderson School written on the side of it, so we took it off," solidified the teacher. A loud bell rang, and we all exchanged quick glances and good-byes, except for the boy with the punk hair, who walked out as silently as he had remained.

I didn't want them to leave. I didn't want to go, but I knew this was just a brief hour of the past I had been given—no more, no less.

As they were leaving, a younger girl in stringy cut-off shorts came sauntering in, her stiff-gelled hair shooting up into the sky. "Ya used to go he-ere?" she asked.

273

"Yes, I did," I said, turning around to face her.

"I'll bet they didn't restrain ya when you was he-ere."

"What is restraining?"

"It's when they grab ya hands behind ya back and throw ya ta the floor and step on ya face, so's ya can't git up. Some kids git a bloody nose or face, but they don't give a shit."

"Who's *they*?" I wanted to know.

"The teachers."

"Why would they do that?"

"Because ya git out of hand 'n throw things. To me, five times."

"You? Why?" I wondered. She gave me no answer. I watched as she began pacing around the room like a tethered pony. I didn't want to lose her. "Why would you want them to? Why would you do things to make them mad enough to hurt you?" I asked, stressing the *you.*

She quickly turned around, whoever she was, and walked silently out of the room. I, of course, knew why someone would do that. Acting out. *I knew why.* Hate. Anger. Frustration. Nobody cared. I knew too well why someone would do that. The physical pain felt better than the emotional confusion. No one taught you the anger inside would destroy you, if you let it.

After everyone had left, I sat in the library and looked over old yearbooks, searching for more memories. Soon I began having a difficult time concentrating. I could hear men's voices back and forth, yelling down the hall. When the tones got loud enough, I tried to decipher the heated discussion. A student, I thought, but didn't hear full sentences until one of the staff members went out into the hall. "I don't care," he yelled. "If he does it again, I'll still do the same thing. I'll just smash his head on the floor. That's what I get paid to do." Then I heard a door slam.

I drifted back to a yearbook I had never seen before, "Dedicated to the betterment of adolescence. In 1924, Doctor

Victor Vance founded the Anderson School to develop the characters and minds of adolescents. No problems too complex to be solved."

Then I read a statement of purpose, written in 1955 by the headmaster of the Anderson School:

Why do I say the things I do? Why do I do the things I do?

Why do I lose my temper, am rude and use uncalled for language?

There is no time for changing the world around you. There is no time for modifying teachers. There is no time for making people fit your formula to please you.

Children were not supposed to change the world around them, but I gathered that the administration was allowed to change the children. Was rebelliousness inherited? If your dad comes home drunk and beats you or your mom, or your uncle sexually abuses you, or if your mom abandons you, or if your parents don't ever say anything nice to you, continually criticize you, wouldn't it be natural to want to change the world around you?

I exhausted the books until Bridget returned and offered to show me around. We walked down the hall toward the "canteen," a tiny room filled with small bags of Lay's potato chips, numerous boxes of candy bars, gum, cigarettes, and sodas. Once the hub of everyday social life, now relegated to a closet. The three-hundred-pound secretary sat behind the counter in a bizarre composition with some of the girls I recognized from the library. As if I were walking through a fun house with too little time to absorb every lurking corner, I followed Bridget. She pointed out the detention room and other offices.

We left the building and entered one of the coed dorms. There were no rugs, no curtains, no mirrors, no pictures. An occasional poster about safe sex hung on an otherwise barren bulletin board. The cement walls of the hallway were painted robin's-egg blue. Everything was streaked with grime. A dingy film that could have been there for twenty years covered the windows. I noticed the locked doors, the sign-out sheets to keep track of everyone's whereabouts, and the duties list I remembered so well. My mind traveled quickly, comparing the past to the present.

"Want to see my room?" Bridget asked.

"Sure," I answered, wanting every bit of information anyone would offer. She unlocked her door, and we walked into a cell-size room with a few posters on the wall and closets with no door. I looked at a few photos on the wall, and she told me about her brother and a few friends who were in the pictures.

We went outside again and into the science building, the same science building I had flunked my senior chemistry test in. I recognized the teacher from the library during lunch. As we entered the open door to the classroom, the teacher warmly said hello and introduced me to the class.

"Do you know *her*?" darted a tall, spindly, anorexic girl with ebony eyes and skin. She stood behind her desk, pointing her long finger accusingly toward the teacher.

"Yes, we met in the library during lunch," I told her.

"She a bitch, and she can't teach a fuckin' thing. I don't know why she's even here—she should git the hell out," ranted the girl. I looked at her, then over to the small sandy-haired teacher, who wore a serene smile. "She don't belong here," the girl continued, "She ought ta git fired!"

The other students joined in, and an explosive din filled the room. I took my cue to leave. As we walked out, I heard the small, gentle teacher say to her class, "What did I do to deserve this today?" *God,* I recalled, *if we ever had that kind of outbreak, we would have been sent to the principal's office, banned from social activities, certainly failed conduct, and maybe even expelled.* Things had changed, some.

"I'd like to get a degree in psychology or something and maybe come back and work here," Bridget confided in me, as we wandered through the rest of the campus, all dirty, all unkempt and timeworn.

"Great," I told her, thinking how fine the line was between needing help and being the helper. "Graduation is a very emotional time here. Everybody cries a lot," she reminded me. "They're sad to leave, to say good-bye to friends. And afraid."

"I cried at my graduation," I told her. I was scared to go on, petrified to face the world—which was sane, when I was not. "The main thing I've learned, I guess, is that looking back from as far as I am, three years is not a very long time compared to the rest of your life. Three years is not the end of the world if you manage to stay alive." Three years when you're a freshman in high school can be an eternity.

I didn't cry when I climbed back into the Mercedes, my soul still solidified inside the time warp. The clouds had closed in, and occasional drops of rain fell onto my hands and knees as I sat halfway inside the car. I didn't want to leave. I wanted to know more, or I wanted to help more, or I wanted to change everything, because there were still so many kids, too many years later. How could I leave now, when I knew how much pain these kids lived with? Maybe I could save them. Maybe I could stop the insanity. But how?

No. My time was up. I would defy the inertia, climb into my car, and drive away. This time I understood the difference between past, present, and future. Nobody would follow me, and I wouldn't be punished. I pulled my legs into the car and closed the door. If I had had that power when I was a child, I wondered what would have happened.

# BIBLIOGRAPHY

The poems that are not cited are common poems we knew growing up, jump-rope rhymes, etc. However, a source that can be cited, if need be, is:

Hastings, Scott E. Junior, editor. *Miss Mary Mac All Dressed in Black: Tongue Twisters, Jump-Rope Rhymes and Other Children's Lore From New England.* Little Rock, Arkansas, August House, 1990.

Miller, Olive Beaupre, compiler. *My Book House, Volume 1, In the Nursery.* Chicago, Illinois: Bookhouse for Publishers, copyright 1920.

Morgenthau, Henry. *Mostly Morgenthau's,* New York, New York: Ticknor & Fields, 1991.

Naumburg, Philip H. *Personal Reflections. (unpublished)*

Many letters, yearbooks, reports, and memories.